Imprint

Bibliographic information from the German National Library: The German National Library lists this publication in the German National Bibliography; detailed bibliographic data are available on the Internet at dnb.dnb.de.

2nd edition (2025)
© 2024 Tim Stegmann
Publisher: BoD · Books on Demand GmbH,
Überseering 33, 22297 Hamburg, bod@bod.de
Printing: Libri Plureos GmbH, Friedensallee 273, 22763 Hamburg

ISBN: 978-3-8192-2869-8

Layout, typesetting: Lukas Ullrich, kleinlaut.biz
Cover image: © IMAGO (Photo: Sven Simon)
Cover design: Lukas Ullrich
Photos: private (p. 12)
ABS (Aktueller Bilderdienst Schwarz), Michael Schwarz (author photo)
Clarification and animation of the game moments screenshots:
Tim Stegmann, Lukas Ullrich
Explanatory graphics:
Own illustration. Design: Lukas Ullrich and Katja Großpietsch, Katika Design

All other photos: © IMAGO
p. 15: IMAGO / Sven Simon
p. 20: IMAGO / BSR Agency
p. 53: IMAGO / Alterphotos
p. 66: IMAGO / Marca
p. 85: IMAGO / AFLOSPORT
p. 88: IMAGO / Revierfoto
P. 138: IMAGO / Beautiful Sports
P. 274: IMAGO / Beautiful Sports
P. 277: IMAGO / Pro Sports Images

Note on the use of language: For reasons of better readability, the masculine form is used in the text. However, it includes the female and diverse forms. All personal designations apply equally to all genders. Therefore, when referring to coaches or players in the context of a general explanation, female coaches or players are always included.

Some sources have been translated from Spanish or German into English by the author to the best of his knowledge and belief, always with the intention of retaining the meaning and essence of the quotation. This book has been prepared very carefully. However, all information is provided without guarantee. Neither the author nor the publisher can accept liability for any disadvantages or damages resulting from the contents presented in the book.
Furthermore, no liability is assumed for content that can be accessed via links to third-party websites, as the content of these websites is not adopted as one's own, but is merely intended to indicate their status at the time of publication of the book.

To Mi,
Samuel Quique,
Isaiah João.

Power,
inspiration,
and home.

Thank you for everything.

"When we look at the present moment with all our senses, we invite the world to fill us with joy. The pains of the past are behind us. The future has yet to unfold. But the now is full of beauty and awaits for our attention."
　TARA BRACH

"Every team needs a Basque."
　JOHAN CRUYFF

Table of Contents

Foreword Martí Perarnau

"You park it!" Xabi yelled as he jumped out of the still-moving car. He ran like a madman through the Allianz Arena until he reached the changing room. He'd arrived to hear the final pre-match talk. Just in time.

This is the character of Xabi Alonso: calm, rigorous, serious, and concise — yet simultaneously capable of going against the current just to arrive before his teammates. Fast and furious.

It was March 11, 2015, and Bayern were playing the second leg of their Champions League round of 16 tie in Munich. Their opponents were Shakhtar Donetsk — a rugged team featuring talented Brazilians such as Douglas Costa and Fred. The first leg had been a difficult one: a goalless draw, with few scoring chances, a rather conservative tactical approach from Pep Guardiola, and Xabi Alonso's sending off. The Catalan coach hadn't wanted to expose his team to the risk of the Ukrainians' rapid transitions, so he left Lewandowski on the bench and minimized any potential dangers. His experience told him that the round of 16 often proved far more dangerous than most imagined — and he didn't want to concede any goals in the first leg. His reasoning didn't spare him the unanimous criticism from the German press, which deemed the goalless draw a poor result for Bayern.

The atmosphere in Munich for the second leg was tense. Xabi Alonso's suspension left the team's midfield somewhat exposed, and they were also without their other great pillar, captain Philipp Lahm, who had fractured his ankle in training. In this context, Guardiola adopted what became known as the Cambridge Pyramid as his system of play. The 2-3-5 was an explosive idea because it grouped all the team's attackers at once: Coman, Ribéry, Lewandowski, Götze, and Robben. And at the same time, it was a high-risk system against Shakhtar's counterattacks.

When Bayern's daring lineup became known, Xabi Alonso was on the Sky Sports television set, sharing the analysis desk with Franz Beckenbauer. Everyone present received Guardiola's decision with skepticism, and some with harsh criticism, as they understood it to be too risky. Xabi had known the lineup for a few days, as the coach had started practicing it in training, and he defended Pep's idea with arguments and passion. He explained that the five men at the back—two central defenders, the holding midfielder (Schweinsteiger), and the two fullbacks—would form a wall that would cut off any opposing counterattack, while the five men up front would relentlessly pepper Shakhtar's goal. Despite Xabi's extensive explanations, no one in the Sky Sports debate panel seemed overly convinced by the idea.

Xabi left the set quite angry, got into his car, and looked at his watch. The match was half an hour away, and we weren't far from the stadium, but very soon we realized there was a big problem: the roads to the Allianz Arena were gridlocked with fan vehicles. At that moment, the "fast and furious" version of Xabi emerged. He wanted to get to the final pre-match talk, scheduled for five minutes before they took the field. He didn't just want to get there: he "needed" to get there. He felt he had to support his teammates, be with them, back them in those risky moments, and tell them to play without fear and with passion.

He grabbed the wheel and began driving against the flow of traffic, inciting the fury of other drivers. Luckily, no one was heading in the opposite direction to the vast crowd moving towards the stadium, but this didn't lessen the storm of horns from enraged fans who watched a black vehicle speeding, overcoming obstacles and traffic jams, even if it meant driving in the forbidden lane. The conversation inside Xabi's car was limited to a few brief onomatopoeias and the player's monotonous comment: "I have to get there on time." Neither his wife Nagore nor I had anything to say about it. In fact, we had no choice but to close our eyes to the obvious driving risk and cover our ears against the huge commotion brewing. Three minutes from arrival, with the stadium already in sight, we had to descend a rather steep curve, and Xabi didn't hesitate to launch himself in the opposite direction, as if an important trophy of his career were at stake.

With a furious brake, he swerved the car right to the stadium's entrance and left us with the task of parking the vehicle, while he bolted towards the private meeting. He arrived just in time, as Pep was giving the final instructions and the huddle of players embraced before the battle. Xabi was sweatier than the footballers who were about to play, a result of the tension experienced inside the car. Before the talk ended, he let out a shout: "¡Vamos!"

For Xabi, arriving on time and fully participating in the talk with his teammates was like playing the match and winning it. He would have to be in the stands, biting his nails due to the suspension, but he wasn't absent from the team; instead, he was an intimate part of it. His teammates would play knowing that Xabi was with them.

This is the character Tim Stegmann portrays for us in this splendid book: a man measured and calm, rigorous and serious, diligent and honest, respectful of collective internal rules, yet at the same time passionate, volcanic, and transgressive. A polyhedral Xabi, cold and ardent, ice and fire simultaneously. A model family man, "Fast and Furious" driver... an outstanding player, a superlative coach.

On that night in 2015, Bayern crushed Shakhtar 7:0. Pep's idea, which Xabi had so fervently defended on television, was brilliant.

Martí Perarnau

Prologue

On October 5, 2022, the world of football in Germany was about to change forever: Xabi Alonso was appointed as the new head coach of Bayer 04 Leverkusen and introduced one day later at a press conference before the 9th matchday against Schalke 04. Almost a year earlier, there had been rumors about a move to Germany to join Borussia Mönchengladbach. Now, the Basque actually decided to gain his first coaching experience in Germany's top division. The fact that Xabi Alonso, after a very successful playing career, would now also make history as a coach, was something that José Mourinho, his former coach at Real Madrid, had already expressed little doubt about in 2019: "His father was a coach, he grew up similarly to me. Then he became a player – much better than me, of course."[1] Xabi has outstanding positioning and knowledge of the game and was trained by the best coaches of his time, so Mourinho concluded: "If you put all that together, Xabi has the best prerequisites to be a very good coach!"[2] The Portuguese was not alone in this assessment: Carlo Ancelotti also shared his confidence: "If I had to bet on a player back then who would become a coach, it would have undoubtedly been Xabi. Someone who has played in midfield has more advantages on the bench. A midfielder (...) must have the quality, be tactically clever, have a good view of the game... And Xabi Alonso was one of the best midfielders I ever coached, very intelligent, with fantastic feet and extraordinary professionalism."[3]

---

1   Mourinho quoted in Bundesliga online 2024.
2   Ibid.
3   Ancelotti quoted by Romero 2021.

For me, having spent a lot of time in Spain since 2021, particularly in Barcelona and Madrid, it was clear that a new level of coaching was likely to arrive in the Bundesliga. After the first rumors about a move to Germany in spring 2021, I had already taken a closer look at coach Xabi Alonso. At that time, Alonso was coach of the second team of his hometown club Real Sociedad San Sebastián and had gained his first "professional experience" as a coach. The young coach Xabi Alonso quickly achieved something special with his team: In the 2021/2022 season, *Sanse*, the second team of Real Sociedad San Sebastián, was the only second team in *LaLiga2*, the second Spanish division. For me it was obvious: I didn't just want to use video to analyze the team's goals and playing style, but also to experience the game alive. Once it was in my mind, I have started making it happen: During my master's degree in Madrid and my internship at the youth academy of Real Madrid, a window of opportunity arose for a visit to a second division game between Fuenlabrada (a suburb of Madrid) and *Sanse*. So on May 7, 2022, I was sitting with my friend from the course on the regional train from Madrid to Fuenlabrada to watch LaLiga2 bottom table duel (21st against 19th) enjoying the best afternoon sunshine. Alonso's team showed a lot of energy, dynamism and passion right from the start, but also demonstrated why they had not collected many points up to that moment: As with many second teams, the issues of experience, maturity (one would call it "ruthlessness") and efficiency played a big role. It almost seemed that Xabi Alonso's team, which still had a realistic chance of staying in the league, would (again) not be rewarded for a good performance, because at halftime the score was 1:0 for the home side of Fuenlabrada, even though they had not contributed much to the game until then. In the second half, *Sanse* finally equalized – but it was clear that Real Sociedad would need a win to maintain a realistic chance of staying in the league. Long before the myth of "Laterkusen" was born, Xabi Alonso's team managed to score the much-celebrated winning goal with a lot of heart and increasing pressure in the 95th minute. In fact, it was this moment, which I captured in a photo (see chapter image), in which all the energy and joy culminated in the jubilation of finally being rewarded for the effort and the good, proactive play.

So when Xabi Alonso was introduced as the new coach at Bayer Leverkusen at the beginning of October 2022, my interest and curiosity were reignited. I was eager to see how a Spanish coach, who had played under so many outstanding coaches during his playing career, would enrich the Bundesliga outside the context of Bayern Munich. When I spoke about Pep Guardiola with some of my Spanish coaching colleagues, for example, they were relatively quick to say: "Yes, but you also have to see: Pep has always had good players. Now at City he even has the best...". While none of them intended to downplay the achievements and in particular the coaching quality of the outstanding Catalan, there was always a certain doubt as to whether a similar performance would have been possible with other players. A coach heavily influenced by Guardiola, among others, arrived in the Bundesliga, taking charge of a struggling team. From that moment on, I followed the games with increasing intensity and attention - an interest whose findings now flow into this book. This is not about declaring Xabi Alonso as a coach or of filtering out the unique influences of the many successful coaches in his career (starting with his father, Periko Alonso, and including Rafael Benítez, José Mourinho, Pep Guardiola, Carlo Ancelotti). Rather, it is about explaining my point of view to the tactical concepts and details his team has mastered and I have studied and deepened through my Master courses and visits, my exchanges and conversations with dozens of Spanish coaches. These concepts not only have a high recognition factor within Spanish football but can also serve as a source of inspiration for any other coach. At the same time, many things are based on those perspectives that have not only shaped Spanish football to a considerable extent but also world football: We are, of course, talking about FC Barcelona's methodology, its view and its interpretation of the game.

So at no point is it about an absolute "truth claim" in the analysis (if such a claim can even exist in football, especially from an external perspective), but rather about enriching our understanding of tactics and shared intentions to help our teams and players in reaching even higher level and offering the coaches a new perspective to football game. The aim is not always that the situations shown will reveal a wealth of previously unknown information, nor will they provide maximally innovative new knowledge. Rather, it is often the fundamental details, the skills that are nowadays overused under the term "basics", to execute simple actions and principles successfully and effectively (and efficient), that are a quality feature that can make the difference in any game.

All of the situations analyzed were interpreted and implemented exceptionally well by the players themselves, guided by their own intuition and feelings and in response to the specific game situation. But as with all things that are "interpreted", these are existing concepts or ideas that, when paired with a special talent (like all the players in the Leverkusen squad) or even a specific genius (think of Florian Wirtz or the free-kick skills of Grimaldo, among others), can become something wonderful and create special moments in football. Some of the concepts or tactical situations may be new to the viewer, while others may feel more "old school". Ultimately this just goes to show that this highly successful Leverkusen team can cover the full spectrum of outstanding behaviors on the pitch - and, as always, in this game where chance plays a significant role - they were also able to rely on the necessary luck in the 2023/2024 season (or rather, earned it through hard work).

Xabi Alonso's career has been shaped by four key influences. First, his upbringing in San Sebastián, where being Basque and playing for his boyhood club was central to his development. Second, the meticulous approach of Rafael Benítez. Third, the relentless winning mentality of José Mourinho. Finally, in the later years of his career, the influence of Pep Guardiola, the leading figure in positional play, alongside the composed leadership of Carlo Ancelotti—whose impact extends far beyond just man-management. To understand Alonso's football philosophy, one must consider both the Spanish perspective on the game and, more specifically, the methodology of FC Barcelona. No other club has had a greater influence on Spain's playing and training approach, the style of the Spanish national team, and, ultimately, football worldwide. This chapter is therefore about the origins and the specific concepts which, as already mentioned, recur in Spanish football (as well as in world football), even if they may be expressed in different ways. What helps us is that Spanish is a very lively language where it is possible to convey a particular intention or feeling just by choosing a particular word or term.

A particularly good example of this is the wide range of descriptive words that are now used for the word "pass" in football within the Spanish language:

jugar	→	to play
"hacer" un pase	→	"to make" a pass
"dar" un pase	→	"to give" a pass
connectar	→	to connect
entregar	→	to deliver (like the post office), ensuring that the ball arrives (in optimal conditions)
asociar	→	to associate / to connect / to unite
relacionar (!)	→	to connect / to build a relationship with someone
interrelacionar	→	to interrelate / to connect with each other (with a stronger emphasis on TOGETHERNESS)
comunicar	→	to share / to communicate / to transmit
interaccionar	→	to interact
enlazar ventaja	→	to combine with the advantage / to link with the advantage *(Note: enlazarse means "to marry")*
encadenar	→	to connect / to join together

More specifically:

filtrar	→	"to filter" – in a figurative sense the interface pass
limpiar	→	"to clean" – in a figurative sense "clearing" as a defensive action

The Pass in Spanish Football

The special thing about almost all of these expressions is that each one can express an intention and an image, and that each individual expression forms a (game-tactical) invitation to interaction. If you look at the German verb "passen", the basic idea of making this "pass" "fit" is hidden in the root of the word – however, the deeper, socio-affective (connecting, community-building) meaning of the action remains hidden. There is also another layer of meaning in the English word "to pass" - the socio-affective meaning of the Spanish expressions remains still remains concealed in this sense. In addition to the simple "play" and the creative "make", the word "give" already implies the basic idea that the pass should be a gift that brings joy to the teammate. If we look at passes from this perspective, some teams have very few gifts to exchange between teammates. All other terms that do not already express a specific action (such as an interface pass that "filters" through the opponent's lines) are clear, connecting terms that encourage interaction and networking, which then automatically merge into a synchronicity that allows the team to play according to the same thoughts and intentions.

Therefore, especially in Spanish football (although, in football history, this idea is certainly not limited to Spain but – like many other such concepts – also has its origins in the Netherlands), the pass *is* the medium by which two or more people connect to achieve a common goal. The pass is the essence of the collective game. The pass is more than a mere technical action: it is the foundation and ultimate reflection of the collective and associative play in any team sport. Accordingly, the pass is also understood as 'sharing the ball among teammates', through which players can communicate with each other and experience the emotion and pleasure of dominating the game through possession of the ball. The connection between players created by the pass requires both to adapt to the characteristics of their teammate. The more the players in the team know each other, the better their communication through passing becomes. At its most extreme, all technical actions in football can be understood as passes: as a pass to yourself (dribbling), as a pass to a teammate, as a pass into the net

(finishing). All variable components of the game are summarized in the overall organization of the team, whose reference points are the ball and the pass. This is not about playing a pass for the sake of passing. Passes have one purpose: to eliminate opponents. If that is not possible, we keep the ball, dribble with it (take on defenders) and look for pressure from the opposition so that we can play a pass.[4]

The pass is the systematic, constant and deliberate repetition of interaction between all team members, using the ball to organize the team itself, disorganize the opposing team and achieve the ultimate goal: to score!

> *"In other words, when you pass the ball, you don't just pass the ball, you give an intention, you give space, you give time, you give energy, you give joy, you give trust - words that really make a team a team."*[5]
> **PACO SEIRUL·LO**

> *"When I make a pass, my goal is for [my teammate] to have the best possible path, with his right or left foot, to have an advantage. (...) Of course [my teammate] has to be in the right position - that is his job. But if I pass to the left, for example, he might have more trouble turning, so I pass to his right foot. That's my idea: to play a pass that brings an advantage and not to create a problem."*[6]
> **XABI ALONSO**

The atmosphere at the introductory press conference on October 6, 2022, was far from that of a team fighting relegation. Rather, Xabi Alonso spoke right from the start about the great honour of being at this club and the ambitious goals that the club had set. None of his words seemed artificial or staged – here was someone with great ambitions who spoke about them clearly. Nevertheless, it might have seemed confusing given the league table at the time: Bayer Leverkusen was second from botton in the table with five points from eight games. For the German media, however, it was a real spectacle that a coach was being introduced who did not even know the German word "relegation battle" ["Abstiegskampf"] and who also left little room for doubt: "If you don't dare to take risks, you won't achieve anything. Nothing is certain in life and even less so in football. If you don't try, you'll never achieve it. I am happy to be here and motivated

---

4   Fernandez 2012.
5   Seirul·lo in Guasch 2024.
6   Alonso in Sports Illustrated 2016.

because I believe we can achieve great things.'"[7] The energy, confidence and the sense of anticipation that this coach exuded at his introduction was certainly infectious and formed a strong contrast to the team's position in the league at the time. In the end, it was one of football's coincidence that his start - just like his Bundesliga debut as a player - was again against Schalke 04, although his debut as a coach was far more successful (his result as a player had been 1:1).

7   Alonso 2022 (recording of the first press conference); and Cáceres 2022.

Excursus: What is a Game Model?

"The game model is determined by the context in which players, coaches, club ideology and environment constantly interact."[8]
DANIEL GUINDOS

"Football is a communicative and social game. It is therefore not recommended to remove the player from the context that affects his performance, since the functions of each player depend on a common function and are the result of constant interaction."[9]
ÓSCAR CANO

In order to delve deeper into Xabi Alonso's coaching philosophy and to gain a comprehensive understanding of the playing style, I will provide a detailed overview of the "game model" in the following section. The term "game model" is often oversimplified, neglecting crucial elements that are essential for coaches in developing a team's playing identity. By establishing a strong theoretical foundation, we can better comprehend the complexities of the game model and its impact on team performance. Even though the concept of the game model and all its facets will be explained in more detail in the following pages, we as coaches should always keep in mind: "The game is played by the players. (...) It's not just about the game; it's about people."[10] Consequently, the primary goal of this theoretical framework is to facilitate the game for coaches and their players. Juanma Lillo, Pep Guardiola's assistant coach, offers a valuable perspective on coaching philosophy, stating: "I want to make it easier for the players to become aware of who they are and what they do. (...) It's about everything. Nothing can be decontextualized. How one lives, what one is, what meaning one gives to relationships, behavior, interaction... All of this affects how a team plays."[11]
Two things are essential for a basic understanding of this book: Firstly, it is undeniable that in a circumstantial, chaotic and unpredictable sport like football, there is no *single, irrefutable* truth. This also applies to the choice of playing style that each team selects. That is why it is not possible to say objectively what constitutes "better" or "worse" football. Each coach chooses the approach they believe will produce the most success, and often this approach depends on their

8   Guindos 2015.
9   Cano 2010.
10   Lillo 2011.
11   Ibid.

own strengths as well as the perceived capabilities of their team. Therefore, this book is not about putting one particular type or interpretation of football above another. For one thing, my research and reviewing countless games have shown me once again: Even in a more direct interpretation, as seen occasionally with Union Berlin under former coach Urs Fischer or Union Saint-Gilloise in Belgium with its former coach Karel Geraerts, all of these teams had a very good and clear idea that, when implemented well, was very difficult to play against making it difficult for opponents to find solutions.

Furthermore, when this book looks at football, it does so from the angle and perspective of complexity. This means that the things we observe often have complex reasons and are rarely attributable to linear, causal relationships. For Juanma Lillo, the role of the coach is crucial: "Science tries to turn us into machines. As far as my work [as a coach] is concerned, empathy is crucial. In any work environment, a person performs better in a good atmosphere than in a bad one. You have to make players aware of things they may not be able to see."[12] In football, due to the sport's great tradition, certain traditional patterns of thinking are still deeply rooted, such as the belief that football performance can be measured solely by data and values. Frequently, metrics like total distance covered, number of accelerations, and sprints are used to assess a team's performance. It is frequently overlooked that all these values have to be contextualized, which means they must be examined in specific circumstances: Who played against whom? Where? Was it a normal league game or a cup game? What was the league standing of the teams at the time? How was the situation? What is the playing style of the two teams? What point of the season was it? All of this information influences the quantitative data that is collected in almost every game in professional leagues today. Therefore, performance cannot be reduced to individual, simple elements, as this would be more in line with the understanding of a machine in which individual parts that do not work can be replaced. Spanish coach Juanma Lillo once said that it almost seems as if what cannot be quantified does not exist in football.[13] All this results in football players behaving in a rather "robotic" manner and only acting to a limited extent. Fortunately, the best of the sport show us almost week after week that football can work differently. As Italian coaching legend Arrigo Sacchi noted, football is "born in the brain, not in the body."[14] This goes hand in hand with the request to the coach to stimulate neural plasticity through training with variable content and thereby ensure the creation of new synapses and connections in the central nervous system of the

12 Lillo 2011.
13 Lillo in Mallo 2020.
14 Sacchi quoted in Mallo 2020.

players. We will look at what this could mean in practice in the chapter on Training Proposals.

"Nature is very complex, but the laws that govern it are very simple." [15]
JUAN MARTÍN MALDACENA

Complex Systems

In his book *La mente bien ordenada* (roughly translated as *The Well Ordered Mind*), the French philosopher Edgar Morin defines a system as something that is "represented by a set of elements that interact to achieve a specific goal."[16] In his book *Complex Football* Spanish athletics coach Javier Mallo explains further: "The characteristics of a system depend on the way in which the components are configured , and they have four categorical properties: Interaction, Totality, Complexity and Organization."[17] The properties of a system cannot be explained by looking at the individual parts, since not only does every change in these components have an impact on the whole, but they are also shaped by the connections between each part and the overall structure.[18] A part of the whole therefore cannot be reduced to be understood in isolation from the totality to which it belongs. To illustrate this point, consider the human heart. While a scientist can study the physical properties of an isolated heart, they cannot fully comprehend its function without considering its role within the entire organism. The specific function of the heart can only be observed when viewed within the body examining the interaction with the other organs. Therefore, properties (or characteristics) that single parts do not have arise which Aristotle pointed out already a long time ago with the statement "The whole is more than the sum of its parts". In football, this manifests itself in a different way, as Juanma Lillo explains: "It's not just that what works with one player doesn't work with another; it's that what works with one player doesn't work with the same player at a different time and under different circumstances."[19] Professors Natàlia Balagué and Carlota Torrents summarize the properties of complex systems as follows:[20]

15 cited in Pol 2021.
16 Morin 2000.
17 Mallo 2020.
18 Morin 2000.
19 Lillo 2011.
20 Balagué & Torrents 2011.

→ **Unpredictability:** The behavior of a complex system cannotreliably be predicted in the long term.
→ **Wholeness:** The whole is greater than the sum of its parts.
→ **Interdependence / Interrelationships:** There is an constant interaction between all parts.
→ **Spontaneous emergence:** The interaction of all parts creates a new whole that is distinct from the sum of all parts.

In addition, former Barça directors Isaac Guerrero and Xavier Damunt mention further characteristics of complex systems:[21]

→ **Interrelatedness:** A system is constituted by its relationship to subsystems and suprasystems.
→ **Irreducibility:** Despite being related, a system retains its unity, identity and autonomy due to a specific internal organization.
→ **Dynamism:** Although a system naturally tends toward disorganization— ultimately leading to its decay and disappearance— it manages to maintain its internal equilibrium through negentropic processes (the reversal of the entropic process so that chaos returns to order) of reorganization and adaptation.
→ **Adaptability:** A system reorganizes itself while maintaining its internal structure in response to disturbances that act on it.
→ **Variability:** Since emergent properties cause permanent changes, a system is never completely defined or adapted.

Complex systems regulate themselves through continuous exchange, interaction and internal feedback loops in order to remain in balance.[22] Spanish scientists Balagué and Torrents further argue that our knowledge of the individual components of living organisms is less important; without understanding how they interact and create relationships among themselves, we gain little insight about their behavior.[23] Portuguese coach Marisa Silva puts it this way: "To understand the team as a whole, we must understand the relationships between the players and, in the same way, we must know these relationships in order to understand the team."[24] For Davide Ancelotti, assistant coach and son of Carlo Ancelotti at

21 Damunt & Guerrero 2021.
22 Capra 1996.
23 Balagué & Torrents 2011.
24 Silva 2008.

Real Madrid, the "real challenge [for a coach] is to identify, among the countless bonds that are created between them [the players], those that need to be
strengthened."[25]
This once again underlines the interconnections that exist within a complex
system. Each individual player can therefore be described as a complex system
which, depending on and together with the network of interpersonal relationships with their teammates, forms another (larger) complex system — the team
— through joint training and a common (tactical) identity.[26] The collective acts as
a whole, generating different synergies and leading to different behaviors that
constantly emerge.[27] In its entirety, not just in football terms, a football team
is first and foremost a social system that "can display extraordinarily complex
behavior based on the possible combinations of the numerous possibilities offered by each of the different components that compose it."[28] This should also be
taken into account in the team management off the pitch.

In order to understand the phenomenon of football, both the broader context
and the interactions between the players — as well as their interactions with
their environment — are crucial. Javier Mallo puts it this way in his book *Complex
Football*: "For this reason, quantifying and modeling team performance using
objective data is an irresistible temptation for people who live in the environment of the sport but do not really understand it." But the main focus for a coach
in competitive sports is actually to get the players to "work together to achieve
tactical organization."[29] This requires a holistic view, as Juanma Lillo explains:
"The game is an indivisible unit, there is no defensive moment without an attacking moment. Both create a functional unit. (...) The thing is, you have to be able
to reduce without impoverishing. And that applies to everything. You can't take
things out of their context because they're no longer the same, even if you then
intend to put things back together. You can't take one arm of Rafa Nadal and train
it separately. If you have done so, reinserting it may cause an imbalance, a rejec-
tion of the organism. (...) Football is associative, combinatorial."[30]

25 Ancelotti quoted by Gagliardi 2023.
26 Mallo 2020.
27 Balagué & Torrents 2011.
28 Ibid.
29 Mallo 2020.
30 Lillo 2011.

"Stupid are those who, without belonging to us, look at us with derision and laugh at our unique habits. Fools, because although they examine us closely, they see nothing. Other experts want to advise us and explain how our team works. They will observe our behavior on and off the pitch; they will collect hundreds of pieces of data and classify everything that happens to us, comparing and evaluating it with other benchmarks. On the last day, they will summon us and show us their diagnosis of what we need to change or improve on a large, bright board. Our team is broken into a thousand pieces. And these scholars will believe they have discovered our secrets. But the team was never merely the sum of different elements, but rather a common spirit that dominates everything and in turn connects it. The team is a home, not just a house."[31]

ANDREU ENRICH IN COACHING MEDITATIONS

Football can be understood in terms of "self-organizing dynamics".[32] This means that the course of the game was not "imposed" or "prescribed" by anyone else. Rather, the course of the game is created by the interactions of the players in specific environmental contexts—that is, by the information provided by each individual, tactical action of a player.[33] Therefore, tactical behavior can be understood as the individual and collective adaptation of players to the requirements of the task within a dynamic environment.[34]

The topic of adaptability is fundamental not only in football, but also in evolution: when we talk about "survival of the fittest", we do not mean the survival of the strongest. In fact, the most adaptable survives, which also explains why humans (the supposedly weaker) survived while dinosaurs (the supposedly stronger species) did not. They became extinct instead. Adaptation usually occurs through the development of functionally advantageous synergies (cooperation amongst individuals). The extent to which this process is beneficial within football, and in particular in actual gameplay, will be explored further in the "Shared Intentions" section. What is clear, however, is that versatility is far superior to one-dimensionality. Cooperation and competition are therefore not only pillars of biological evolution, but fundamental principles in sport.[35]

---

31 Enrich 2024.
32 Ric et al. 2016.
33 Ibid.
34 Ibid.
35 Pol et al. 2020.

In order to ensure that the interaction between players does not occur arbitrarily, the **principle of organization** is crucial in this sense, since without the existence of organizational relationships between players, they could only be considered a group.[36] When observing a team, one can often recognize certain patterns on the pitch that reflect the unique nature of the team's organization. In this sense, one can speak of habits, which, however, arise from certain relationship conditions.[37]

The relationships between the players influence and determine the game interactions, which must be shaped by the coach so that the intended collective dynamic (as envisioned by the coach) can be consistently by the team during the games.[38] Vítor Frade, the "father of Tactical Periodization", also points out that the type of play that a team achieves results from the interaction between the players and that these relationshipsmay carry different meanings depending on the team's overall identity.[39]

This process does not happen immediately, as the system (or in our case, the team) "must go through unstable phases until a more effective organization finally emerges."[40] Training plays a decisive role here, in which appropriate behaviors should be stabilized without being fully automated, as situational flexibility is always required in football to adapt to the various game situations — and, by extension, in training.[41] Instead, it's more about the players internalizing of the game idea and feeling secure in it so that they can subsequently act with more freedom and increasingly intuition (embodiment of the game idea).[42] This is particularly successful when the players can identify with the coach's game idea.

Spanish coach and tactical analyst Enric Soriano cites the example of Pep Guardiola when describing this process, which is crucial for the implementation of the game model: "He has managed to bring the collective game to an excellent level by getting each of his players to recognize themselves in the game and to recognize the others, so that the socio-affectivity [connection between players, author's note] is much stronger and the game is harmonious and effective."[43]

36 Couto 2018.
37 Cano 2012.
38 Silva 2008.
39 Frade in Silva 2008.
40 Mallo 2020.
41 Balagué & Torrents 2014.
42 Cano 2012.
43 Soriano in Ballesteros 2020.

"The creators like themselves, the destroyers like themselves, but not that much."[44]
ÓSCAR CANO

The organized interaction of a team can therefore be described as tactical organization, since the players work together toward a (common) game objective. Teams with good organization help individuals to appear "better": players seem faster, always get the ball at exactly the right moment and (falsely) seem fitter.[45] All this happens through the interaction of the players, which is why the training itself should not consist of repetitiveexercises, since the intended purpose of each action is crucial for retention.[46]

The coach is the one who, depending on the characteristics of his players, has to develop and configure a game idea with different game patterns that enable the creation and implementation of "his football".[47] Based on this, Xavier Tamarit defines the game idea as the *"tactical culture"* of the coach, who is constantly aware of both design and process — in the game and within training.[48]

A team begins with a prescribed, already known and prepared organization, and then reorganizes itself in each new space and each new phase of the game according to certain rules and guidelines, depending on the unforeseen events that may arise. The ability to self-organize allows the team to adapt to each game situation, which is by definition unique and incomparable, and enables different actions in response. This adaptation to the changing context is essential and allows the player to perform optimal motor actions based on his abilities, traits and characteristics, regardless of whether he is in possession of the ball or in the process of regaining it.

Understanding certain concepts is essential for structuring your team as desired. It is also important to understand that in order to play the game as a team, each individual must be active and act as a functional unit, given the unpredictability and chaos that the game itself brings.

The idea of basic organization, combined with the coach's idea of the game, gives rise to the concept of the game model, which, however, is frequently misunderstood in football. It is often referred to as a system or scheme of play or even a basic formation, but this refers more to the positional arrangement at the start

44 Cano 2012.
45 Mallo 2020.
46 Ibid.
47 Martín-Barrera & Martínez-Cabrera 2019.
48 Tamarit 2010.

of the game (basic formation) or in different, predictable, phases of the game (build-up phase, defensive moment like pressing, etc.) and is only visible for a brief moment. While this does address the positional organization of the players and thus the team, it does not do justice to the concept of the *"game model"*.[49] In this respect, it is important to distinguish between **structure** (in the sense of a basic formation) and **function**, since **structure** alone represents a very rigid side of a system, whereas the **function** takes into account the relationships between all elements. Therefore, the **interaction of all players within a game system** is more important than the skills of an individual player outside the system.[50] At the same time, it is not the system itself that is important, but rather the meaning that the players give to the system.

Other authors, with regard to the game model, refer to the formulation of the coach's ideas, which is composed of overarching principles in conjunction with further sub-principles that articulate certain behaviors for different game moments and are thus intended to ensure a a cohesive, identity-forming organi-zation.[51] There are differing views on the elaboration of this *"tree of principles"*, as some proponents of the methodology of **Tactical Periodization** perceive a fragmentation in this subdivision and multitude of sub-principles and further sub-(sub-)principles, which they argue violates the principle of the '*unbreakable wholeness*' and is thus classified as a linear reductionistic approach that is alien to the game (because it is unnatural). Overarching, it can be stated that **game principles** should provide the team with reference points and guidelines and thereby shape the game model. The successful Portuguese coach José Mou-rinho, for example, affirms that through the clearly defined and prioritized prin-ciples that he has implemented in his team, he has given it a certain DNA (in the sense of identity).[52]

Portuguese coach Nuno Amieiro sees a team's identity as nothing more than the consistent reaffirmation of the organization that defines it up.[53] This organization is displayed by the team at every moment of the game and recurs consistently.[54] At the same time, this organization and thus the game model as a whole should be dynamic and constantly questioned, since "the future must be maintained as

49 Martín-Barrera & Martínez-Cabrera 2019.
50 Mallo 2020.
51 Martín-Barrera & Martínez-Cabrera 2019.
52 Mourinho 2014.
53 Amieiro 2005.
54 Tamarit 2010.

a causal element of game behavior."[55] The flexibility of the game model is essential, as different interpretations and needs arise depending on the different context, players and game conditions.[56]

Davide Ancelotti, currently assistant coach of Real Madrid, sees **organization** as a possibility of "creating a situation in which a certain connection can benefit the collective."[57] He views the game model—and thus the idea and organization—as a fundamental decision of the coach, who can draw on the entire pool of resources (existing and still to be invented or developed) to decide which "outfit" he wants to dress the team in. Therefore, it must be well understood and carefully studied. When describing the nature of a coach, Ancelotti likes to use the example of the chameleon, an animal capable of constantly changing color to escape the dangers that surround it, to adapt to the reality that surrounds it. It is not tied to an identity. Nowadays, two completely different games can take place between the first and second half, just as one and the same team can play completely differently depending on their opponents.[58]

The Spanish author Martí Perarnau, who has spent a lot of time with Pep Guardiola in the course of his book projects, seesthe idea of the game as "not set in stone, but is constantly influenced by the competition, the opponent, incidents and adversities within the team, by fitness, technique and well-being, both individual and collective, by the calendar and its requirements. The game ideas are flexible and changeable throughout the entire time."[59]

Spanish coach Óscar Cano's view on the player organization indirectly refers to the idea of **complex systems**: "It is exactly (...) [the] network of relationships that determines the dynamics of the organization. It organizes the system and also enables the production of new elements that become part of the system."[60] The main task of the coach is to recognize and strengthen these relationships and to ensure maximum outcome for his own team through the resulting synergy.

Every idea of a coach is highly dependent on the players and the interactions and interpretations that emerge from that idea.[61] For Vítor Frade, it is essential

55 Frade 1985; Martín-Barrera & Martínez-Cabrera 2019.
56 Martín-Barrera & Martínez-Cabrera 2019.
57 Ancelotti quoted by Gagliardi 2023.
58 Ibid.
59 Perarnau 2016.
60 Cano 2012.
61 Martín-Barrera & Martínez-Cabrera 2019.

that the game first takes shape in the minds of the players, by highlighting and improving their characteristics.[62] Óscar Cano views the game model as the organization of conceptual tendencies that arise from the interaction of the natural abilities of the players.[63] Juanma Lillo, Pep Guardiola's assistant coach at Manchester City, comments: "It's about awakening what the player already has. It's not about them incorporating it, which is what the coaches' vanity leads us to believe. The footballer is a reality in his own right. There are coaches who are annoyed that the team plays more like the players and not like themselves."[64]

> *"But my assistants are subject to the tyranny of the boards and argue that the game is only okay if the actions conform to the guiding principles of the model. A model that takes shape like a stencil through cutting and folding. And through its precision, it amputates the player's uniqueness to turn him into a mere pattern"*[65]
>
> ANDREU ENRICH IN COACHING MEDITATIONS

While Cano sees the role of the coach as more of a "facilitator" and "enabler" with a focus to the natural talents and abilities of individual players, he at times takes an extreme stance. However, it isundeniable that the game model reflects "the way players relate to each other and how they express their view of football".[66] Former Real Madrid U18 coach Fran Beltrán makes it clear that this is fundamental: "When a coach leads a team, he must understand the nature of the players and the contexts in which these players can make the difference."[67] Therefore, for Miguel Lopes, a Portuguese coach and professor in the Master of "Tactical Periodization" program, the game model emerges from the characteristics of the players within the context shaped by the coach.[68]

Italian coach Antonio Gagliardi sees another future competitive advantage in acknowledging the individual characteristics of each player: "This combination consists in bringing dynamism, fluidity and greater freedom into more rigid systems, taking into account the different characteristics of the available players."[69] Óscar Cano follows a similar approach, seeing the coach's focus as "finding the strengthening bonds that arise when his players combine their characteristics.

---

62 Frade 2004.
63 Cano 2012.
64 Lillo in Cano 2012.
65 Enrich 2024.
66 Portolés 2007; zit. n. Martín-Barrera & Martínez-Cabrera 2019.
67 Beltrán 2013.
68 Lopes 2024.
69 Gagliardi & Bordin 2024.

Rather than arranging a pre-determined procedure, the commitment focuses on composing a style that (...) [natural] characteristics of the players are taken into account."[70]

In any case, the game model reflects "the personality of the team (...) and thus the character of the coach".[71] The Spanish author Martí Perarnau compares the game model to a piece of music: "The music always sounds similar, but if we compare the piece as it was at the beginning with how it is at the end, we notice that rhythm, harmony and interpretation have changed greatly. (...) A game model is ultimately a fixed and movable frame at the same time. It is a score that changes daily due to the opponent, the experiences and the evolution of the idea itself."[72] Despite all the emphasis on flexibility, the aforementioned point of the "personality of the coach" is essential: a coach like Xabi Alonso or Pep Guardiola will always pursue and try to implement a certain game idea due to his character and basic attitude and values. Some coaches act more pragmatically, while others may be more idealistic—however, the core identity will only rarely change completely.

Overall, it can be said that the game model is reflected in the players' actions on the pitch. However, it is created by the interaction between the coachs's game idea and the individual skills of the players. It can also be influenced by external factors such as the club, its history, or the league.

Looking at Xabi Alonso's Bayer Leverkusen, a certain three-dimensionality can even be seen: within his game idea and his playing system, the players always take on the same roles, which, regardless of the individual player, are relatively fixed, binding and clearly defined (1st dimension). At the same time, the specific approach regarding how each position should be played depends on the opponent and the space they provide. There is therefore a strategy or a *match plan* that influences the execution and interpretation of the position or player role (2nd dimension). Finally, the personal attributes of each player influence how they execute their actions. There is a clear difference depending on whether Andrich or Palacios plays alongside Xhaka in midfield or whether Xhaka does not play at all. There are fewer qualitative differences between these variations, as Xabi Alonso has clearly demonstrated through his frequent squad rotation. Rather, it is about the typical tendencies, characteristics and behaviors that influence the coach's decision: whether it is Boniface's tendency to repeatedly

70 Cano 2012.
71 Perarnau 2016.
72 Ibid.

drift to the left wing and thus open space in the center or the corresponding counterpart when Patrik Schick plays as a traditional nine. The dynamic shift when Borja Iglesias takes on this role and the clear clear contrast when Adli, Wirtz and Tella create havoc in the front with maximum flexibility—all this does not change the fundamental system but shapes the team's overall approach to the game. Nuances evolve due to the individual attributes, tendencies and abilities of the players, but also due to the interactions and the emerging synergies that develop between them.

Spanish coach Abel Mourelo particularly highlights the connection between the coach's idea and the players, as well as the resulting synergy: "You not only have to understand the game, you also have to know your players. You have to know the game. Observation skills make the difference when it comes to getting to know the player—how he thinks, his abilities, his potential... And then we introduce him to the game. The player should recognize the game and recognize himself in the game."[73]
This is where the coach comes in:

> "To create connections without losing one's identity, without losing the backbone of everything. (...) He gets the most out of the game and empowers his players. He brings out hidden talents. He causes players to break the limiting beliefs they have acquired through previous life experiences. (...) He creates potential, but also limits. He is able to convince and seduce the player and show him that he can be better. How does he get player X to run under pressure? Well, because this player previously enjoyed what he did. He creates connections so that the player does something he wouldn't normally do because something happens beforehand that makes him happy. If I have the ball, I'm happy, if not, I run quickly."[74]

Mourelo's comment is crucial because it refers to a central point that Xabi Alonso has also stressed time and again, not least at his very first press conference: "The most important thing I have learned from all my coaches is that the players have to follow you. They have to believe what you say and you have to 'feed' them. They need to feel that they are improving because of you. They need to know that you are there to help them with your knowledge, your guidance, your motivation. The first thing is to lead the group and then you can talk about the

73 Mourelo in Ballesteros 2020.
74 Ibid.

tactic and the strategy."[75] Mourelo now combines two key aspects: the leadership of the group and the development of the content—the individual "approach to the player" in connection with the practical implementation of one's own idea. He also shows how important it is for the players themselves to be convinced of the trainer's core philosophy, to be fully engaged in it or at least to execute it with great enthusiasm. This ensures that even the physically demanding or challenging aspects of the idea arecarried out with joy and commitment—a mindset that may not have existed under another idea. Xabi Alonso himself defines football as "a question of emotional states." Depending on the team, there are different ways of dealing with doubts and setbacks: "There are teams that digest such things naturally; others find it more difficult to find their way around and they have to learn that sometimes it really hurts if you want to be successful."[76]

This, along with the previous point about synergies resulting from player interactions, brings us to another exciting topic within the broad framework of the game model: player roles.

The Italian coach Antonio Gagliardi has stated in a particualarly interesting article that, after the change of perspective from **position** to **function**, a further development has now taken place and "the 'role' (...) is no longer a (more or less specific) function, but the interpretation of an individual within a 'relationship'— it is the constant and continuous movement of the ball, the teammates and the opponents that determines the free spaces around the player in possession of the ball."[77]

The concept of "relationships" between players—currently being discussed with great enthusiasm under the term "*relationism*"—is becoming increasingly important in modern football. However, as we have already seen in relation to Spanish terminology for passing, the idea of "networking" and the socio-affective aspect of technical actions within Spanish football has existed for some time. This was the case long before discussions about a "relationship-based game." Rather, in football it was and is always to have a strong onfield understanding within the team—of both tendencies and typical behaviors of one's teammates. We will explore this concept further in the chapter on "Shared Intentions". However, Gagliardi tries to further define this term:

75 Video recording of Xabi Alonso's first press conference in 2022.
76 Alonso quoted in Cáceres 2023.
77 Gagliardi 2023.

"It is clear that the entire game of football is full of relationships, and every game model involves relationships. The big difference, however, is that in positional play the potential relationships develop from the positions, whereas in relationism play the potential positions develop from the relationships. This seems like a philosophical difference, but it is not. Quite simply, in positional play the most important element is the position of the players. The defensive structure of a team is planned beforehand (i.e. positioning), and in general the same applies to the offensive structure. The focus in positional play therefore remains on the positions; it is from here that the movements and relationships develop.
[We can, however, state that] (...) building a more fluid and dynamic team with more freedom for the players and a greater focus on the individual brings, and will bring better result. In relationism football, the focus is on the characteristics of the players and their relationships with each other. This paves the way for new positions that players take on the field."[78]

Presently the best example of this type of football in the world is Fluminense (Brazil), coached by Fernando Diniz, but there are also some examples in Europe that are developing independently, such as Thiago Motta's time with Bologna, in Italy, Henrik Rydström's Malmö in Sweden or even, at the time, the Hungarian national team coached by Marco Rossi. These tendencies can also be seen in Bayer Leverkusen's football under Xabi Alonso.

However, one should respect and understand the steps within the development process: In order for an idea to become increasingly flexible and to be implemented in changing contexts, a stable foundation is firstly necessary, which does not mean that it has to be set in a restrictive way.

Xabi Alonso himself puts it this way: "On the pitch I was encouraged to make my own decisions. This is something I really want to develop and something I tell the players again and again. They are not robots."[79] "They have the knowledge of what can happen and the qualities to decide. And if they make a bad decision, we will try to do better," explains Alonso, who sees himself as a supporter of the players. The decisive factor is the players' awareness of having "their own judgment on the pitch."[80]

The evolution of Xabi Alonso's style of play, which can be observed up to this point, also shows a change towards more flexibility and intuitive play after the

78 Gagliardi & Bordin 2024.
79 Alonso cited in France 24 online 2023.
80 Ibid.

team's stable foundation and the security has been achieved. However, the fact that this is a gradual process and occurs as a natural evolution is crucial, because in the challenging situation Bayer Leverkusen found itself when he took office in autumn 2022, probably only a few players would have been helped by terms such as "freedom" and "relationship"—regardless of whether Xabi Alonso actually uses these terms today or probably does not.

However, relationship-based play and clear interaction were key in his game, as we will explore in later chapters. Gagliardi further focuses on the concept of "relationship" in a way that helps us to understand Xabi Alonso's approach, and the interpretation and implementation of his players more clearly: "It is therefore the 'relationship' with the ball, with the teammates, with the opponents—the relationship with the environment—that determines and influences the movements, the decisions, the game of each player."[81] Xabi Alonso himself said in an interview that they would talk less about individual formations or game systems. Instead, the focus would rather be on the things that would probably happen in the game and where the advantage would emerge.[82] The focus is clearly on the qualities of the team's own players. Alonso continued: "The more passes we play, the more of them in their half, the better positioned we are for counter-pressing. If we play too quickly and too far into the other half, it will be impossible to counter-press."[83] Therefore, only the relationship to the ball organizes the game in every aspect, be it spatially or in interaction with the other players. Antonio Gagliardi succeeds in giving a fantastic description of the game of Xabi Alonso's team, albeit unintentionally and without knowing it:

"This style of football is able to highlight the qualities, characteristics, and emotions of the players, especially the more technical ones, also because the connection between the players makes everyone a little happier. This style of football is not afraid to adopt an asymmetrical form, and does not want to dominate possession through tactics and predefined spaces, but through technique and dynamic spaces. The focus shifts from the space to the ball, and to the players. In positional football, the space occupied is fundamental to achieve a better performance; in relationship football, it is individual performance that determines the space."[84]

81 Gagliardi 2023.
82 Alonso in video clip on X; 2023.
83 Alonso 2023.
84 Gagliardi 2023.

As already mentioned at the beginning, clear demarcations, as well as extreme statements such as "always" or "never" are often difficult and counterproductive in football. The same applies to the clear distinction between the supposedly "outdated" positional game and the "modern" relationism game: When we speak to the coaches themselves, very few of them have the intention of coining exactly this term. Rather, their ideas and decisions depend on what they see as most promising for their team in the given situation and context.

Therefore, I would like to make the reader aware that both positional play and relationship play have many faces and expressions, and that there are many interpretations of football in between, as the question of belonging to one camp or the other is less relevant than the question of how the next game can be won in conjunction with one's own idea, one's own players and one's own team. However, it is worth taking along some overarching key ideas.

Current Ajax coach Francesco Farioli notes that the key concept is "dynamic equilibrium". One can speak of a "dynamic equilibrium" when things or organizations are balanced, but react extremely adaptably to changes, and then try to establish a (new) equilibrium again in the course of their self-organization. For Farioli, the challenge is to get players "more and more used to exploring different areas of the pitch, with increasingly diverse skills. (...) Today, the dynamics of the game, the contrasts, the constant changes of modules, and the training itself lead players more and more to less specific but definitely broader knowledge."[85] Farioli also refers to the approach, already expressed with regards to complex systems, of competitive advantage gained through improved adaptability to changing circumstances by his team.[86]

An additional approach to the game model and game mode, that has not yet been discussed much, is the idea of shared values and their influence on the effective interaction of a team, and how this can be further exploited. This particularly concerns instructions, restrictions or rules that influence the interaction of a team and the actions of an individual. Each actor is influenced by the "character of the social institution (e.g., club, government, etc.) and the social order (culture) in which he lives."[87] These influences interact and act on different time scales.

In summary, it can be said that "personal values and competition rules (...) can

85 Farioli quoted from Gagliardi 2023.
86 Ibid.
87 Vaughan et al. 2022.

change over decades, but the fatigue and behavior of fans (...) can change within days or months, and the internal load and the game situation (...) within seconds or minutes."[88] The same can be said for the individual motivational states of the players: "The goal of having a successful sports career, for example, takes longer to achieve than the goal of winning a championship, winning a game or gaining possession of the ball during the game."[89]

There are several aspects that the coach can take away from this, because with a view to the more or less dynamically changing conditions or clues of the players, it can make sense to rely on something that already exists collectively, such as shared values, and to live by them. Clear sporting actions can also be derived from this. The principle of "We support each other" can be applied to many different areas on and off the pitch: Not only is clear mutual support required off the pitch in the event of any problems, but this value or principle is also visible on the pitch in a way that there are always a variety of passing options for the player in possession of the ball or that no one is left alone to defend when the opponent is in possession of the ball, but that every defensive action is supported accordingly and absorbed by their own compensatory movement. Interestingly, this approach was also part of the training of one of the best football teams in recent history, FC Barcelona. As Barça's long-time head methodologist, Paco Seirul·lo, writes in his book *ADN Barça*, there is "the double idea: 'I help my partner, I help myself, and we help our team', which should activate the initiative of the teammates in that moment, and throughout the rest of the game."[90] This clear reference to shared values, which are translated into football actions, can also be found in other successful football teams: For example, the motto "Everyone is responsible for everything" at Liverpool FC during Jürgen Klopp's tenure helped the players, among other things, to make independent decisions when pressing, regardless of whether the opponent acted in the predicted mode or not.[91] Fairly often, it is not decided in the first action whether the approach is 'right' or 'wrong', but depends on whether the teammates pick up the thought or intention of the action and pull along accordingly. Analogous to theater, where a deviation from the script goes unnoticed thanks to good improvisation and can even reveal better content than what was originally conceived, the same applies here. However, in order someone preferred - for someone to be able to improvise, it often helps to maintain a

88 Balagué et al. 2019.
89 Ibid.
90 Seirul·lo 2024.
91 Matos 2021.

certain level of confidence in the basic actions and behaviors. The moment our decision-making is based on shared values, we can follow and implement them even under maximum stress or in situations of extreme fatigue.

The second aspect relevant for the coach relates to training: As Balagué et al. note: "it makes little sense to propose tasks detached from the game to activate specific metabolic pathways (e.g., aerobic/anaerobic), since physiological/bio-chemical activation occurs as a consequence of a context of conditions when players respond to task characteristics. Trainer instructions (...) should primarily relate to processes that develop over longer periods of time, e.g., values, goals and strategies. Instructions that prescribe specific action solutions (e.g., in relation to technical skills such as dribbling, passing, shooting, etc.) which can change in very short periods of time during a game, can compete with the actively perceived possibilities of the players and be counterproductive."[92] However, if the coach appeals to the common goals and values, that is, the overarching, less quickly changing aspects within the conditions that shape our behavior, the players are more quickly ready to carry out certain actions and acts. This is especially true if the players see this as useful for achieving their personal, over-arching goal, that was addressed by the coach or if this central value (e.g., "We help each other") is important to them personally. Subsequently, it depends on the coach's ability to repeatedly address these values *through action* to emphasize the connection between the formulated value and the action played, and not to allow the formulated values to degenerate into empty phrases.

Juanma Lillo uses very figurative language when describing the way his team should play football and the process to get there:

> *"The move is not always the same, the opponent changes. That is why I speak of culture (...). You know that a deep, round bowl is useful for soups, and a spoon too. For a steak, you need a flat plate and a sharp knife and fork. But you need to know whether what is being served to you is actually soup or steak. You need to understand what you are dealing with before you can decide which tools to use.*
> *Another example: you confuse a map with the territory. I know where to go to get home; I even have a satellite navigation device to help me. But that's the map, not the area. It doesn't tell me if there are construction sites or if a*

---

92 Balagué et al. 2019.

dog is running out in front of me. That's what I mean by culture: you have to know how to react, when to brake, and when to swerve. The map shows you where to go, the route you can take, but not how to get there. (...) We build a common language through which we understand what we do. Often this language is not even conscious; it is an understanding."[93]

In summary, the following can be said about the game model:

→ The game model is based on the coach's game idea and depends on numerous external factors.

→ The game model should fit the culture lived by the coach (and ideally the entire club) and express this in football terms.

→ The game model depends on the individual characteristics, qualities and abilities of the players.

→ The game model organizes the interaction of a team according to certain rules and behavioral patterns that follow a decision-making hierarchy. These rules are usually called "game principles", but can also be generally described in terms of the "intentions" of a team.

→ The appropriately organized style of play gives the team a dinstinctive identity within its playing behavior and, basically, aims to simplify the organized interaction of the team. In particularly successful game models, emphasis is also placed on bringing out the unique qualities of each player.

→ The game model is reflected in through the implementation or interpretation of the game idea by the players.

→ Each game model is intended to provide orientation and, on this basis, is flexible and in a state of continuous change as part of future-oriented development.

→ A game model fundamentally includes the organizational design of all game moments and summarizes them into higher-level behaviors. In a successful game model these behaviors should fit together and interlock, as the different game moments are interdependent and linked. For example, counter-pressing is difficult when the team in possession of the ball operates at extremely large distances.

93 Lillo 2011.

"Be aware that during the attack process, I generate the future defensive conditions and vice versa."[94]
ÓSCAR CANO

→ Even if the general principles of the game or common intentions of the team are formulated as broadly as possible, this does not preclude going into more detail in certain areas and further defining concrete, position-specific behaviors. The crucial point is that the game model always serves as an orientation and decision-making aid for the players, and does not restrict their actions or slow down their intuitive, quick decisions.

→ Every coach is able to develop his own game model based on his individual characteristics, preferences and ideas. This game model remains changeable and must be adapted to the current team (and other external factors), but will retain its core over the years.

The founder of **Tactical Periodization**, Prof. Vítor Frade, once said about the concept of the game model that the *"model"* is like the dress of a model walking down the catwalk: everyone around would admire it and subsequently try to copy it, however, without deciphering the actual idea and intention behind it.[95] The same applies to the coach's game idea and the resulting game model as an interpretation of the players in relation to their personal characteristics and their individuality.[96]

94 Cano 2012.
95 Frade 2020.
96 Ibid.

A Tactical Dictionary – Basic Understanding

A famous quote by Spanish football philosopher and Pep Guardiola's current assistant coach, Juanma Lillo, which is very popular among his supporters, is: "There is no better tactical book in football than the official rules."[97]
The rules, as long-time Barça coach Joan Vila says, are fundamental because they define the space (the playing field), the objectives (scoring one goal more than your opponent), the actions, the consequences of these actions, and the restrictions (everything that is not allowed).[98] In the hierarchy of rules, the offside rule in football is by far the most important as it determines the available playing space. At the same time, there are (tactically speaking) several ways to "play" with the offside rule, since being offside is not punishable *per se*, but only if you touch the ball or actively intervene in the game. It is also essential to know when the offside rule does not apply (goal kick, throw-in and corner kick). A striker can become "invisible" to the defenders through his clever positioning, for example by deliberately placing himself offside and simply observing his team's passing and waiting for the right moment. Through his positioning he conditions his opponents, who must constantly keep an eye on him to be able to control him, which means that they are less able to keep an active eye on the ball. At the same time, this often causes the space between the lines to become larger. Should the defending players of the last line still be more focused on the ball (because the ball is a strong "magnet" of attention)[99], this enables the striker to move unnoticed from an offside position, where he can receive a pass and become a goal threat. Alternatively, if the defensive line is bypassed, he can use his advanced position and movement advantage to threaten the goal with a second action.

97 Lillo 2016.
98 Vila 2023.
99 Ibid.

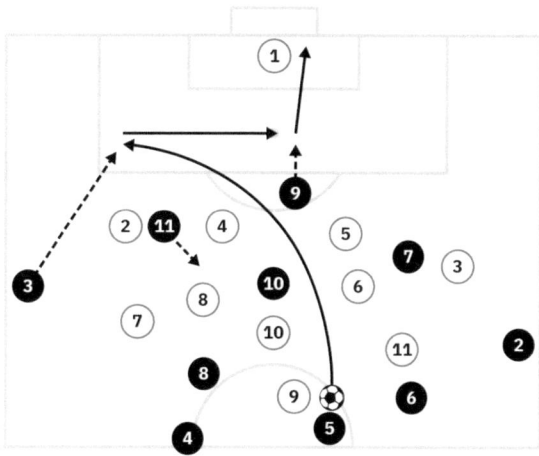

The striker deliberately positions himself offside in order to exploit the positional advantage in the next phase of play.

It helps the striker if he is constantly in a diagonal position to both the ball and the nearest defender. To ensure this, the striker can move against the ball's movement, thereby simultaneously evading the attention of the opposing defenders.[100] It is advisable not only for the striker but also for all other players to position themselves in such a way that they can overcome the opponent directly through their ball control and their first contact with the ball.

All players are positioned diagonally to the ball and their opponents to minimize the opponents' reach as effectively as possible.

100 Ibid.

Playing with the opponent's attention is an art for the teammates who offer themselves when they have possession of the ball: There are moments when players consciously try to draw their opponent's attention to themselves to give a teammate elsewhere has an advantage. Then again, there are moments when players remain active in the game even though the opponent has almost "forgotten" them, such as after a deep run where they didn't get the ball. Repositioning and reorganization at this point can help create the next advantage, since the opponent's attention is currently elsewhere.

In football, viewed as a game of positioning and spaces, the spaces play a major role in the "typically Spanish" view, some of which can also be found in the view of Xabi Alonso's game philosophy and are of great importance.

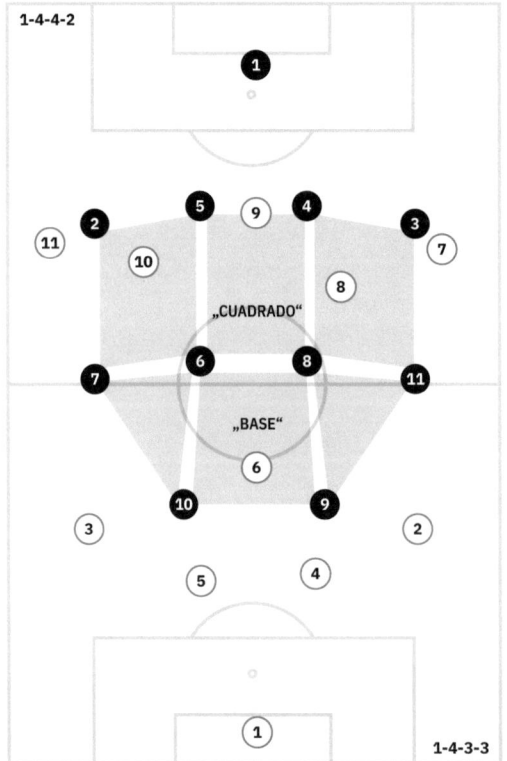

Dynamic spaces "Base" & "Cuadrados" for the white team (own illustration):

The "base" is always located behind the opponent's first defensive and must always be occupied. When No. 6 moves out, someone else must take his place.

"Cuadrados" are created behind the midfield line and in front of the opposing defensive line whenever these lines can be pulled apart. When I position myself, I should be careful not to block a passing line through my positioning.

When talking about tactics and spaces on the field in Spain, two central spaces are given priority: the so-called *base* and the *cuadrados (squares)*. The *"base"* refers to the holding-midfielder (6) space, which is always behind the opposing strikers or the opponent's first line of defense. Accordingly, the positioning of this space is dynamic, as it is dependent on the opponent. This space is the most important space for all advocates of possession-oriented play, as it gives the team stability, balance, and the best options for ball circulations. Regarding Bayer Leverkusen's game, we can see that this space is also always occupied, often by two, and at times even by three players (such as Wirtz, Hofmann, Adli).

"Cuadrados" are the squares that form the space between the midfield line and the opponent's defense line. If you draw the squares in both the opponent's half of the field and your own half, you get a total of six zones in the midfield. In the classic interpretation of FC Barcelona's 1-4-3-3, these six zones are always occupied either in a 1-2, 2-1 or 2-2 formation. This does not always have to be done by the central midfielders, but can also be done by dropping full-backs, wingers, or the central striker in order to create an imbalance for the opponent. Bayer Leverkusen frequently and strategically utilizes this space from a variety of positions, thereby repeatedly creating positional advantages.

Within possession, a distinction is made between three basic objectives when playing a pass: The ball is moved to "give continuity" to the game *("dar continuidad")*—i.e., to allow the ball to flow; to advance play *("progresar")* or to threaten the opponent *("amenazar")*.

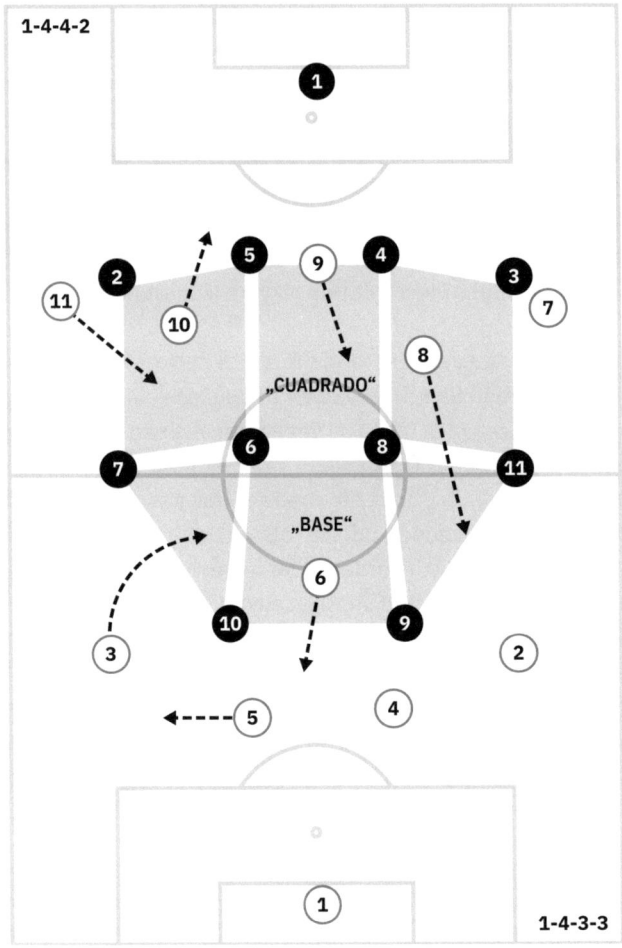

Dynamic scope of the White Team (own representation): With structural changes (1-2, 2-1, or 2-2).

The most frequently used game principles are often understood in Spanish football as metaphorical expressions with an inviting character, which, however, is often not position-bound.

Here are some examples:

→ *Winning the back* – Especially within the squares we want to be played in the back of our opponent.

→ *Fixing* – Means binding the opponent, especially through strategic positioning. However, this can also happen by stopping the ball (e.g., with the sole), provided the intention is the following:

→ *Attract* – I want to draw the opponent out of position, for example through the concept of the "repeated pass" (*repetir pase*) or by stopping the ball with the sole.

→ *(Line)breaking free runs* – These are deep runs through the defensive gaps. The space between the central defender and the full-back is particularly preferred. This is sometimes referred to as "piercing".

→ *Threaten* – Through my positioning and body alignment, I constantly threaten the opponent, especially because my actions can potentially make me a goal threat.

→ *"Causing damage"* – This is the basic task and intention that every player on the pitch should pursue and must fulfill.

→ *"Follow the shadow"* – Means using the covering shadow of the approaching opponent by positioning ourselves in it and then stepping forward to become playable. By following, we also evade the reach of our next opponent, who will normally not pursue us. A more proactive formulation could be *"use the shadow"*.

→ *"Change line"* – Means that we, as the offering player, adjust the passing line or passing axis to become playable.

→ Delayed one-two – A one-two that is not played directly, but which has a significant tactical value due to its time delay. For example, it allows the teammate more time to run to the next position while the opponent's attention is focused on the new ball carrier. This player can attract more defenders, who are then bypassed, while the recipient of the delayed one-two has moved almost unnoticed into a better position. In Brazilian football, there is also the term *"tabela"*, which means "to build a table together" or "to sit there together", like a family sitting together at the table while eating.[101] This already implies a special connection between them. In addition, the term does not necessarily mean a "direct one-two" but can, as already mentioned, be delayed to give the teammate more advantages.

→ Pass against the direction of movement of the opponent (*jugar contrapie*) in order to surprise the defense.

→ *"Pausa"* – A brief delay to acelerate the game afterward. Example: I hold the ball briefly so that the opponent sets both feet, bringing him to a stand-still, before generating speed with the next action.

→ *"Foot and space"* – Passing options in the attacking third, allowing the ball holder to play both *"into the foot"* and *"into space"* (deep into the run).

→ Support – in Spanish football terminology, this refers more to as passing option, since "support" can be expressed in various ways. Additionally, support can mean reinforcing a movement or dribble by having a second player just behind the ball carrier, creating an outlet while simultaneously acting as a feint for the opponent. The latter struggles to control both the dribbler and the supporting runner. At the beginning of 2019, DFB analyst Dr. Stephan Nopp discussed an example involving Leo Messi and Luis Suárez during a lecture, describing an "asymmetric 2v2 situation" that was merely impossible to defend. In this sense, it is beneficial to create these situations repeatedly when in possession.

→ Connecting actions/situations (*encadenar acciones*) – Follow-up actions, in the sense of "play and go". Start the next action directly and become an important factor in the next moment of play. The goal is not only to be a passing option for my teammate but also to challenge the opponent through positioning, fullfilling at least two functions simultaeously, such as:

    ↳ Provide continuity and security.
    ↳ Offer and create a thread for the opponent, or at least attract defensive attention.
    ↳ Change line to enable continued play.
    ↳ Anticipate the next passing connection and act as the third or fourth target player.

101 Hamilton 2023.

The goal of ball possession is always to disorganize and destabilize the opponent. It is not the number of passes that matters, but rather how effectively and efficiently the overarching goal of creating a high-quality goal-scoring opportunity is reached. The flow of the ball continually creates new spaces that can be used by the players in possession and leads to a certain fluidity through position changes. At the same time, these emerging spaces can be attacked by deep runs, allowing a shift in pace and rhythm for the team in possession.

Xabi Alonso himself sees this as a key factor. In an interview with the Spanish newspaper *El País* following the World Cup in Qatar, he said: "The ball must be played inwards-outwards-inwards and from left to right. If it only goes horizontally... If they [the opposition] defend with two back fours and move horizontally, they don't tire, but if you pass inside and outside and move them from front to back, it creates space. The problem is not the short pass, but that you only play with the ball and forget to attack the space. The problem is how to attack the space to get the ball there. Sacrificial runs are becoming increasingly important, those you make when you know the ball is probably not coming to you but that serve to create space."[102] Alonso emphasizes the tempo (or ryhtm) shift as a key element within possession-based play: "The problem is not possession, but the lack of change of pace and depth. If you have too many players behind the ball, it becomes difficult. Because it's about creating spaces and attacking. In my opinion, spaces are created through what are called 'sacrifice runs'. By luring the opponent out of their reserve through possession of the ball and being well positioned to defend if the ball is lost and to be able to attack again once the ball has been regained."[103]

The tactical means used for this are independent of the specific design of the game idea, and are consistently observed despite the most diverse formations and systematic arrangements. As former Real Madrid U18 coach Fran Beltrán explains: "in the first attack phase (...) it is about creating an initial numerical superiority and paying attention to the distances between the goalkeeper, central defenders and central midfielders. The players near the ball holder should not be more than fifteen to twenty meters away. Repeated passes ['*repetir pase*'] and variability in the initial passing sequences to attract one or another player and release the following [players] [find the free man]. [Players should not be positioned on the same](...) axes (...) and should play at different heights to open up the previous lines."[104]

102   Alonso in Torres 2023.
103   Alonso in Cáceres 2023.
104   Beltran in Ballesteros 2020.

Within the Spanish football methodology, there is a clear expectation that players understand what they can provoke or trigger in their opponents through their movements and positioning on the pitch, opening up a range of alternative options.[105] Spanish coach Rubén de la Barrera instructs his team to prioritize occupying certain key areas to unsettle the opposing organization, "by trying to prevent them from recognizing direct opponents. It is a game of references and stimuli, and identifying certain stimuli to change the references is the key to influencing and destabilizing the opposing organization. Everything is moving while we remain stable."[106]

Recognizing these cues and references within the game and reacting to them according to one's own intentions also aims to sustain one's own structured and consistent behavior patterns, remaining independent of the opponent's game idea and as adaptible as possible. This requires a high level of knowledge and a fundamental understanding of the game from the players, as their perception and attention are constantly challenged.

105 Cano 2012.
106 de la Barrera in Ballesteros 2020.

A Typically Spanish Element – Positional Play

"You never play if an opponent doesn't come out."[107]
PEP GUARDIOLA

"Don't pass if you don't want to create anything. Pass to overcome lines! Look for the third man and the second action; give the ball to the furthest away. Create superiority in the next line. Don't pass sideways if you don't want to create anything."[108]
JUAN MANUEL LILLO

An association that is used almost synonymously with *"Spanish football"* is the idea of positional play. As we have already seen in our analysis of different game models, there is also a broad spectrum within this interpretation of football. There are now various nuances of the idea of positional play, ranging from the traditional interpretation, in which the players operate strictly "within their positions" and wait for the ball there, to the highly dynamic interpretation in which the players travel together with the ball and, in constant interaction, try to create

107 Guardiola quoted in Fernandez 2012.
108 Lillo quoted in Fernandez 2012.

advantages through their positioning and attack the opponent's goal. This requires a high degree of synchronization, which is why the relationships between the players also play a major here. This style of football cannot be interpreted by a team that does not support each other well or lacks a basic level of footballing empathy.

Before Pep Guardiola' tenure in Munich, only a few Germans had a clear idea of what lays behind positional play. Guardiola's then-assistant coach Domènec Torrent remembers: "(...) in Munich they thought it was a method to keep possession of the ball. No! It's about much more! It's about learning how to position yourself when you have the ball, where to move when you don't have it to apply pressure. (...) Positional play exercises contain everything, and they are so important to Pep because positional play adds pace and meaning to a game. (...) What they were doing was the essence of football: losing the ball, pressing, regaining it, spreading out—the ball is back to us again."[109]
Abel Mourelo describes the essence of positional play as follows: "It is a feeling for the game. It's *the* game. I want the ball and I want to possess it with the intention of causing you damage. I don't want to play to have it; I want to have it to play. I want to hurt you [with the ball]. And if I can hurt you with three passes, then I will. If I need twenty, I'll play twenty. (...) And when I (...) [have the ball], I work on certain movements and balancing situations so that if I don't have it, I can get it back as quickly as possible—and that I am protected. That my attack and my compensations in attack change the game cycle the moment I have it, trying to achieve the advantages in the most ideal way and with the necessary passes."[110] In particular, Mourelo's emphasis on feeling for the game—which defines positional play at its best—stands in contrast to the perception of positional play as a rigid and automated system that some coaches believe it to be. There are no absolutes: long balls are also part of the repertoire of positional play, as the game is based on creating and exploiting advantages for one's own team. Mourelo explains: "(...) And if there are no [advantages], we have to create them—like free spaces. You create them, recognize, and exploit them. Where do I have advantages? If I have them there, then they are there. The difference is how I get there, which is in two ways: how I get the ball there and what I do when the ball gets there. In this way, you often change the flow of your opponent's game."[111] The successful Italian coach Luciano Spalletti emphasises this

109 Torrent in Perarnau 2016.
110 Mourelo in Ballesteros 2020.
111 Ibid.

evolution: "There are no more patterns in football. The spaces are no longer between the lines, but between the players, and the art is to find these spaces."[112] This further reshapes the classic interpretation of positional play, which once saw players simply holding their positions and waiting for the ball.

Spanish coach Carles Martínez, who currently works for Toulouse FC in the France's Ligue 1, describes the idea of positional play as follows:

"For me, positional play is more than a position and ensuring that everyone occupies one—it is about reading the spaces. We have to use these spaces, occupy them, clear them or create them to our advantage. If the opponent gives you little space to cause damage, at some point, you have to attack the back, attack from the outside, or position the key players in areas where they will draw attention—so that the spaces you want to exploit, which were previously small, become large. The problem with everything we've discussed is that, in the end, timing is everything."[113]

To understand positional play, it is crucial to study its defensive counterpart and understand key defensive concepts. It's about knowing how the opponent will respond to your attacking movement within his defensive intention and being able to anticipate and counteract.

"That's why training is very important—so that the player understands the timing, the moment,, and (…) [so] the 'before' ."[114] Due to the importance of timing, as mentioned above, the concept of "space-time" has developed in FC Barcelona's methodology. In a sport like football, speed alone does not lead to success. Opportunity is the precise moment in which one intervenes with a specific action at the right time. The goal in football is not to act quickly, but at the optimal moment.

"Time is determined by space and vice versa. Space, time and opportunity are three closely related variables. One variable cannot be understood without the other. The time allotted for a particular player's intervention is reduced if they are closer to the opponent's goal. In most game situations there is little time to intervene."[115]

ROBERT MORENO

112 Spalletti in Gagliardi 2023.
113 Martínez in Benedetti 2020.
114 Ibid.
115 Moreno 2013.

Control of space is an essential variable for occupying and creating space. Looking at the player profiles, it is worth considering which type of player and character I,, as a coach, want to have in specific areas of the pitch against different opponents, each with their own individual characteristics.

Carles Martínez places particular emphasis on a player's behavior before receiving the ball, as this "before" moment is fundamental for what happens afterward:

"A very clear situation: The center-back has the ball, and a [own] winger is perfectly positioned, creating doubts in the opposition winger—this is essential. For example, if you are at a distance where you know you are drawing attention to your target, what do you generate? Space for an inner player [8]. On the other hand, if you see that your opponent's outside player is entirely focused on the inside player, your positioning must change because you will be the one to advance play. Then small details are coming: If the outside player is marking the man, and you move into space [or 'break' an opponent's positional line], the outside player will almost always follow you.

But there are certain key moments. For example, when the winger in a defensive situation The moment the ball unconsciously shifts inward— because the ball attracts attention—the winger turns his body and looks inward. When that happens, it's the perfect time for the outside player to say 'now' I can surprise, I've arrived in my outside lane, while my opponent is no longer attached to me.' The same principle applies to center-backs. Some center-backs wait for the pass to react to the opponent's movement, unaware of what came before. Others position themselves perfectly with the [opposing] striker and surpass him—but at a height where the striker can nitiate movement, creating space for the No. 6. Most importantly, what they gain from close interaction is time.

If, in the end, we manage to attract the [opposing] outside player, if the center has been positioned exactly right, if the inside player has moved in front of his central counterpart to pull him along and create an attraction, and if the outside player times his movement perfectly—what have we built up little by little? Everyone has created time and space—space-time—so that this player receives the ball exactlywhere we wanted, but with time and space. And at this moment, the player must have the freedom to say: Do I play from foot to foot? Do I pass? Do I open up for the wide lane? (...) The

'before' is very important and is sometimes not given adequate considera-
tion. If the ten players on the pitch concentrate on understanding what to
do in the 'before', the 'during' (...) and the 'after' become much easier."[116]

The specific sequence that Martínez describes focuses on the chain of actions
and the off-the-ball interaction in the game, which ensure that the opponent is
destabilized and thrown off its organization and that one's own advantages are
created to execute one's intended game plan.These actions are interconnected
and mutually dependent. Therefore, the players constantly interacting through
both, verbal and non-verbal communication and must remain highly attentive to
one another. This allows them to execute corresponding and coordinated movements and runs, which do not necessarily have to be pre-rehearsed but rather
follow the structural rules and principles of the team as defined in the game
model and to support their own game intention.

The implementation of positional play is often misunderstood because it is not
about passing for the sake of passing.[117] Juan Manuel Lillo, one of the most influ-
ential figures in modern positional play, expresses the essential goal as follows:
"This game consists of creating superiority behind the line that puts you under
pressure."[118]
The idea is to use ball possession and quick combinations in tight spaces to free
up teammates positioned further away. Several aspects should be taken into
account here:[119]

→ To facilitate the creation of different passing routes, players should be
   positioned at varying heights ("levels" or "floors").

→ If necessary, wide players must stretch the field to creat space in the
   central areas.

→ The concept of the "free player"—often found through a third-man pass—is
   essential.

→ Players don't pass aimlessly but recognize when the game requires a pass
   versus a dribble.

116 Martínez in Benedetti 2020.
117 Fernández 2012.
118 Lillo in Fernández 2012.
119 Fernández 2012.

→ Dribbling can lure the opponents and create space for "free players".

→ Superiority should be created behind the first pressing line, targeting the ball carrier.

→ Diagonal positioning creates "passing triangles", allowing progression and maintaining fluidity in play.

→ Superiority must be built from the back, making a clean build-up phase crucial.

→ The ball carrier should always aim to destabilize the opponent, "eliminate him", and impose his team's playing style.

→ The team travels together with the ball.

→ If possession is lost, compact positioning enables an immediate ball recovery. The way we attack determines the way we defend and therefore the way our opponent plays.

→ Constantly scanning for deep runs and goal-threatening opportunities.

"We must travel together, not just on the same train, but in the same carriage."[120]
JUANMA LILLO

When executed effectively, positional play has a number of key consequences:[121]

→ A maximum number of teammates are drawn to the opponent's half around the ball.

→ Counter-pressing and regaining the ball together become easier by positioning close to the ball.

→ By maintaining our own game flow, we minimize the opponent's actions as much as possible.

In the pursuit for the best and most precise definition of the elementary components of positional play, Juanma Lillo reflects:

"We call it positional play, but this term is not very precise. We can ask ourselves: Can one be well positioned but stand poorly? Or the other way

---

120 Lillo in Perarnau 2016.
121 Cano 2012.

around: standing well but poorly positioned? Naturally! So it can happen that you have the right posture but are in the wrong place. Or you are in the right place, but with the wrong attitude. Both aspects are related to the sequence of actions—what happened just before, and with what you intend to do next to maintain the game's flow. Therefore, it might be better to speak of 'positioning play', because this term implies a tactical intention."[122]

Within positional play in training, the coach typically sets an intention regarding the task, positioning, and roles that players should adopt within a given space. However, at the same time, players are given the freedom to adjust dynamically to the situation and optimize their positioning based on the game context, thereby bringing the training form to life.[123] The same principle should apply in matches, as football is unpredictable, and the players must make independent decisions based on the game situation. In the chapter on training proposals, we explore some ideas for training contexts that help players develop the best positioning together.

A key technical action in positional play is the pass. This not only connects two players but also involves further technical and tactical actions: in the "before", the pass offer and in the "after", the ball reception or the follow-up action, direct forwarding or finalization.

Within the various ways to create a passing option (*apoyo* in Spanish, meaning support or help), longtime Barça coach Joan Vila distinguishes eight different types:[124]

→ *"Appear" / "Emerge"*– Move into space to offer a passing option that surprises the opponent. Goal: help the teammate!

→ *"Continuity"* – Maintain possession and keep the game flowing without immediately advancing towards the opponent's goal. Goal: Retain ball possession!

→ *"Overcome"* (horizontal or vertical axis) – Break through opponents through positioning—either by a forward pass or a lateral switch of play. Goal: Break opponent's lines or bypass defenders!

→ *"To finalize"* – Create a direct scoring opportunity. Goal: Score!

122 Lillo in Perarnau 2016.
123 Torrent in Perarnau 2016.
124 Vila 2023.

→ *"Third Player"* – Use a third player when no direct passing line is available. Joan Vila distinguishes between vertical and horizontal third-player involvement. Goal: Facilitate progression for the second player!

→ *"Support as a Magnet"* – Draw defenders toward you without intending to receive the pass.

→ *"Attraction"* – Position yourself as a goal threat, forcing your direct opponent to focus on you, freeing up time and space for the ball carrier.

→ *"Simulate" / "Block"* – Deceive your opponent or impede him (e.g., by making a run) to create time and space for your team.

In his book *ADN Barça*, Paco Seirul·lo lists further indirect passing options and support movements:[125]

→ Suppressing (*the opponent's actions*)
→ Predefined / rehearsed routes
→ Deceiving (the opponent):
  ↳ Blocking
  ↳ Unanticipated "appearance"
  ↳ Feinting
  ↳ Two players occupying the same space, creating uncertainty for the opponent.

All this applies in particular to the "stage spaces" of mutual support and cooperation (see chapter on stage spaces). The following basic requirements apply:[126]

1. Every passing option must have a clear intention (ideally for the collective). The guiding principle here could be: "Always anticipate the next action." There is a strong connection here to the concept of shared intentions, which will be discussed later in this book.

2. The goal is always to provide the ball carrier with the best possible solutions—ideally at least two options at the same time.

3. Offer passing lines ("communication channels"), preferably diagonally, to stay open to the game.

4. Pass recipient: Offer the best possible support based on the most effective, situation-appropriate intention. Manage opponent pressure (through feints,

125 Seirul·lo 2024.
126 Vila 2023.

deceptions, etc.) to receive the ball in the best possible situation. To do this, it is essential to understand the different types of support and how to improve them. Recognize the ball carrier's intentions.

5. Ball carrier: After passing, immediately position yourself as the next passing option in a different direction to maintain the game (follow-up action).

6. A positioning in the triangle—both in depth and width—simplifies and optimizes passing options and support. (*Author's note:* It is often easier for players to discuss diagonal positioning relative to the ball, as the concept of the triangle, while simple for coaches, can be more abstract for players.).

7. When considering the best passing option, take the following into account:

   ↳ Approaching the ball carrier is not always beneficial (useful only for repeating the pass, e.g., a "bounce pass", or to lure the opponent; *repetir pase*).

   ↳ Turning your back to the ball without checking your surroundings is never a good idea.

   ↳ Position yourself laterally with a good posture/alignment to enable a diagonal passing option when advancing play (orientation).

   ↳ Keep your heels off the ground to improve your agility and coordination.

   ↳ Master the entire cognitive process to choose the best technical action when receiving the ball (scan in all four directions – complex perception).

   ↳ Adjust your timing when making off-the-ball runs to align with your teammate's actions.

   ↳ Vary your movement paths to make it harder for opponents to track and defend.

   ↳ Ensure players are positioned both in "immediate support spaces" and "cooperative spaces" (see chapter on stage spaces).

Within this process, it is crucial to maintain heightened awareness of teammates' actions (synchronicity) and to clearly communicate or anticipate intentions. In this context, FC Barcelona's so-called "4 P's" also play a central role in the implementation of the game. From *"Percepción"* (perception), *"Posición"* (position), *"Posesión"* (possession) and *"Presión"* (pressure; after losing the ball) there is a high focus on the first P, which conditions the following factors: Perception. It allows players to identify and interpret all variables on the playing field, and leads to interaction through the absorption of perceived information.

A better perception leads to better positioning, which in turn facilitates effective possession. Compact positioning makes it easier to apply pressure after losing possession, increasing the likelihood of recovering the ball quickly.

All these principles ultimately serve to create one of five different types of advantages in the game, as defined by Paco Seirul·lo:

→ Positional superiority / positional advantage (*I am in the better position.*)
→ Numerical superiority / superiority in numbers (*We outnumber the opponent.*)
→ Socio-affective superiority / socio-affective advantage (*We are better connected / we have a 'blind' (intuitive) understanding of each other.*)
→ Qualitative superiority / qualitative advantage (*I am technically or tactically superior.*)
   ↳ Within the qualitative superiority, we can also highlight a fifth type of advantage: dynamic advantage or dynamic superiority (*I am faster.*), as it plays a crucial role in potential qualitative advantages.

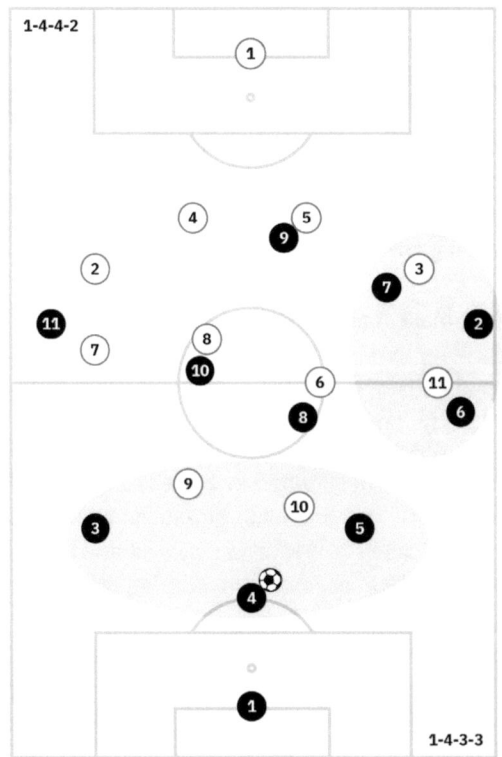

Figure: Types of Advantages in the Game (Own Illustration)

In the highlighted field areas, the black team gains a numerical superiority through smart positioning, creating a tactical advantage over the opponent.

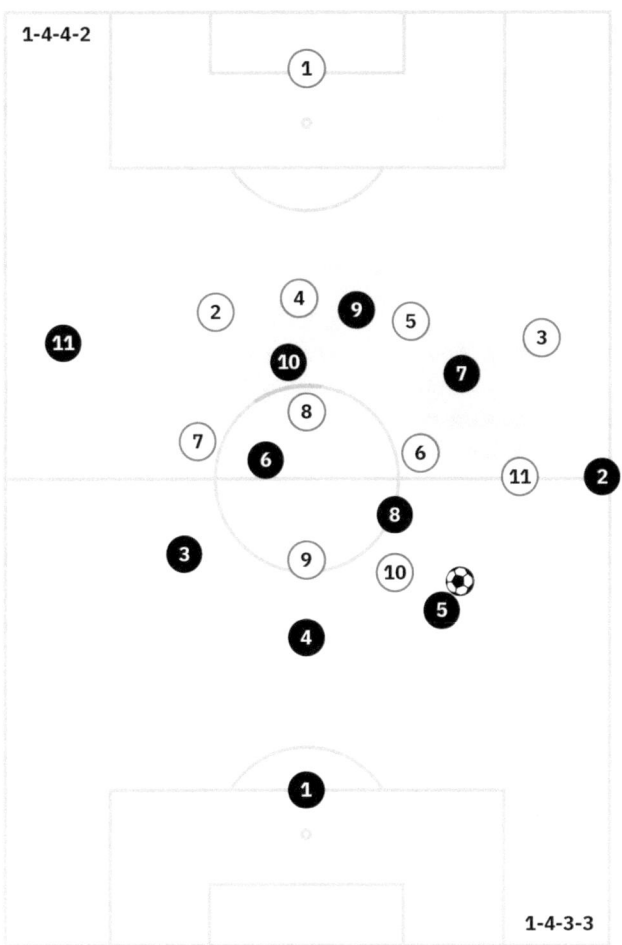

Illustration of Game Advantages (Own Illustration)
Although the black team lacks numerical superiority, the players have positional advantages.
Our right winger (7 black) stands inside the "square", staying out of reach of four opponents.
If the opposing full-back (3 white) steps forward to mark him, the space can be exploited by a
deep run from our full-back (2 black).
Our strikers and attacking midfielders (9 & 10 black) are strategically positioned, making it diffi-
cult for the opponents to control them effectively.
If play shifts, our left winger (11 black) is already positioned at "optimal width", ensuring that
when the ball is switched, he can immediately bypass the opponent.
This shift should be prepared with short passes to attract defenders and create time and space
for teammates. Optimal width means that our left winger (11 black) is positioned in such a way
that, in the event of a shift in play into space, he can immediately overcome the opponent.
Similarly, our defender (4 black), who is positioned on the same axis as his immediate oppo-
nent (9 white), allowing him to bypass the defender with his first touch.

However, Paco Seirul·lo sees "a better relationship between and among the players" as the foundation for these advantages. This involves the spatial-temporal-situational organization of our players both in both in possession and during ball recovery, as well as simultaneously in both phases, to achieve the intended tactical goal."[127] Seirul·lo explicitly refers to "relational advantages," instead of "superiority," arguing that "superiority" implies an innate characteristic.[128] Instead, he highlights the collective dimension that arises from through players' shared relationships within game spaces.[129]

Improved interconnectivity and synchronicity are also key aspects for Spanish coach Rubén de la Barrera, who defines the concept of "supra-superiority" (suprasuperioridad). This is closely linked to players recognizing how they can contribute to the team's success independent of their functional role at any given moment. The idea is to "become a functional unit where, although you play with eleven players, the team always functions as a whole. It's about collectivity, plurality, presence, and constant connection before, during, and after every game action."[130] What de la Barrera defined aligns with Vítor Frade's concept of **Tactical Periodization** as the "embodiment of the game idea", since the team is able to make flexibel decisions based on the same criteria, achieving a form of collective identification and coordinated perception in every game situation.[131]

The increasing flexibility and dynamism of football also play a major role in this evolution. In the game model section, Davide Ancelotti already highlighted adaptability as a key strength in modern football, linking it to a chameleon's ability to change color. Similarly, Professor Vítor Frade, the founder of **Tactical Periodization**, uses the same metaphor.

"A chameleon changes its color, but it never forgets that it is a chameleon."[132]
VÍTOR FRADE

This concept underscores why football training should not be limited to isolated situations. Instead, the game idea must always be trained as an indivisible whole, ensuring that the team—with all its individual qualities and unique characteristics—always functions as a conscious collective. Recognizing the roles

127 Seirul·lo 2024.
128 Ibid.
129 Ibid.
130 de la Barrera in Ballesteros 2020.
131 Reis 2021.
132 Frade quoted in Smith 2017.

and distances between players allows collecitve play to manifest fully.[133] This requires deep tactical knowledge of the game and strong game awareness from coaches and staff so that they can answer the "questions the game raises". By successfully guiding players, coaches can build trust - both in themselves and in their game idea.[134]

Spanish coach Martí Cifuentes, currently under contract at Leicester City in England, sees this as a critical factor for future success: "The ability to adapt to new demands from the opponent during a game will lead to more flexible and dynamic teams. And that requires intelligent and spatially aware players: they have to understand that the ball, opponents, and teammates all create advantages—and and that these are dynamic factors"[135]

Positional play — and the desire to dominate through possession — will remain a central pillar in modern football, regardless of its tactical variations.

At the same time, a clear trend toward a more fluid, adaptive interpretation has emerged, as demonstrated by the teams of Fluminense (Fernando Diniz, Brazil), Bologna (Thiago Motta, Italy), Malmö FF (Henrik Rydström, Sweden) and Bayer Leverkusen (Xabi Alonso, Germany). In the following chapters, we will explore how Xabi Alonso implemented this evolution at Werkself.

133 Soriano in Ballesteros 2020.
134 Soriano in Ballesteros 2020.
135 Cifuentes in Ballesteros 2020.

CHAPTER 1

Apprenticeship at home – Alonso's time at Real Sociedad San Sebastián

As with all decisions in his career, Xabi Alonso took his time to carefully think through his decisions regarding his "second" career start and did not allow himself to be seduced the allure of opportunities stemming from his status as a highly decorated former player. Alonso, who started out in Real Madrid's academy with a U14 team and quickly learned to love coaching there, explained his move to Real Sociedad San Sebastián's second team, *Sanse*, as follows: "Because I could work under professional conditions, but without the urgent need to deliver results first and foremost. I had the peace and freedom to get to know and try out myself as a trainer. I was allowed to make mistakes and learn what made me feel comfortable. You have to have a good understanding of yourself to be authentic."[136] It is this modesty and overly cautious self-assessment that not only earns the Basque a lot of sympathy, but also allows him to grow organically over time, even if, as an outsider, one always hasthe impression of seeing a coach who already appears more than ready for higher tasks. For San Sebastián's sporting director, Roberto Olabe, it was "the logical meeting place. (...) After everything he accomplished as a player, he had the humility to recognize that he needed time—time to learn."[137]

Xabi Alonso was not only helped by the fact that he was "at home", but also by his experience as a player. Roberto Olabe, who was his coach at Real Sociedad in 2002, recalls: "I remember we were in a bad situation, close to relegation to the Segunda Division, and he showed his strong personality. Even as a young player, he spoke to important players such as Darko Kovačević, Nihat Kahveci, and Mikel

136 Alonso in Cáceres 2023.
137 Olabe quoted in Romero 2021.

Aranburu. He told them what to do."[138] Xabi Alonso attributes this ability, which is now an important quality as a coach, to his upbringing and the values he learned from his father, Periko, who was once a player himself and later became a coach: "It has a lot to do with character, looking at the collective and taking responsibility to achieve the best. I learned that right at home."[139] Neither as a player nor as a coach is Alonso too shy or too prioritize succes above all else. He had to constantly adapt to make his way as a player, as Roberto Olabe remembers: "Xabi played very good football, but he was never a fast player. So he had to find his own way, and his way was knowing the game, understanding his strengths and weaknesses, and knowing how to compensate for his lack of speed."[140] In terms of Xabi's future path as a coach, Olabe sums up: His game was based on intelligence, and that can only help him as a coach."[141] The coach under whom Xabi Alonso made his debut at Real San Sebastián, Welshman John Toshack, speaks similarly about his former protégé: "Xabi was not like most boys of that age. He was incredibly mature grown-up, and disciplined. He lived football, breathed it and was utterly obessesd with ist."[142] The football-specific intelligence or the decisive speed for football, which was to make Xabi Alonso one of the best midfielders of his time, Toshack already saw in Alonso's perception: "And there Xabi was faster than everyone else. He saw things earlier, he understood situations faster. Before he got the ball, he knew what he wanted to do with it."[143] At the age of 20, Xabi became his captain.

Many years later, Xabi Alonso took his first steps in the professional field as a coach and made the conscious decision to coach the second team of "La Real": "I was starting a new career and I knew that here I would learn, that I would find the patience and support of so many people. There is a very clear model here, with support, facilities, communication—everything is very natural, very fluid. The process helps me to get to know myself, to correct things and to make mistakes. This is a place where you have a little more space to learn. The players also teach me a lot about what it means to train, play, communicate and explain."[144] Alonso quickly became very successful: He managed a stable first season in the third divison of Spanish football, and in his second season 2020/2021 he led *Sanse* to promotion to *LaLiga2*, the second division of Spanish football.

138 Olabe cited in Jones 2023.
139 Alonso quoted in Torres 2023.
140 Olabe cited in Jones 2023.
141 Jones 2023.
142 Toshack cited in Saller 2023.
143 Ibid.
144 Alonso quoted in Corrigan 2021.

As coach of the second team of "La Real", Xabi Alonso sees two tasks as particularly important: "First, to support the first team so that the players who are needed at the top are ready. But at the same time, we are in the Segunda División [at that time; January 2021, author's note] and we want to be competitive. It is a very demanding challenge, but that is what we want. It pushes us to the limits in our daily work to try to optimize the decisions we make, the meetings, the plans."[145]

Xabi Alonso's plan to learn and mature as a coach under *Sanse* is definitely working, as he revealed in an interview with Javier Cáceres in 2023: "I am not the main actor. It also helped me to train a reserve team in the shadow of the first, and away from the headlines. This allowed me to focus on the relationship with the players. When asked how I can improve young players like Turrientes, Pacheco, Karrikaburu, or Zubimendi. I realized: 'Xabi, it's not about you. It's about them!' It's about giving them the tools to get better. If they succeed, a better coach."[146]

His basic approach is shaped by his experiences as a player, but also clearly by the influence of his father: "Not in the sense that I studied him, but rather that I was born into it. I learned from him that the priority is teamwork and that were instilled at my hometown club, Real Sociedad. I was a midfielder, a six-man, and for me, the game was about generosity, not individual brilliance. The goal as a player was to have as many great players around me as possible and to make them look even better. Because if I was the best in a game, that necessarily meant that the playmaker, the attacking midfielder or the wingers hadn't been at their best. I always saw my job as providing them with good balls so that they could do things near the goal that I couldn't do myself. Now, as a coach, my role remains the same: making players better and teaching them this philosophy - just from the other side of the game."[147]

The style of play of the second team of Real Sociedad San Sebastián, coached by Xabi Alonso, was by no means the classic possession game with which the Spanish national team became world champions in 2010. Here, one team took the initiative, played dynamically forward and wanted to have the ball the whole time. The temperament and personality of the players obviously allowed for this exciting mix of game control through ball possession and maximum speed up front.

---

145 Alonso quoted in Corrigan 2021.
146 Alonso in Cáceres 2023.
147 Ibid.

Mikel Recalde, sports editor of the Spanish regional newspaper *Noticias de Gipuzkoa,* remembers: "His team was very flexible. Every game was a new world for him. Often he even left out some of the players who had stood out the most in the previous game."[148] When the opposition had the ball, Alonso was already very influenced by José Mourinho's approach, adapting to the opponent in order to gain the greatest possible control.[149] Nevertheless, even then, playing in possession of the ball was the essential aspect of coach Xabi Alonso's game.

In the 2020/2021 season, Alonso's team had an average possession of 59.8% per game, the second highest of over 100 teams that make up Spain's regional third division.[150] This is all the more remarkable for a young team that never kept the ball just for its own sake, but always attacked the opponent with a high passing frequency and vertical passes.

Sanse also achieved an extremely high pass density statistic (13.9) under Xabi Alonso, which was only slightly below Barça B's rate and was the fifth highest of the over 100 teams.[151] The next value, further reinforces the game model already established at that time, is the number of "line-breaking passes", which, at 6.41 passes per game, was the second highest value of all teams in the Spain's third division.[152]

Last but not least, Alonso was brilliant at making individual players better through detailed coaching: One player who particularly benefited from Alonso was Martín Zubimendi, who now plays for the Spanish national team. Recalde said: "A midfielder like Xabi himself, who was always there to give advice."[153]

Some of the basic ideas of his style of play, which can now also be found at Bayer Leverkusen, could already be recognized at this time, although the basic training and characteristics of the individual players were different compared to Leverkusen. Some of the concepts presented have already been explained in the introductory chapter of this book.

---

148 Recalde quoted in Weber 2022.
149 Weber 2022.
150 Ibid.
151 Ibid.
152 Ibid.
153 Recalde quoted in Weber 2022.

Structure 3-2-4-1 in possession. Compared to Leverkusen, the half-forwards have a different profile (more 8s than 10s), which is why the interpretation of the position and their role is adapted to their abilities. The central players form a square together hile positioning themselves behind their opponents, allowing them to evade their opponents' grasp. The focus is on occupying the center in order to be able to continue diagonally forward. The striker's position provides depth in the game and ties up opposing central defenders, while the wingers pin the full-backs wide. The opponent already has no access to the area between the lines and is even outnumbered there (5v4).

"Xabi is still a midfielder. And I think midfielders want to control the game. If they don't have that, they suffer greatly. He wants his team to have the ball, to be balanced, to control the space when in possession. He wants to build that midfield zone, and he wants that pivot player who can help him do that."[154]
   ROBERTO OLABE

154 Olabe cited in Jones 2023.

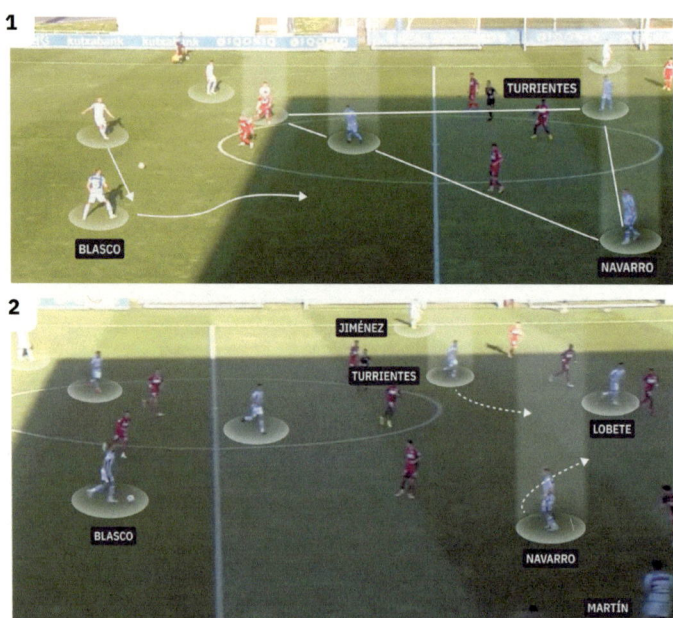

Image sequence 1/2: Blasco, who is positioned as a half-back in the three-man line, uses the space available to enable the game to progress. The space is only made possible by the positioning of the central players, who are arranged almost in a square - both 6s are very close to each other (thus tying up the strikers). Between the lines are two 8s / 10s—Navarro and Turrientes, who have the chance to immediately speed up the game by receiving the ball behind the opponent.

Image sequence 2/2: Blasco dribbles and uses the space. Navarro and Turrientes move toward the center to be close to striker Lobete and to enable a connection between the lines. Navarro feints to the outside to keep the ball in motion and speed up the game, while wingers Martín and Jiménez ensure with their wide positioning that there is enough space in the middle for the others to interact. Turrientes cuts into the back of his opponents and becomes the second striker, while Lobete consistently runs into the interface from the deep position and scores 1:0 for RSO B after a perfectly timed pass from Navarro.

There are also clear parallels to Leverkusen's opening over the halfway line: the right-sided central defender (often Kossounou in Leverkusen) dribbles intothe space. Both central midfielders are positioned close together and in the center circle. The full-back on the right (here Martín) is wide. The 8s / 10s posiion themselves between the lines and, in this situation, pin the opposing full-back, freeing *Sanse's* right sided wing-back (Martín).

There are clear parallels to Leverkusen's opening play: the right centre-back dribbles and finds the central midfielder. At the same time, the striker and the hanging forward/ intermediate player move in the opposite direction: while the striker drops back (thus drawing out the opposing centre-back), the intermediate player runs directly into the space created in the deep area. The positioning is very similar to Leverkusen.

Compared to Bayer Leverkusen, the central midfielders take on slightly different roles here: While the 10-man overloads the ball-near side, generating numerical advantage and offering passing options to sustain play or break through on the right, the second central player runs the next gap offering a close passing option. The third central mid- fielder (no. 4 / marked) attacks the depth from the centre. He benefits from his start- ing position between the lines ('cuadrado'), which makes it difficult for the opponent to pick him up (unlike, for example, Wirtz or Hofmann at Leverkusen, whose movements - though also between the lines - start from a more advanced position and are therefore easier for opponents to track. *Sanse's* positioning is also a good example of the multi-tude of promising options available to the ball possessor.

A detail that the Bayer Leverkusen players would later adopt: *Sanse's* players constantly look for the opponent's back and often position themselves between the lines, in the so-called "square" *('cuadrado')* between the midfield line and the opponent's defensive line. This positioning allows players to immediately turn when they receive the ball and increase both the sharpness and tempo of play. The teammate does not always have to be found with a diagonal pass - often a straight pass forward is enough if the players are well positioned between the lines and can be passed to in a gap.

Immediately after regaining possession of the ball, it is not rushed forward without pre-paration. By passing the ball laterally to an open player (with the whole field in view), the teammates are given time to take up their positions. At the same time, there is hardly any access by the opponents. Due to the high technical level, the small distances are sufficient to allow quick passing sequences, leading to a shot on goal within just two passes through the center. At the same time, the pass shows the communication—pass to the inside foot—as a non-verbal cue to turn and play forward.

Note the positioning of Real Sociedad B, especially when comparing it to Bayer Leverku-sen: in a 4-3 structure (from 1-3-4-3), *Sanse* penetrates into the final third. The strikers Lobete, Navarro and Alkain occupy the interfaces of the last line and are therefore all at a positional advantage ince they remain outside their opponents' defensive coverage. Also interesting: Lobete, who mainly plays the role of center-forward, drops out to the left (similar to Boniface two years later); Navarro, who has more of a number 10 profile, repeatedly makes deep runs into the attack (similar to what a certain Florian Wirtz will do later), and Alkain is agile, a strong dribbler,and always looking for the half-space (a certain similarity to Adli's behaviour is noticeable).

Real Sociedad B (RSO) positions many players between the lines - some requesting the ball to feet, others making runs into space (right players). The concept of feet and space: the deepest player has just pulled the defensive line back with his run towards the goal, forcing defenders to shift backward while staying oriented toward the ball carrier, ready to react to his next move. At the same time, RSO managed to get completely in the back of the midfield line creating numerical superiority in the space just ahead of the opoo-nent's five-man defensive line.

Image sequence 1/4
Navarro (no. 24), the eventual scorer, receives the ball in midfield, turns and accelerates. You can also see the positioning of the players in relation to each other: great proximity for combination play, diagonal passing options, and also two deep players who occupythe opposing back four.

Image sequence 2/4
Navarro draws several opponents towards him with his dribbling (*conducir para fijar*) and passes the ball to the right at the last possible moment. Both strikers occupy an interesting position close to each other, which makes it difficult for the opposing central defender to control both of them in such close proximity - especially because the follow-up movements are almost impossible to anticipate.

Image sequence 3/4
The new ball carrier feints to the right with his body and has his sole on the ball—almost stopping play and attracting opponents with this movement*(atraer)*. The entire attention of the defenders locks onto the ball, so that the full-back furthest from the ball (no. 16) can anticipate the next situation (and thus the pass) into the penalty area without an opponent. The pace increases due to another shift. We remember: the ball came from the center to the right in order to then "turn" the game back (*girar*). A striker (no. 9) engages his direct opponent through physical contact, while the other defenders are still in the space but not firmly assigned. Navarro (no. 24, highlighted) runs into the box.

Image sequence 4/4
The full-back (no. 16) who ran into the box creates a technically demanding first-touch cross into the center. There we can already see that all defenders have a positional and dynamic disadvantage and have no real chance to intervene their direct opponents. The first-touch cross is converted by Navarro from five meters into the goal to make it 1:1.

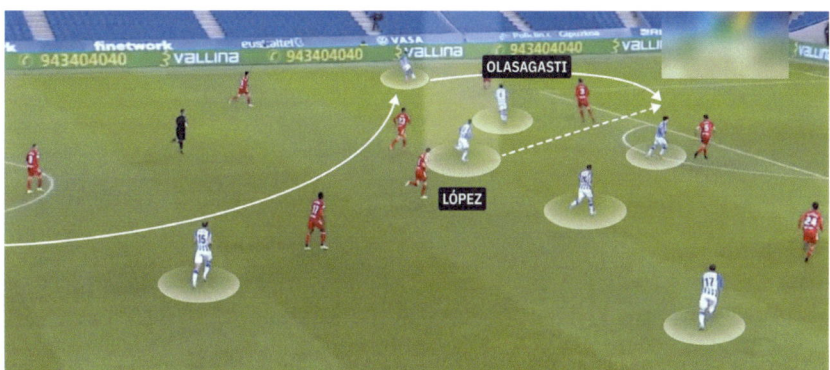

After a long ball to the wing, Real Sociedad has not only a numerical but also a positional advantage: the position of the central striker occupies the opposing defender (no. 5), while the advanced eight of *Sanse* (Olasagasti) in the space between the full-back and the central defender (no. 3) engages them, drawing out the opposing central defender. The resulting gap is filled by the eventual goalscorer López, who directly converts the precise flat pass behind the defensive line.

Flat passes behind the defensive line will also be observed later in Leverkusen as a successful means of setting up goals.

As was the case later in Leverkusen, Real Sociedad's second team defends with a man-orientation in attacking pressing: They try to make the game predictable and lie in wait for the first pass to then hunt down the opponent. However, the striker does not quite manage to position himself correctly and is subsequently simply easily bypassed.

Standard situations and especially corners have also become a successful means of scoring goals in Leverkusen. The corner kick is delivered directly into the goal area. A total of
six players are in the box. The players close to the goal try to "open the door" by moving
apart and pulling their direct opponents with them. Three more target players (headers)
make their runs. In particular, the marked player (no. 23, Sangalli) plays an important
role: He drops back and occupies the far post to cover any deflected balls. Such a case
happens now: The header from the center is not powerful enough and flies towards the
far post, from where it is then pushed over the line.

In *Sanse* 's scenes under Xabi Alonso, several stylistic elements can be observed that were later also used in Leverkusen: The fundamentally dynamic, proactive style of play with a frequent "play and go" right from the opening; the
structure and organization in a 1-3-4-3, passes preferably through the center,
overloading the center, exploiting the space behind the opponent's defense
(*attacking the backs*), players running through into the penalty area, players
close to each other for short passes and consistently attacking the box.

This is combined with the intention of making the game predictable in the opponent's possession and, in particular, pressing directly in the opponent's half.

Excursus: How the Academy of Real Sociedad San Sebastián works

The academy of Real Sociedad San Sebastián has earned an excellent reputation in recent years. Unlike rival Athletic Bilbao, they do not have the self-imposed restriction of only relying on Basque players; however, the main focus is still on regional talent. The club has therefore set its key performance indicators to make the success of its work visible. 80% of all players in the academy are expected to originate from the immediate region of Gipuzkoa, were live around 700,000 people. The remaining 20% is distributed across the rest of the Basque Country (10%) and the slightly more distant regions, including neighboring France, as San Sebastián is only 20 km from the border.[155] A path that French World Cup winner Antoine Griezmann also took as a young player because he was considered too small and slight in France.

The regional context is also unique: between the third and sixth grades, school sports play a special role. Three individual and three team sports are practiced, trained and compared in competitions. This also means that the youth academy does not have an official team in these age groups and provides oly limited training opporttnuities: Up to the age of ten, training is limited to once a week at the club. From the age of eleven, players train at most twice a week, as there are no official leagues before the U13 level.

Instead, they work extensively with partner clubs and collaborations to improve the training quality across the region and to bring the most promising talents to "La Zubieta," where they can be be developed into top-level players. The poly-sportive training in schools gives children a broad range of motor skills and prevents early specialization. This is likely one reason why the highest number of Spanish Olympians come from the Gipuzkoa region.[156]

Sport holds an extremely high status within the culture of the Basque Country and is firmly embedded not only institutionally but also historically. Basque football legend Mikel Etxarri, who worked for Real Sociedad San Sebastián for many years in the youth academy, explains: "I see football as an expression of the characteristics of this country. The sport developed here from daily work, from what people had around them: lifting stones, handling animals, using their hands. The values of the competition came from everyday life."[157]

---

155 Corrigan 2021.
156 Iriarte 2022.
157 Etxarri quoted by Corrigan 2021.

This connection with the universal values that are reflected in football in the Basque Country is repeatedly emphasised by different people and seems to be another key factor behind the teams' success and their "typical" characteristics. Sports director Roberto Olabe mentions commitment, honesty, and a sense of responsibility and emphasizes: "Seriousness is the basis of everything for us."[158] Mikel Etxarri shares his own expierence: "Everyone had to work. At 14, I worked in a factory, played football on the beach, and studied for exams. Not only me, but everyone around me. The culture of effort, hard work, and getting ahead in life is widespread in the Basque Country."

For this reason, it is a logical consequence that such a remarkable high number of successful coaches currently come from the small region of Gipuzkoa. In addition to Xabi Alonso, these include Mikel Arteta (Arsenal London), Unai Emery (Aston Villa), Julen Lopetegui (former West Ham United), Andoni Iraola (Bournemouth FC) and Imanol Alguacil (Real Sociedad).

For Mikel Etxarri, culture and common character are the decisive factors: "As coaches, they have nothing in common. Each of them has developed themselves. But as people they integrate a certain culture. Life in Gipuzkoa is continuous. (...) There is a foundation of solidarity, of camaraderie, and cooperation for a common economic good, which is a very important value in football. (...) Effort and competition are rewarded with money. All this is ingrained in the education of the Basques and also into football. It's about survival. This culture, instilled in children, is the only explanation I see for why there are so many good coaches in Gipuzkoa."[159] The president of the Gipuzkoa Coaches' Association, Josu Zubia, explains the impact of this mentality: "When we come to a club, we become rooted in it—its coat of arms, its model, the city, the language, and its people. That's because we experienced it ourselves."[160] As a result, these coaches not only have an easier time adapting to the identity of their respective clubs, with it, but also possess outstanding qualities as "group managers": "Close to the players. They demand, but they also argue. If you need a scolding, you get it, but with a constructive pat on the back afterwards. They are coaches with whom players feel comfortable."[161]

These are impressive figures when you consider that the Basque Country has a comparable area and population to Schleswig-Holstein in northern Germany. And it's not about the coaches: There are currently 70 professionals from the

158 Olabe quoted in Biermann 2024.
159 Etxarri quoted in Torres 2023.
160 Zubia quoted in Saller 2023.
161 Ibid.

entire Basque region playing in one of the first, top European leagues, followed by around 250 second- and third-division players.[162] Regarding the coaches who come from the region, according to Etxarri they are above all pragmatic rather than following certain dogmas, and he should know it, after all, he has trained some of them himself either as a player or as a coach: "If a team scores a lot of goals, it has good strikers; if it concedes a lot of goals, its defenders are not the best. But if all games end 0:0, 1:0, 0:1, 1:0, then it's down to the coach and the organization of the team."[163]

For this, a "solid" foundation is essential in order to subsequently achieve strong results in conjunction with the "typical Basque values" of unity and a high work ethic.[164] The first team of Real Sociedad San Sebastián, mainly known as "La Real" in Spain, is currently implementing all of this almost perfectly. In the last Champions League season (2023/2024), they remained unbeaten in the group stage and received numerous compliments, even from their opponents. Inter coach Simone Inzaghi, for example, praised the team and their style of play, as well as the "clear principles" of the "fantastic team".[165]

The focus of the training is not only on sporting development, but is holistically oriented toward personal grow. The club's homepage states: "We work in an environment that combines enthusiasm and frustration. Dealing with this reality is one of our greatest challenges."[166] The training is therefore not limited to sports-related topics alone—it is also about values and a fundamental orientation in life outside of football. Roberto Olabe, San Sebastián's sporting director, says: "Every player is a project."[167] It is obvious that this statement is not just a cliché, but is actively lived at every moment by those involved.

The Spanish word most commonly used for the term "youth academy" is "cantera", which means "quarry". In fact, this term perfectly fits La Real's approach to youth development, as youth director Luki Iriarte explains: "[For us, it's not so much about] signing players, but training them and developing them over time. Our first-team players stay with us for an average of seven years. The average with our local players is eleven years. It is important to show players in all youth teams that they can make it to the first team. And we must help them

162 Biermann 2024.
163 Etxarri quoted by Corrigan 2021.
164 Corrigan 2021.
165 Haupt 2024.
166 Homepage Real Sociedad Fundazioa online.
167 Olabe quoted in Biermann 2024.

achieve this goal with patience and perseverance."[168] This is probably also why the building for the youth teams is called "Gorabide", which in Basque translates to "from bottom to top".[169] Everyone at the Zubieta Academy is aware that players should stay at the club for a long time. Since long-term development is paramount, "La Real" is even committed to keeping youth players in its own teams for at least two years. Head of Young Talent Luki Iriarte about that: "We try to build up the teams step by step. If there is a mistake, it is ours. We signed him [the player], so he should not suffer. So we let very few players go until they are older, and then you have to put teams together or make other decisions."[170]

The holistic approach taken in youth training helps to underpin not only the sporting but also the social importance of the Real Sociedad San Sebastián club. Attention is not only paid to football training, but also to school and further education. This has a long tradition—in fact, Xabi Alonso had already completed a degree parallel to his first years as a player, and even national players like Mikel Oyarzabal take advantage of the educational opportunities and the invitation to engage with content beyond football.

The club's goals within training are defined as follows:[171]

→ Increasing the opportunities to optimize players' individual skills with the aim of producing well-prepared players for the Real Sociedad San Sebastián first team.

→ Preparing players for a professional football career in other clubs.

→ Ensure financial stability to make the club sustainable.

Within this process, stability is extremely important. Youth players stay at the club for an average of 7.4 years. 80% of the second team (*Sanse*) and about 58% of the first team come from the youth ranks. This means that by 2022, the club was already very close to the defined target of 60% with regard to the proportion of self-trained players within the first team.[172] In the same season, 18 players who had come through the club's youth system had already played in the first team, which had the lowest average age of all *LaLiga* teams, including four first

---

168 Iriarte quoted from Corrigan 2021.
169 Corrigan 2021.
170 Iriarte quoted from Corrigan 2021.
171 Iriarte 2022.
172 Biermann 2024.

division debuts—and this is not at the expense of sporting success.[173] Quite the opposite: Over the past four years, the team has remained stable in the top 10 of LaLiga (worst ranking: seventh place), and even won the Copa del Rey, the Spanish Cup, in the 2019/2020 COVID season. There were eight players on the pitch who had been trained at "La Zubieta" since the U15s, such as winning goal scorer Mikel Oyarzabal.[174] Academy director Luki Iriarte remembers this moment particularly: "You can imagine what it was like to see them win the Copa. This was the work of all of us here. It was a huge satisfaction for anyone who plays in the first team or the youth team, now when they win the Copa del Rey. But also the children who did not make it into the first team, but are still important for the province of Gipuzkoa. I'm not just saying that—we are very happy and aware of the responsibility we have and what Real Sociedad means in this province."[175] The fact that these players not only serve to fulfill the (self-imposed) requirements, but also play an important role within the team, is also evident in the numbers: The CIES Football Observatory confirmed in an international comparative study from November 2023 that at "La Real," 45.4% of the accumulated playing time had been completed by players from the club's own youth team. In the Champions League, this number was only surpassed by the Ukrainian team Shakhtar Donetsk.[176]

This is also reflected in the signing policy of the first team. Sporting director Roberto Olabe explains that the club always looks to its own academy first when it comes to filling a position: "Our goal is 80-20 in the youth sector, but 60-40 in the first team. We sign players who not only think about the present, but also about the future. When we sign a left-back or a goalkeeper, it is because we need some time to prepare for the goalkeepers that come through our system. In recent years we have tried to bring more speed and explosiveness to the team, because our children are more long-distance runners than sprinters. Our own pool of talent offers us many opportunities, but also some limitations."[177] Olabe gives an example of the added value that can be offered by signing an external, more mature and experienced player like David Silva: "With David Silva, we felt that we needed to look for someone for a key position who would activate everyone else and make them all better. We are waiting for people like Robert Navarro and Roberto López to come to us. For these players and the surrounding

173 Corrigan 2021.
174 Ibid.
175 Iriarte quoted from Corrigan 2021.
176 Haupt 2024.
177 Olabe quoted in Corrigan 2021.

positions, it is great to play and train with David. These are the elements—like Alex Remiro [the goalkeeper] or Alex Isak [a striker at La Real at the time]—who come to us to make us better."[178] Ultimately, however, the focus of the entire club is on successful youth work, as Olabe emphasises: "We feed on ourselves, and that is very good in terms of loyalty and social feeling. But that also limits you. Sometimes we also need what I call a 'bomb' from outside, which is hard to get used to, but we have to do it."[179] The interplay of these influences and the respect for the first team's own youth development is certainly a key success factor for the recent development of the entire club.

The focus when selecting young players is on technical strengths and a good understanding of the game. Added to this are resilience, speed and dexterity. The typical Zubieta player demonstrates personality, actively seeks the ball to make decisions, and communicates effectively. He plays intensively with and without the ball and constantly strivey to improve. Mistakes are considererd an integral part of the learning process.[180]
The training plan is implemented by the coaches, who are expected to be coaches of "the club" and not of an individual team. The plan is highly structured and is based less on training frequency and more on qualitative impulses to advance the necessary development goals. On the path to the first team, a strong emphasis is placed on "playing." Additionally, there are specific development phases based on age group: "Play and Enjoy" in the basic development phase, "Play and Learn / Compete" in the advanced phase and, "Play and Win" in the performance phase. The club tries to be less active in the area of youth signings and transfers in order to "make fewer mistakes." Instead, players are given space and time to develop in cooperation clubs, which is expressed through playing time and close supervision. The issue of "playing time" is even firmly anchored in the youth rules in the Basque Country: if a substitute does not play at least 20 minutes, the game is considered lost.[181]

Within the style of play, the primary focus is on one's own game, but this is deliberately varied in the training process, so that 75% of the training time is focused on vertical (forward-facing), fast combination play, but 25% of the training time is also allocated to training a more direct game (alternative style of play,

178 Ibid.
179 Ibid.
180 Iriarte 2022.
181 Ibid.

e.g., counterattacks, long balls, etc.).[182] The tactical concepts in each age group are basically the same, with only variations in complexity and execution. The coaches are given a great deal of autonomy to achieve the club's goals, but "We have a game model that we fight hard for. Passing, transition play, and dominance of space are our three pillars," explains sporting director Roberto Olabe. At the same time , he emphasizes the autonomy of the youth academy: "If the coach understands this way of working, then we give him the brush to give it his shape."[183] The philosophy is to "want to be the best from Monday to Friday in order to earn exceptional results at the weekend," says Olabe.[184]

From Real Sociedad to the 2024 European Championship title: Merino, Oyarzabal, Remiro, Le Normand and Zubimendi.

In order to advance players individually, there are three different approaches and options in the training of the "La Zubieta" teams: This can happen through individual training, but also through collective training contexts that are tailored so that a player can achieve or at least make progress toward his individual development goal. In this case, one coach leads the training session, while

182 Ibid.
183 Olabe quoted in Romero 2021.
184 Olabe cited in Haupt 2024.

another is assigned exclusively to the player, providing targeted feedback and observations to support his development. Likewise, the individual can a generic training form intended for the collective. All this depends on the momentum of the individual and the needs of the team in the respective game situation and training phase.

The coaching teams, which can sometimes consist of up to ten people, are all part of the development process and have a defined role at every moment of training, helping to push players to the next level.

The content and training methods are statistically recorded, as is the focus on specific players: which players were the primary focus and how frequently, as well as the specific learning objectives of each training method, ensuring that each player receives adequate opportunities to maximize his potential.[185] Everything at "La Zubieta" serves the goal of bringing players into the first team. Therefore, the playing style is also constantly evaluated using data, and an approximation of the decisive parameters regarding the playing style is sought. Within this comprehensive analysis, the aim is to support the development process and generate useful insights, rather than simply collecting data for its own sake. The goal is to create actionable knowledge that can be used to challenge existing beliefs.[186]

Within the training process, "*Sanse*", the second team of "La Real", is the "jewel in the crown of the club, the place of ultimate transition", as Roberto Olabe says.[187] Therefore, Xabi Alonso's time with this team was extremely important; not only for him, but also—and especially—for the team itself in preparation for the highest level of performance: "His leadership qualities, his ability to 'give feedback,' his understanding of the game (...)... [What Xabi gave us] is the art of convincing the boys that they are ready and that it is not so much about winning, but how you win."[188] Alonso himself described his role at "*Sanse*" as follows: "*Sanse* is the last step in the entire work of Zubieta. The player comes to me as a product of all, having learned very good concepts. And this is the last, very important step in preparing them to become professionals. We want them to know professional football, the competition, the training sessions, the habits and you need to make it happen. It's like an assembly line, and we put them in the box to prepare them for the first team and we have to do it right."[189]

185 Iriarte 2022.
186 Ibid.
187 Olabe quoted in Romero 2023.
188 Ibid.
189 Alonso quoted in Corrigan 2023.

The club has also already made impressive progress in the women's sector. In a national comparison, the number of active female players (with the corresponding active playing authorization; in Spain, this authorization is referred to as a "player's license rather than a "player's passport").

The formation process does not stop with the players. The club is already scouting for potential future coaches and has even implemented a UEFA B license exclusively for women. The training of local talents extends beyond players, serving both as a means of fulfilling the club's social responsibility and as a foundation for long-term success.

CHAPTER 2

A pragmatic start

Xabi Alonso took over Bayer Leverkusen in second-to-last place in the table in October 2022. It was obvious that the team was not living up to its potential, but quite often in Bundesliga history, teams that considered themselves "too good" for the relegation battle found themselves dragged into it, sometimes barely avoiding relegation—and some didn't. At the same time, Xabi Alonso already saw the outstanding potential of the individual players and had clear ideas about how he wanted to stabilize and further develop the team. The view and analysis of this first season does not examine each game individually, but instead highlights key matches to trace the team's development throughout the season. From the very first games, typical elements of Xabi Alonso's game idea appear repeatedly, forming the foundation for the team's playing style in their championship-winning season. The focus here is primarily on bringing the concepts already mentioned to life and using examples to illustrate how the team had already incorporated specific aspects of Alonso's philosophy. The team took a huge step in development during the World Cup break between November 2022 and January 2023, which certainly facilitated the process for Alonso. But more on that later, because every journey begins with the first step—and in this case with the first game against Schalke 04.

Home Debut: 08.10.2022

Leverkusen starts in a 1-5-3-2 formation, which changes to a 1-3-4-3 in pos-session. In defense, the wingers Bakker and Frimpong move inside alternately to form a back four. When in possession, the 1-3-4-3 is played with hanging strikers, i.e., forwards who are positioned centrally but interpret their roles dif-ferently. What is particularly noteworthy in the interaction between the players on the right side: with Tapsoba, as the right central defender, always positioning himself slightly wider in order to better access depth via the fast wingers. The interplay between Tapsoba, Diaby, and Frimpong on the right side already shows a very good (socio-affective) connection between the players, which clearly out-performs the left-side combination of Hincapié, Bakker, and Hudson-Odoi. As a result, Leverkusen's right side generates significantly more danger and regularly threatens Schalke's goal.

Positional advantage ("We Are Better Positioned") of Leverkusen. The Leverkusen play-ers occupy the spaces between Schalke 04's defensive line, limiting their movement. Schalke is not numerically outnumbered there, but has no direct access to the players between the lines. In the marked area, Schalke is not outnumbered either, but is fun-damentally in a weaker position, as a pass to the outside or a quick combination play can generate numerical superiority on the wing and increase attacking momentum due to the players' profiles.

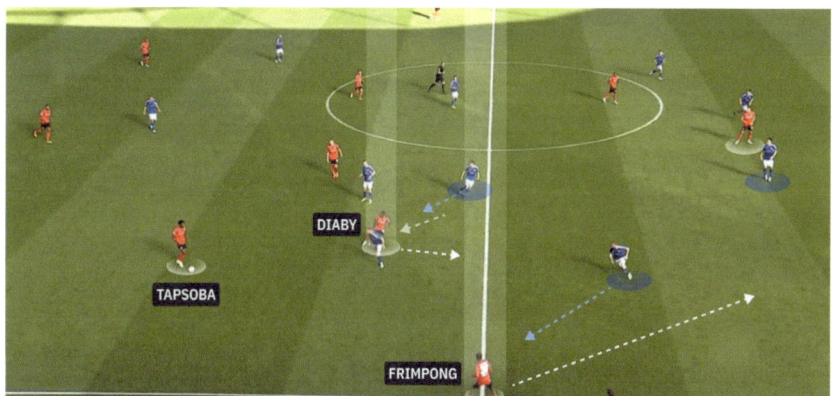

Diaby briefly runs behind Tapsoba's next opponent, who could actually press him, thereby granting Tapsoba additional time. Tapsoba with the option to play a short pass to Frimpong or into the freed space to exploit his pace. Good lecture / perception of Frimpong's posture and intentions by Tapsoba, who is then able to create a goal-threatening situation. Schalke 04 has allocation problems, as there is no pressure on the ball and the next opponents, and no clear decision-making hierarchy whther to protect the center, close down opponents, or cover space - resulting in unclear responsibilities.

Structure of Leverkusen's positional play: The *BASE* zone is occupied. 8s / 10s on the side of the opposing 6s, creating decision-making problems in the responsibility split between the opposing 6 and full-back. The Leverkusen striker deliberately stands offside behind the defenders, forcing them to constantly checkover their shoulders to know his position and control his movements. Leverkusen's full-backs positioned very wide to stretch the defensive shape and create space. The team in possession has many open passing lines and communication channels, while the opponent struggles to gain access to a player.

Leverkusen maintains close distances in defensive moments. They establish basic access to all "playable" opponents. Leverkusen makes the opponent's game predictable. This allows Hincapié, the left center-back from the five-man line, to step forward aggressively and defend his opponent, who is positioned closed (facing his own goal), without Schalke being able to exploit the space behind his action. Schalke 04 fails to provide a corresponding or interacting free-running movement to take advantage of this opening.

Game Conclusion

The game ends with a win for Bayer Leverkusen, primarily because they maintain defensive control against a Schalke team that is offensively unimaginative. Schalke never gets a grip on Leverkusen's right side and suffers from decisive speed and positioning disadvantages. Leverkusen already displays a certain level of security in possession and a stable tactical structure (1-3-4-3), which remains a key factor throughout the rest of the season.

At the Bottom, 15.10.2022

During the week, Leverkusen had to bury nearly all hopes of advancing in the Champions League after a 0:3 defeat against FC Porto. Now they face Eintracht Frankfurt, whose approach to the game, formation mirroring (1-3-4-3 from Leverkusen vs. 1-3-5-2 from Frankfurt) and constant search for individual duels aim to disrupt Leverkusen's rhythm. Frankfurt exploits Leverkusen's tendency to "defend forward," as described in the previous analysis, repeatedly attempting to break past the Leverkusen defenders. Leverkusen struggles to create strong attacking moments of their own.

Leverkusen with an overload of the right half-space. Diaby, acting as a half-forward/hanging striker, rotates outward, while Frimpong moves inward from the wing, positioning himself between the lines. At the same time, the left hanging striker (Paulinho in this game) shifts to the right between the lines. As a result Leverkusen now has two players positioned "in a square" between the opposing lines, allowing them to interact closely. There are now multiple passing options for Tah, who has the ball. In this situation, he continues with a pass to Frimpong, who accelerates play with a speed dribble.

Game Conclusion

Eintracht Frankfurt plays with intensity, speed, and aggression, causing Leverkusen significant problems, especially in the early stages of the game. The player positioning is similar to the previous league game, but the build-up players do not yet dare to play forward consistently and struggle to find opportunities between the lines.

Defensively, the agile Kolo Muani from Frankfurt is particularly difficult for Lever-kusen to contain. Leverkusen struggles to find their rhythm, and their counter-pressing in the opponent's half is not effective. The Werkself plays too many lateral passes in possesion, despite available vertical options. The goals conce-ded result from avoidable individual errors, which Frankfurt ruthlessly punishes. At this point, Eintracht is in a different state and on a higher level. Leverkusen lacks confidence in their own actions and fails to establish the connection to their teammates, preventing them from building up on promising sequences.

Immediately after the game, Alonso was already very clear in his conclusion: "We got into problems right from the start. We didn't have the intensity that is needed at this level. It's our fault, no one else can help us—no excuses. To be competitive, we must improve. We now have an intensive week ahead of us."[190] At that time, the press had already begun to question whether "the aura" and the "worldly demeanor" alone would be enough to fix Leverkusen's "system crash".[191] However, Xabi Alonso did exactly what he had announced: he worked on improving the team. Of the seven games remaining before World Cup break, Leverkusen lost only to Leipzig, secured two draws in the Champions League (against Atletico Madrid and Club Brugge) and one in the Bundesliga against Wolfsburg—and then began winning games, securing three consecutive victories.

Looking back, Xabi Alonso remembers that moment in Frankfurt and his start: "I think there comes a moment for every young coach when they look around the stadium and think: 'What am I actually doing here? How did I get here?'"[192] All the "ideas," the entire match plan, the countless notes and hours of video - "all useless. (...) The result [5:1 for Frankfurt] never lies."[193]

According to Alonso, the foundation for winning a title was laid in that difficult moment. From the game against Atletico, where the team fought back to a draw, he saw something that made him confident: "I could just feel that we had a spe-cial group. The players had this look in their eyes – *Belief.* If you've ever been a coach, you know that you can look your players in the eyes in the first two or three minutes and just know if it's going to be a good day or a difficult day. Either the faith is there or it is not. We had faith, even in defeat."[194]

190 Alonso in SZ online October 15, 2024.
191 SZ online from October 15, 2024.
192 Alonso in Robles 2024.
193 Ibid.
194 Alonso in Robles 2024.

Unburdened, 06.11.2022

Even after coaching change to Xabi Alonso, Leverkusen did not immediately show improvement - at least in terms of results. However, the team was already making progress, even if it was not yet clearly visible to outsiders. The matchup on that 13th matchday is unusual from today's perspective: Leverkusen, ranked fourteenth in the table, faces Union Berlin, who sit third in the Bundesliga standings. Bayer made some changes to their personnel for this game: While the team still operates from a 1-3-4-3 in possession, Bakker in particular shifts into a left-back role in a back four when the opponent has the ball, while Tapsoba remains mainly in the center, likely due to his strength and heading ability to counter the opponent's long balls. At the same time, Frimpong positions himself further forward , allowing him to pose a direct threat to the opponent with his dynamism.

Union Berlin looks for direct duels and try to cause Leverkusen problems with long balls, physical battles, and numerical superiority in the final third. In this situation, Bakker and Hincapié show strong defensive access, while Leverkusen's defensive unit maintains a compact structure. In contrast, Union Berlin, lacks immediate supporting options for their forwards, who are tightly marked.

Leverkusen's three-/five-man backline is well prepared for Union's long-ball approach: They compress the spacetogether, and already have potential recipients of Jordan's header under control. Hincapié steps forward to contest the duel, while Bakker and Tapsoba close the space behind him. This creates a 3+1 defensive structure, ensuring a numerical advantage to secure the second ball.

Game Conclusion

In the first half, Union had more possession but consistently opted for long balls. Up to that point, Leverkusen had not created any chances in the penalty area, with their best opportunity coming from a counterattack. In possession, their distances were sometimes too large, though an adjustment to Union's five-man defense was structurally noticeable. The Werkself's 1:0 lead came from a corner and was almost unexpected (46'). The second goal was also gifted—this time by the goalkeeper, who made critical error with the ball far outside his box. As a result, Union saw more of the ball in the second half but failed to create significant danger. This is where Xabi Alonso's pragmatism becomes evident: instead of dominating possession, he lets the opponent have the ball to neutralize their threat, controlling the game from a stable defense, which gains confidence through repeated successful defensive actions.

The win against Union Berlin was followed by derby successes against 1. FC Köln and over VfB Stuttgart. With these results, the Werkself entered into the World Cup and winter break with a positive outlook. This marks the end of an intense opening phase for the young coach. Alonso reflects on this period: "We had little time to go into depth, but had to deal with ten games in six weeks. It was just a matter of concentrating on one thing and doing it right. The most important thing for me was to give the team back their self-confidence and create a positive atmosphere again."[195] Therefore, he focused on having many personal conversations: "It was important to get to know and understand the players and how I can 'catch' them. But also because I am deeply convinced that the best way to create a sense of commitment is through personal bonds."[196]

With the return from the winter break, so comes the return of a player whom all of Leverkusen had been eagerly awaiting: "Florian is a gift for me as a coach. He is a player who is... different. But we cannot rely on him to fix everything on his own. This would not do justice to him or to ourselves. In order for his extraordinary abilities to flourish, we must give him a foundation. For this we need structure, a lot of stability and a clear self-image."[197] Wirtz is not a key, but he is very important. What is also interesting about Alonso's statement is that he emphasizes the overall team organization—which is crucial for Wirtz's skills to come into play. Working on the team's game model therefore plays a central role in bringing out the abilities of the individual (exceptional) player.

Further Development, 15.01.2023

After the winter break, Bayer Leverkusen plays test matches against AC Venice and FC Copenhagen, winning both. However, far more important than the results are the developments emerging at the Werkself. It is immediately noticeable that with the return of Florian Wirtz, every other player also improves. Leverkusen has also changed its collective interaction: In attacking pressing, a man-orientation is now evident, combined with the intention of making the opponent's game predictable. The clear 1v1 in the attacking third evolves into an approach where fewer players control multiple opponents (e.g., against Venice, when two Leverkusen strikers were tasked with covering the opponent's three-man build-up). The goal is to control the opponent's next passing options so that the pass arrives at the same time as the defender comes in.

The team is becoming more adaptable in its approach to games. In the second test match against Copenhagen, Leverkusen repeatedly managed to compactly defend the center (distance between team units approx. 15m). The two forwards primarily try to press the full-backs.

---

195 Alonso in Cáceres 2023.
196 Ibid.
197 Ibid.

In possession, the players' intentions and movements no longer coexist in isolation—targeted movements interlock harmoniously and there is increasing interaction between the players on the pitch e.g., by creating space for each other. This was not the case to this extent at the end of the first half of the 2022/2023 season and represents a clear evolution. Different positions are also more closely with individual player characteristics. Against Venice, for example, Wirtz and Amiri both play as number 8s, yet assume distinct roles. Against Copenhagen, Amiri suddenly operates on the wing, unlocking new synergies.

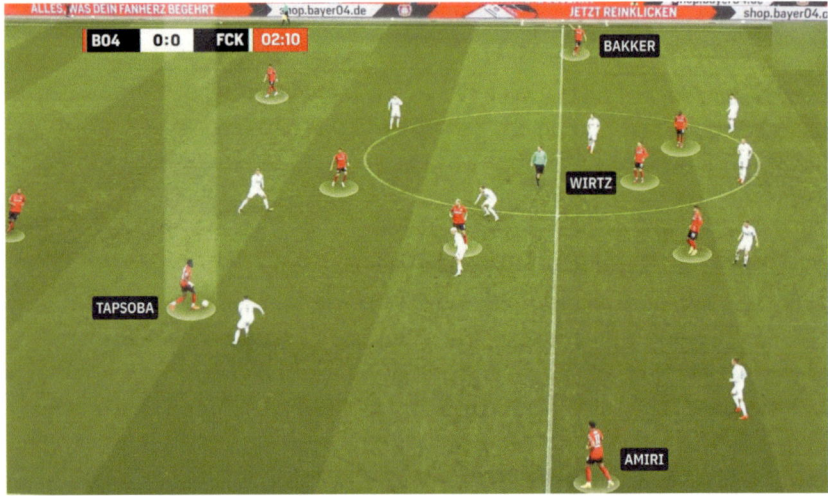

In this situation, the difference between the 1-2 formation (i.e., with two strikers up top) and the 2-1 structure of the last line (previously dominant until the winter break, with two hanging strikers behind a clear No. 9) is clearly visible. Wirtz occupies the No. 10 space, perfectly suiting his footballing characteristics in possession. It is particularly striking in this match that Amiri acts as a full-back, allowing him to utilize his attacking abilities as an additional striker fromwide areas. Leverkusen finds itself in a 1v1 situation against the last defensive line and could create a temporary numerical advantage by increasing the tempo through a switch to the deep-running Bakker. In terms of controlled build-up, a pass into the center to the midfielder positioned in *BASE* is open and viable.However, Tapsoba will immediately opt for another touch while dribbling, closing off the passing lane again.

Leverkusen's central defenders always have the intention to bypass lines and opponents with their passing. In this situation, Wirtz acts as a perfect third player, who immediately has the game in front of him and can continue dynamically. A total of three Leverkusen players position themselves directly behind the opposition's midfield line ("winning backs" concept) and occupy the so-called "square" between the defensive and midfield lines. This is made possible by multiple players staying close to the ball and keeping open passing lanes.

Maturity, 22.01.2023

The second half of the season after the World Cup in Qatar begins for the Werkself with an away match in Gladbach—and one more world champion in their squad: Exequiel Palacios was part of the Argentine national team that won the World Cup and played a total of 50 minutes in the tournament (across three appearances).

Leverkusen sets up in a 1-3-4-1-2 formation with Adli and Diaby as strikers and Hložek as the No. 10, though they interpret these positions flexibly. All forwards have a profile designed to attack depth and generate dynamic movement—which they do repeatedly. At the same time, the three forwards remain extremely ball-oriented and stay close to each other in possession to interact effectively. Throughout the match, Leverkusen constantly looks to run behind defenders and occupy spaces between the lines. The short distances between players in ball possession allow quicker ball flow making it harder for opponents to press effectively.

In counterattacks, the ball is played diagonally whenever possible and consistently combined into the box.

Defensively, the three central defenders work very well together and resolutely close off the center, while the wing-backs repeatedly push forward to put pressure on the opposing wingers. The rest of the defensive line shifts accordingly, "shuttling" into a back four, with access to the opponent.

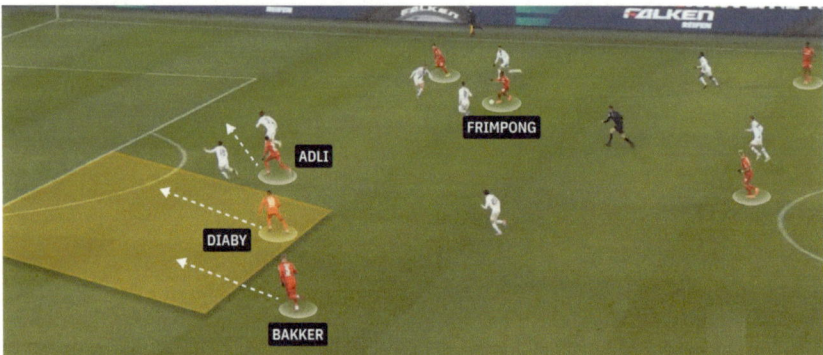

After a strong dribble and an excellent turn from Frimpong, he accerlerates play. It is already evident that Leverkusen is outnumbering the opposition away from the ball, with Diaby and Bakker positioned as advance full-backs. Adli shifts to the half-right space, pulling both defenders with him. This opens the left half-space, allowing for a diagonal switch to create a scoring opportunity.

Leverkusen engages in high pressing with clear man-to-man assignment across the entire pitch. Due to the compact distances, the opponent has only viable passing options are into the space behind the defensive line, which forces them into either a footrace or an aerial duel - both of which favor Leverkusen's defenders.

Game Conclusion

At the start of the match, Leverkusen frequently loses possession, as passing options are limited, and space in the center is reduced due to a lack of staggering (tiers) and a flat interpretation of the forward players' roles. Despite initial struggles against opposing set pieces, Leverkusen enters halftime with a 2:0 lead, capitalizing on well-executed counterattacks.

In the second half, Gladbach improves their structural play and becomes more threatening with deep runs and their effectiveness from set pieces. Leverkusen scores the decisive 3:0 from a counterattack, where Amiri and Adli combined brilliantly in the penalty area. The home side pulls one back with a stunning goal (82'), creating space against the central defenders and executing well-coordinated movement through crossing runs and positional interplay. In the end, thanks to a second exceptional goal (Stindl volley), the result becomes tight again, but not threatend at all as Leverkusen confidently defends all remaing attacks. The Werkself seems to have passed their first true test of maturity.

Pragmatism, 25.01.2023

Bayer Leverkusen enters their next match against VfL Bochum at the end of the first half of the season with a seemingly altered structure, tactical rearrangements, and changes in personnel. However, these adjustments do not fundamentally alter the team's playing style. Analyzing only the varied formations and positional shifts in different game phase makes it difficult to distinguish between the different setups (1-4-2-3-1; 1-4-2-4; asymmetric build-up when opening with a back three and Frimpong pushing forward). This is where Xabi Alonso's pragmatism becomes evident - similar to the first-half victory of the season against Union Berlin - by neutralizing the opponent's strengths and shaping the game to Leverkusen's advantage. In this match, the team usually organizes itself defensively with a back four - a stylistic element that will reappear periodically in specific phases of matches and against particular opponents. However, in possessions, the established tactical interactions remain intact. What is notable about this game is that Amiri moves into the starting lineup and is deployed as a 6/8, a role he has rarely played in his career, having previously been used mainly as a "dribbler". This shows Alonso's imagination in evaluating and utilizing players based on their characteristics and their impact in different areas of the pitch. Compared to other games, this match features a short effective playing time (less than 60 minutes), indicating many interruptions (fouls, balls going out of bound).

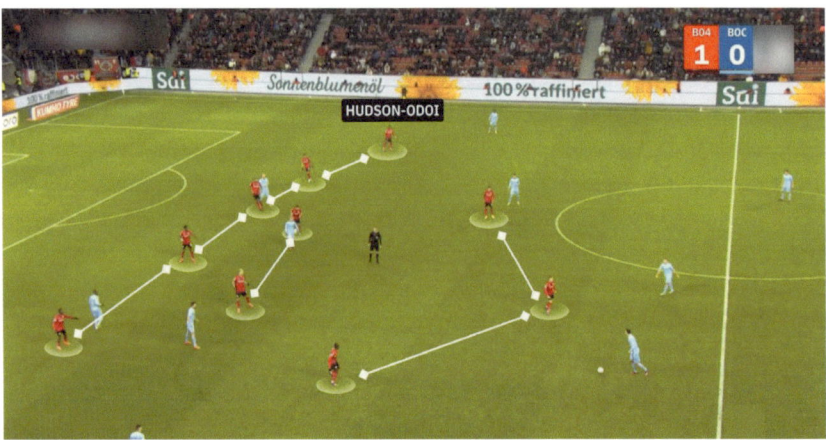

Leverkusen remains Leverkusen: Even though a four-man backline was evident at times in the game against Bochum, Hudson-Odoi repeatedly dropped back into defense as a left-back to ensure a stable center. If the ball shifts to the other side and further forward (or into Bochum's own half), Hudson-Odoi pushes up to exert pressure on the ball—transforming the defensive line into a "swinging" back four. This means that the offensive winger Hudson-Odoi repeatedly takes on the role of a full-back long before a (German) national coach was criticized for a similar idea of using an offensive player in an international match. Although Xabi Alonso has tailored and adapted the match plan to Bochum, there are always game moments in which the team can revert to known and already ingrained behaviors that have already become part of their identity, which is being further developed at the same time.

Leverkusen with an almost perfect allocation in the box defense: All defenders (as well as Andrich, who tracked his opponent and dropped back from central midfield) have their opponent in view (at least peripherally) as well as the ball and can therefore react adequately to any movement as well as to the trajectory of the ball to clear it.

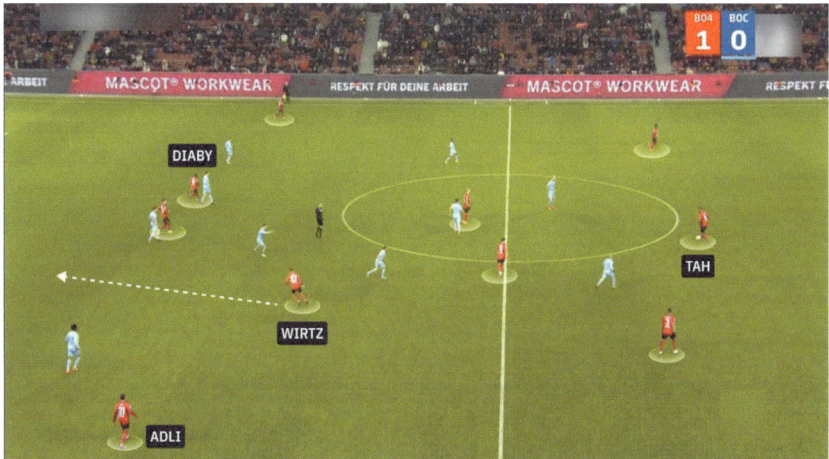

Halftime adjustments: With the substitution of Adli for Hudson-Odoi, a player with a greater goal-scoring threat is on the pitch, who can also interpret the wide position in Alonso's system as a dribbler. Against Bochum's last line, the numerical matchup is now even as Diaby plays like a striker. Both strikers are positioned inside the defenders, which further increases the potential threat to the opponent's goal. These one-on-one situations already threaten the space behind the backline, but they also ensure that players like Wirtz enjoy even more freedom in the space between the lines and exploit it by making runs from this space into the gaps of the defensive line.

Game Conclusion

Bayer Leverkusen has little possession and repeatedly attempts to outplay Bochum's pressing. The Werkself remains dangerous through the mobile Frimpong and Diaby, who are never fully contained by the opponent due to their speed, mobility and agility.

Bochum, on the other hand, struggles to create the ball effectively to generate an immediate goal-scoring threat. The basic defensive orientation and positioning (wingers occasionally dropping back as full-backs) of Leverkusen's wingers provides defensive support in certain phases of the game when it comes to defending. The outside players are used to dropping into the backline and forming a five-man defensive line depending on the situation.

At the beginning of the second half, Leverkusen slightly adjusted the positioning of the forward players (substitution of Adli for Hudson-Odoi), which led to a slight increase in possession and, as a result, a quick 2:0 lead (53' – Hložek).

For the rest of the game, Leverkusen handled the high balls relatively securely. Bochum only created two notable chances to score, including one great chance, while Leverkusen relied on counterattacks to seal the game. Although Leverkusen have occasional periods of ball possession - these are more of a hint than outcome of actual structure. The end result is a pragmatic victory.

Growing, 23.02.2023

The following weeks proved to be a mixed period for Xabi Alonso's team, who managed just one win in their next five games.

In the 0:2 defeat against Borussia Dortmund, Xabi Alonso's team attempted to solve the opponent's high press with a flat four-at-the-back formation but often failed to get past the opponent's next defensive line. However, progress is already becoming apparent in this game: the team demonstrates a lot of quality in possession in the middle third, and can create new space through positional play and off-the-ball-movement and thus attack the depth. Leverkusen demonstrates that they have developed greater punch and fighting spirit than in the first half of the season. At the beginning of the second half, Leverkusen manages shorter distances in the build-up phase, facilitating better team connectivity. In addition, there is better staggering for the second ball if the team decides to play long over the opponent's pressing. Dortmund's first clear scoring opportunity in the second half results in 2:0 in the 54th minute when, after a throw-in and diagonal switch of play, the chasing players were not properly marked and Haller was lucky enough to score directly from the sharp cross (while in a duel with Tapsoba). Officially, this goal was recorded as an own goal. After 62 minutes the *expected goals* (xG) statistic is displayed: It shows 0.83 for Leverkusen and 0.54 for Dortmund. To give the game a positive turn, Xabi Alonso adjusts his lineup and aims to increase presence in the penalty area with his substitutions. Bakker, Bellarabi and Frimpong are brought in to create scoring opportunities for Hložek and Azmoun via crosses. Also, there are additional offensive players on the pitch with Diaby (like Bellarabi in relation with "dribbling") and Demirbay (then in combination with "combining" and scoring from distance).

Leverkusen ultimately loses despite a strong performance. It is difficult to prove, but it seems as though the team lacked the necessary confidence in their play at that time. The game that the spectators saw was a high-quality match, even if the standings at the time did not (yet) reflect this.

In the Europa League, the first leg against AS Monaco takes place for a few weeks later in a very tough February. Leverkusen approaches their opponents' 1-5-2-3 formation, which tends to be slow and deliberate in possession until the tempo accelerates in the opponent's half, with a 1-4-2-3-1 setup in which Hložek plays as a true No. 9, supported by Diaby on the left, Wirtz as the No. 10, and Amiri on the right. The first leg of the Europa League features a high effective playing time (82 minutes), which results from the many extended possession phases of both teams. It is a game with minimal physical duels, and neither team's possession truly generates a goal threat or a decisive change of pace due to the rigid positional structure. A lot of balls are played sideways; the teams rarely manage to play progressive diagonal passes.

Monaco takes the lead after just nine minutes thanks to a very bizarre own goal by Lukas Hrádecký. Leverkusen quickly equalizes after the break when Frimpong plays the ball towards Wirtz and Diaby. Diaby benefits from the interaction with Wirtz, displays all his quality and agility and scores to make it 1:1. Shortly afterwards, Leverkusen even takes it 2:1 lead but ultimately lost this typical "draw game" by two long-range shots in stoppage time, making the final score 2:3.

A few days later the next Bundesliga game follows: Mainz 05 visits the BayArena. Xabi Alonso makes major rotations (bringing in Demirbay, Kossounou, Azmoun and Sinkgraven), although the core tactical structure remains the same, particularly in possession.

Leverkusen struggles to find rhythm and plays with large positional gaps in between, which made team coordination challenging. At the same time, it is clear that the mutual on-field understanding is not yet fully developed, and the early-season struggles have not yet been completely shaken off. Tapsoba misses a penalty (23'); nevertheless, Leverkusen equalizes via a counterattack (Amiri, 32'). However, it remains an unfortunate game for the Werkself: In injury time of the first half, Leverkusen loses a duel in their own penalty box twice and concedes the 1:2 goal. At half-time, Hincapié and Frimpong come shifting the initial 1-4-2-3-1 back into a 1-3-4-1-2 setup. After a counterattack at the start of the second half (58'), Schick levels the score at 2:2 by scoring off a rebound.

Finally, with just under ten minutes remaining, Adli receives a red card for a tactical foul to prevent a goal-scoring opportunity—Mainz scored from the penalty spot to secure the final 3:2 victory.

Overall, Leverkusen's game that day lacks structure, balance and security. Kossounou operates more like a true wing-back, while Adli, as a striker, rarely drops deep.

The second leg against AS Monaco was meant to be a turning point in the season and to bring the team closer together. Leverkusen started with what was considered their best starting eleven, aiming to secure their place in international football next season with a successful Europa League campaign.

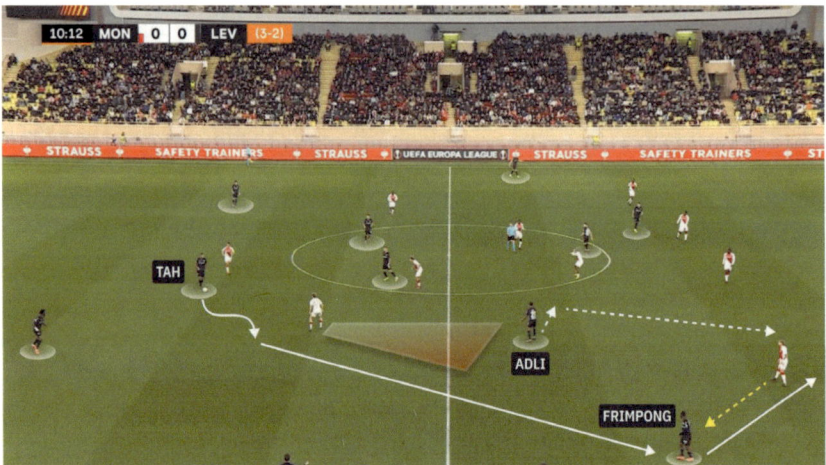

Tah dribbles towards an approaching defender, who takes a step to the right to put Adli in his cover shadow. Adli adjusts his passing line and runs into the space behind his opponent to become a line-crossing passing option for Tah (concept: *cambiar línea* by the pass receiver). This opens the passing route to Frimpong, who has moved away from his direct opponent. Monaco's left-back steps out with Tah's passes to Frimpong, opening the space between him and his centre-back, which Adli immediately runs into. Frimpong notices this movement and delivers the ball perfectly to Adli, who dribbles into the box and scores.

Leverkusen applies the concept of changing passing lines more frequently in this game, especially in the central areas, with the idea of initiating play using both central players on the ball side to bypass Monaco's pressing.

Image bottom left: Leverkusen presses high with a man-oriented approach. Only Hložek covers two opponents so that Wirtz can attack the goalkeeper. Andrich then intercepts the goalkeeper's long clearance with his head.

Leverkusen establishes itself in the opponent's penalty area after a fast counterattack. Palacios and Wirtz display great passing combinations and interactions several times. The attack is completed by Adli, who skillfully heads the chip from Wirtz toward the edge of the six-yard box into the far corner. The moment of Wirtz's vision is remarkable—the brief, instinctive eye contact with Adli, who shares the same imagination and intention for the space and the pass as Wirtz. Adli makes his run from behind the defenders to capitalize the attack.

Game Conclusion

Compared to the first leg, Leverkusen presents a different side: Playing in their usual – and strongest – structure with arguably the best available lineup, Leverkusen immediately applies pressure and takes the lead 1:0 after 13 minutes (Wirtz). Leverkusen is well in control and then concede a penalty, which is unexpectedly converted to make it 1:1 (19'). The Werkself remains unfazed and responds immediately, securing a quick go-ahead goal.

Overall, it is a strong performance, even if at times too many attackers are positioned on the same horizontal line and without propper staggering. As a result, they can often only present themselves as passing options in static position or attack directly from deep—both of which hinder structured build up play.

In the second half, Leverkusen controls the game and scores in the 58th minute after a beautiful through ball from Wirtz to Adli to make it 3:1. Their tactical clarity becomes apparent in the way they execute their game plan but it is also evident that not everything is stable and instinctive yet. Defensively, Bayer struggles with organization at times and does not apply defensive pressure effectively, which results in too many good chances for the opposition even though Monaco is not pressing Leverkusen constantly.

In this phase, Leverkusen pushes for the decisive goal with counterattacks and direct attacking play but fails to capitalize despite numerous chances. Monaco's equalizer through Embolo after a cross from the right wing comes as a result of insufficient marking and weak duels in the box. The game goes into extra time, where Leverkusen gradually gains more ball control although they fail to create any clear scoring opportunities. Shortly before the end, the game shifts again in Monaco's favor—but no more goals were scored. Leverkusen wins on penalties—all shooters convert.

Series, 12.03.2023

The victory in Monaco on penalties served as an initial spark for the team. After a very tough February, it would now take until the beginning of May before the Werkself suffers another defeat.

In the second game after Monaco, the Werkself celebrated a convincing victory against the "Old Lady" from Berlin, but benefited primarily from their own ice-cold utilization of opportunities and the high intuitive (socio-affective) connection between Frimpong and Diaby, who shine as a dynamic duo on the right side. The 1:0 is a joint production, and the 2:0 is scored shortly after. In between, Leverkusen concedes a penalty—their seventh in the 2022/2023 Bundesliga season alone. Despite the decisive result, it was an uneventful game that Leverkusen ultimately won almost effortlessly 4:1, without particularly standing out. On Leverkusen's side, Diaby impresses with his outstanding initiative and agility, as does Wirtz, who repeatedly suggests with his play that he can decide matches single-handedly.

The Werkself is developing an ever better understanding of its own game, which nevertheless remains somewhat fragile. The players are improving their coordination, which is also evident in the equalizer against Werder Bremen:

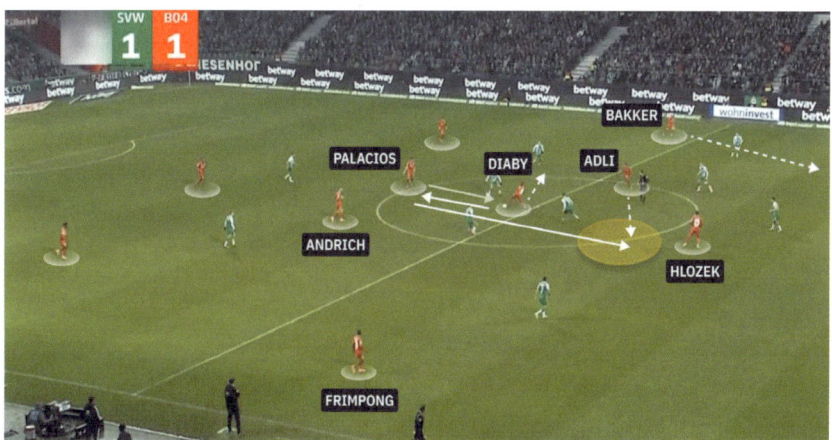

The equalizer against Bremen: Positionally, Hložek and Frimpong provide vertical threat and pin down the opponent. Diaby drops back from his position between the lines into the center circle, pulling one of Bremen's central defenders out of the defensive structure. Diaby, together with Adli, creates a square shape along with the two No. 6s, Palacios and Andrich. He delays Palacios' pass slightly on the return (to lure the opponent even more) and repositions himself laterally. Adli recognizes the space that has become available, makes a diagonal run behind his opponents, and receives the pass through the gap. As the pace of play increases and the box is attacked, left winger Bakker levels the score with a volley to make it 1:1.

Game Conclusion

At the start, the spectators in Bremen saw an evenly contested game, which went into the break at 1:1. Bremen repeatedly exploited Leverkusen's man-to-man marking in the five-man backline with well-timed runs and opening upspaces to attack. This led to danger at times. Leverkusen attempted to control the game, but only managed to do so at the start of the second half and was promptly rewarded with a 2:1 lead through a deflected shot on goal (56' Frimpong – already his seventh Bundesliga goal). Bremen then threw everything forward but Leverkusen held firm. In the 83rd minute, Leverkusen launched the decisive counterattack down the left side, which Hložek headed in to make it 3:1. The handball penalty three minutes later for Bremen did not change anything, although converted to make the final score 3:2.

Hints, 19.03.2023

The win in Bremen was followed by a smooth progression in the Europa League against Ferencváros Budapest, where the Werkself won both the first and second legs 2:0. The biggest possible test of endurance is coming up in the Bundesliga: Leverkusen hosts the German record champions. The atmosphere on both sides could hardly be more different: Leverkusen on a strong run and extending their winning streak with every game, and Munich, seemingly in a constant (mood) crisis. Bayern coach Julian Nagelsmann, who - even though no one suspects it at this point - will coach his final game for Bayern sets his team up in a 1-3-5-2 / 1-5-3-2 hybrid formation. Munich repeatedly pushes players high up the pitch and presses Leverkusen deep (width covered, striker always positioned high, and runs targeting open gaps). Xabi Alonso opts for a tactical approach that will become more common in the following season: A 1-3-4-3 shape without a traditional striker, providing extreme positional flexibility. Several notable personnel decisions: Andrich plays as a center-back alongside Tapsoba and Kossounou. Hincapié who can also operate as a left half-back, plays as a left full-back . Frimpong maintains his usual high and wide role on the right. Demirbay and Palacios form the central midfield pairing, while the forward line remains fluid and dynamic, with the agile and quick trio of Diaby, Wirtz, and Adli, who are constantly coordinate and position themselves intelligently in open space.

The Werkself faces a significant defensive challenge but effectively minimizes the opponent's impact through high work rate and collective defensive organization.

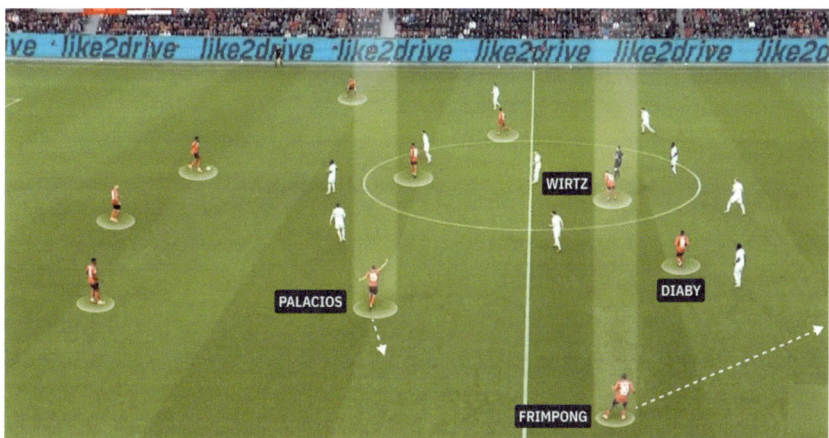

Leverkusen creates both positional and numerical advantages on the right side through positioning: Palacios raises his arm and signals that he will move out to the right. Frimpong positions himself high and prepares to attack the space, while Diaby occupies his opponent inside and Wirtz, with his position between the lines, attracts the attention of the opposing center-backs, who are therefore on the verge of stepping forward.

Leverkusen controls Bayern's very wide wingers with a five-man backline. The center-backs of the back three are always ready to absorb the movements/positional shifts of Bayern's strikers and attacking midfielders, and step out defensively in certain situations. Leverkusen's front three does not press the ball but shifts compactly to constrict space—yet remains alert to pounce on the ball. You can also see from the posture of Leverkusen's last line how they adjust their lateral positioning based on the body orientation and the movement cues of the ball holder to improve reaction speed for the next pass.

Leverkusen presses the ball with Frimpong, while the rest of the team shifts laterally. Kossounou is ready to step out to challenge Mané, while Palacios tracks and defends Goretzka's deep run. In this scene, Frimpong marks Davies on the inside lane and tries to force him onto his right (presumably weaker) foot.

Alonso and Leverkusen make slight adjustments at half-time: With more passing options in the build-up phase (more players dropping deeper), Bayern's pressing routes are stretched. The front row shifts with the ball and can be played deep both to feet and into space. This allows Leverkusen to utilize the pace and movement of the offensive players more effectively in the opponent's half. Bayern attempts to counter this and sets up direct man-marking. As a result, Munich takes a high risk, as one long ball or a lost sprinting duel against the rapid Leverkusen strikers can now be enough to create a clear goalscoring opportunity for Leverkusen.

Game Conclusion

Bayern's first real goal chance—a deflected shot from Kimmich—makes it 0:1. Before that, Leverkusen had been sharp, proactive, and active with and against the ball. Leverkusen entered half-time with a narrow deficit and without creating any clear goalscoring opportunities. On the other hand, Bayern played a strong game without completely dominating. At half-time, Nagelsmann makes three substitutions: Müller, Mané and Cancelo come off— Musiala, Gnabry and Coman come on. In the second half, it becomes apparent that Leverkusen pushes higher up the pitch and presses Bayern earlier.

A remarkable thing about this game: Bayer turns it around after two VAR interventions, resulting in two penalties—both following fouls on Adli, who was twice accused of diving. On Leverkusen's side, Palacios stands out, showing himself to be extremely strong in duel and intercepting numerous passes. In addition, he has the ability to "leave his mark" in his distinct Argentinian style. In terms of performance alone, it is difficult to understand why Julian Nagelsmann was ultimately dismissedd as Bayern coach: The record champions' off-ball movement, positioning and chance creation could have produced a different result; Leverkusen won through two penalty decisions, which were mainly due to individual defensive errors. The few clear scoring opportunities Bayern managed to create are a testament to the defensive discipline that Xabi Alonso has given his team since taking over the office. Leverkusen shows more than just promise and makes it clear that this team will be a force to be reckoned with in the coming season.

Applications, 20.04.2023

Leverkusen's winning streak continues even after the victory against the record champions. Too often in the past, teams have struggled to return to regular league life after a win against Bayern, but the Werkself are already showing an impressive level of maturity that will benefit the team in the next season. Leverkusen wins the games against Schalke and Eintracht Frankfurt before the next Europa League challenge awaits: Belgian surprise package Union Saint Gilloise (USG), a team that had already caused problems for Union Berlin, now poses a serious test for the Werkself. Coach Karel Geraerts has molded the tactically intriguing team into a difficult opponent to face: In a mixture of 1-5-3-2 and 1-3-4-3 formations, the Belgians constantly seek duels and favor direct attacking play. A certain Victor Boniface, their striker, stands out having already scored five times for USG in the Europa League. The direct style of play is also enabled by the fact that, in addition to Boniface's physical presence, his relentless movements in the front row makes it very difficult to control him and defend him effectively. At the start of the first game, he operates more as a left winger, positioned slightly deeper. This changes in the second half when the Nigerian converts his first chance to make it 0:1.

Leverkusen creates their first chance to score in the first leg after just seven minutes with a counterattack. The Werkself plays very wide and have few players between the lines; the middle is virtually empty. In the evenly contested first half, USG proves to bean unpleasant opponent that relies on physicality and direct, long passing. At half-time, Xabi Alonso makes tactical adjustments to reduce the distance between players, allowing for better passing connections and, as a result, better possession control. This remains the case with Boniface's 0:1; however, the game stays complicated: USG performs well and repeatedly threatens on the counter with well-rehearsed attacks. At the same time, the Belgians defend with discipline and structure. It takes until the 82nd minute before Wirtz relives the Werkself and equalizes with a long-range shot after a pass from Azmoun. The goal originates from a fundamental tactical principle: a diagonal shift to the left half, from where Hincapié plays a diagonal pass to the striker who fails to break through and redirects the ball to Wirtz. In the final phase of the match, Leverkusen increases the pressure but fails to generate any clear chances. So it goes, accompanied by another draw in the league, balanced into the return match to Belgium.

Leverkusen controls Saint-Gilloise's possession without actually engaging in physical duels. Amiri's positioning disrupts the opponent's build-up, as the opponent does not dare to go one-on-one and thus cannot gain any momentum. All potential passing stations are blocked or covered by Leverkusen to limit access. Close spacing shrinks the field, while making it difficult to play passes into the space behind the defensive line. For Union Saint-Gilloise, the only remaining option is to recycle possession through the backline.

Game Conclusion

Leverkusen bursts into the second leg like a torpedo: Diaby, sprinting aggressively and pressing high, scored immediately after a second ball won in counter-pressing and a quick pin pass to make it 1:0 after two minutes. Leverkusen remains clinical (second shot on goal) and scores 2:0 after a fast attack by Bakker (37'). Nevertheless, it is a complicated game for the Werkself, with Leverkusen focused on maintaining control and preventing attacks or shots on goal from the opponent. They can always pose the threat through their dynamism and at the same time control the opponent by keeping the ball safe. In the 60th minute Bakker presses the goalkeeper, who, under pressure, played the ball into Frimpong's feet. Frimpong capitalizes and finishes into the empty goal without any problems. After USG pulls one back, Bayer briefly wobbbles and conceded further shots on target (including one off the crossbar), but does not concede again. Instead, it was Hložek who makes it 4:1 after a rebounded effort from Diaby. A well-earned victory against a very difficult opponent, where Victor Boniface in particular leaves a lasting impression on Leverkusen.

The Last Victory of the Season, 23.04.2023

The Werkself celebrates the semi-finals of the Europa League, although they must now face RB Leipzig immediately in Bunderliga again in the run-up to the English weeks. In view of the workload in the Europa League, Xabi Alonso rotates his squad; however, the basic system and positioning remain unchanged. Particularly noteworthy in the game against RB is the movement and role of the central midfielders Demirbay and Andrich, who repeatedly drop alongside the central defender (Tah), allowing the respective wide center-back to push out higher up and creating staggered positioning on the flanks. This is particularly relevant for the right side, as Frimpong is pushed to the highest offensive positionand activated as a winger. Several tactical patterns can also be observed in this game, which also develop their effect in the title-challenging season.

Opposing runs to lure out the center-backs: Adli drops deeper as a passing option, while Diaby simultaneously makes a deep run to exploit the gap between the two defenders. Leipzig defender Klostermann reacts in time and does not follow Adli, but instead cuts off the supposed gap in behind.

The 1:0 for Leverkusen comes through a sudden increase in tempo: Andrich receives the ball from Kossounou in an open stance and, while the ball is on its way, already lifts his head three times. He sees how Diaby identifies the same opportunity in this situation and makes a run in behind. Diaby's direct opponent Gvardiol fails to anticipate the play in time and is still positioned in front of him, which makes it almost impossible for him - not only due tu Diaby's natural explosiveness - to track him or stop his run. Diaby receives the ball in stride and then finds Hložek with his pass, who scores to make it 1:0. In the TV replay of the goal, it almost seems as if the pass was too long for Andrich and forced him to accelerate. He only touches the ball with his toe and nudges it forward toward the onrushing Diaby, with success - and an example of the shared intentions of both players.

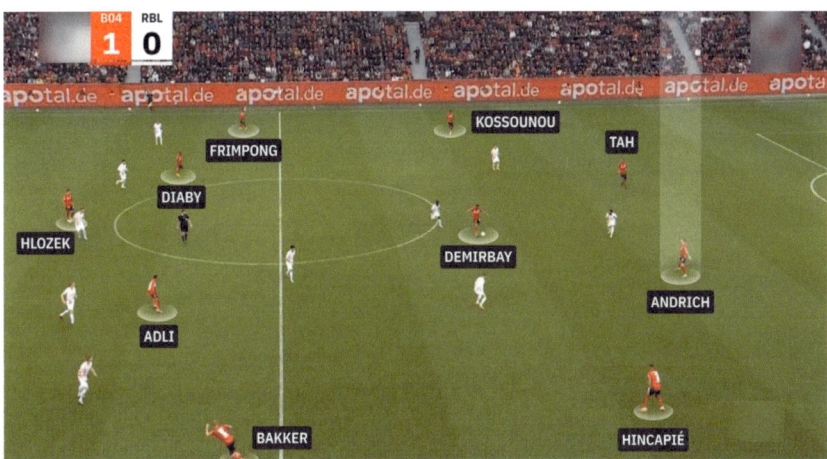

In this frame, you can clearly see the unique positioning of Andrich, who normally acts as a defensive midfielder in front of the backline. He drops alongside Tah and thus creates a temporary back four when build-up play begins or when the ball is circulated from deep. The wide center-backs Kossounou and Hincapié position themselves wider, allowing the nominal wingers Frimpong and Bakker, to push extremely high. With Adli and Diaby occupying the half-space and Hložek leading the line as the striker a 5v5 scenario or direct 1v1 matchups are created on the last line. At the same time, Leverkusen retains control in their own half with the ball.

Game Conclusion

Early on, Leverkusen focuses on defending their own goal and rarely finds relief. At the same time, clear-cut chances from Leipzig remain limited, although they still dominate the game. As a result, Leverkusen grows into the game more, without generating any goal-scoring opportunities of their own. It turns into a highly competitive game in which both teams seek to eliminate each other's threats. Hincapié, pushing forward, makes the first statement with a long-range shot off the crossbar (32'). Leverkusen's 1:0 goal towards the end of the first half arrives unexpectedly. By the 44th minute, both teams are nearly level in *expected goals* (xG B04: 0.25 to RBL: 0.22) – so the game remains tightly contested with few clear chances. Leverkusen has to withstand heavy pressure in the second half before securing their final three points of the season: Leipzig intensifies the pressure, forcing Hrádecký and Co. to make a series of crucial saves. Although they manage brief phases of control with the ball, overall this is far from a controlled performance, but a tough, hard-fought battle for Alonso's team. In the 84th minute, Leverkusen breaks away on their final counterattack, leading to a tactical foul in the penalty area: a red card and a penalty follow, which Amiri calmly slots home for the 2:0 victory. This victory highlights Leverkusen's evolution throughout the season: they can now win ugly, not just with speed or possession, but through multiple approaches. Their once-fragile defense now appears solid at just the right time for the final weeks. What remains unforeseen: It is Leverkusen's last victory in the 2022-23 season.

Derby, 05.05.2023

Leverkusen concludes April with a goalless draw against Union Berlin – and thus sees their impressive 14-game unbeaten run across all competitions come to an end. In the derby against FC, Bakker's advanced positioning is notable, as Leverkusen defends with a back four, particularly in high pressing situations. Here Bakker effectively acts as the third striker alongside Diaby and Adli, while Wirtz drops deeper into a hybrid No. 10/8 role. Meanwhile, Frimpong adjusts to Adli's positioning, deciding situationally whether to operate as a right winger or a deeper outlet. The full-backs are already exhibiting movements that will define Leverkusen's playstyle in the next season: By making diagonal runs toward goal, they consistently position themselves inside the box during their own attack.

Leverkusen's principles on the counterattack: avoid direct duels, but maintain "forward" mode. The preferred direction of play is diagonal, but a lateral pass can also be used if it secures possession of the ball. The basic idea is to practice a "play-and-go" approach, since the player who initiates the pass and is tackled, will subsequently be lost from sight of by the opponents chasing the ball. Therefore, Adli plays the ball wide in the center circle (instead of dribbling past his opponent and thus using his agility and speed advantage) and then continues his run. He is free to finish on Diaby's low-driven cross pass, because all of his opponents are focused on the ball and have lost track of him— and he scores the 1:1 equalizer against Cologne.

Game Conclusion

Leverkusen starts powerfully although with slightlyless control of the game through possession and structured defending. Cologne, playing in an unconventional and direct manner, creates their first offensive move in the 14th minute and scored through Selke, who makes it 1:0. The goal conceded is another example of the defensive vulnerabilities of Leverkusen's back line. In the 28th minute, Bayer equalizes: After winning the ball at their own byline, the team counterattacks diagonally forward, not always immediately playing pass immediately, but briefly linking up to each other until good deep passing options emerge. You could describe it as a slightly less vertical approach, allowing more players to join the attack thus ensuring that the ball is not lost immediately. Instead of engaging in tackles, the ball is played away immediately - especially diagonally or to the side - when pressure aarives. This also means that many players arrive in numbers with force in the opponent's penalty box.

With the equalizer, Leverkusen gains momentum, combines effectively, pressures the opponent even more and thus create scoring chances. The distances in possession immediately tighten, which allows better connections between the players. It was precisely in this phase that Cologne restores their lead through Davie Selke on their second shot on target - again after an attack on Leverkusen's left side (36'). The introduction of Palacios after 60 minutes brings more punch and structure to Leverkusen's play, as they attempt to turn the game around, but struggle to find success. Cologne, on the other hand, positions three attacking players directly against Leverkusen's back three, thus creating a constant threat to Leverkusen's last line. In the second half, Leverkusen's game structure improves, therefore as well their relationships and thus their interactions. However, this does not change the result.

Mourinho, 11.05.2023

In the semi-finals of the Europa League, Xabi Alonso faces former coach José Mourinho once again. The extroverted Portuguese, who has won numerous titles with his pragmatic game management, yet represents a formidable challenge for the Werkself with AS Roma. The Romans are extremely compact centrally and forcefully direct Leverkusen out wide. This causes Andrich and Palacios struggle finding rhythm into the game and becoming actively involved. Only wide-area passes are possible. At the same time, Roma defensive line remains positioned high, making it difficult for Leverkusen to gain momentum. Leverkusen attempts to counter this by attacking down the half-spaces in order to find space in front of the opposing defensive line and to bypass the first compact block. When this happens, Rom's outside players drop deeper, so that the last line always remains occupied by five players. Overall, the team operates in a highly functional and coordinated manner, which makes it exceptionally difficult to find gaps.

Leverkusen relies heavily with a mobile striker (Hložek), who creates numerical superiority and drops deep as a passing option, then lays off the ball so that the game can progress forward again. In doing so, he is generally left unmarked or not tracked by his opponent.

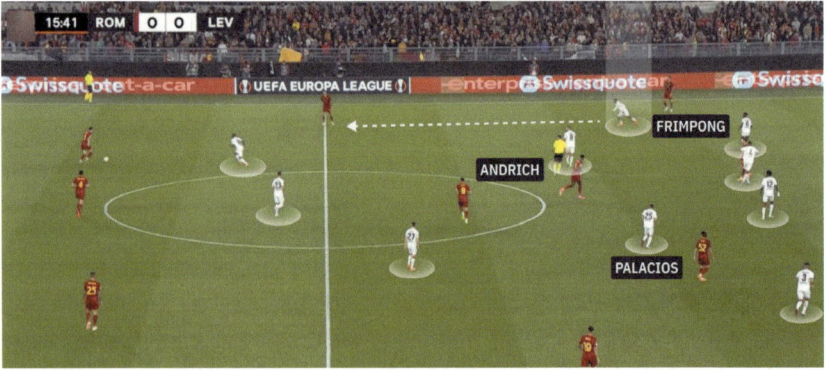

Leverkusen's five-man backline transitions fluidly into a back four: Frimpong steps out to press Roma's left-back, while the remaining defensive four mark the attackers. At the same time, potential defensive challenges for Leverkusen already emerge: With two attackers positioned between the lines, ready to make deep runs and exploit gaps in the defensive line, Leverkusen must react with strong positioning and heightened awareness for the next pass options. Leverkusen's three-man frontline, in conjunction with the central players Palacios and Andrich, attempt to lock down the center and block direct penetration through the middle.

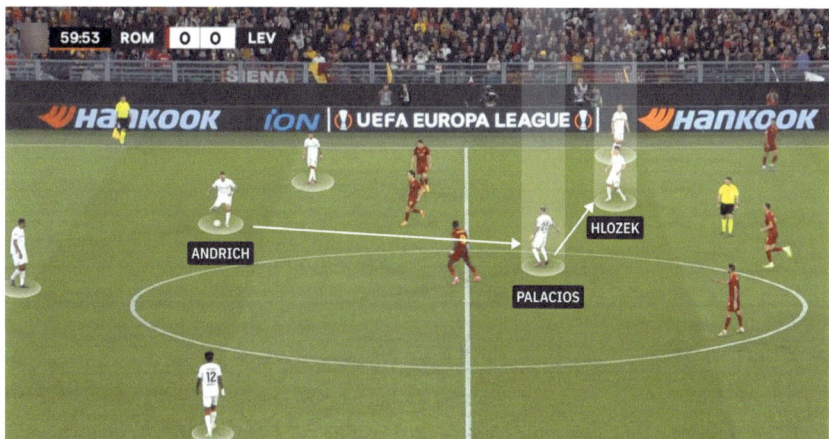

Leverkusen accelerates play against Roma: Andrich disguises his pass—his body position suggests a lateral ball, but he instead breaks through Roma's first defensive line and finds Palacios, who from a tight position, redirects the ball first-time to Hložek in a classic third-man combination. Hložek instantly accelerates play alongside Bakker on the left wing, and together they create a wide-ranging advance to the penalty area. Against Roma's compact defensive structure, changes of pace through vertical passes and subsequent proximity to support quick tempo shifts via vertical passes and immediate close support play.

Game Conclusion

Leverkusen registers the first shot on goal after 43 seconds. The first half remains tight and controlled, in which both teams are highly aware of each other's strengths and do everything to neutralize them. At the start of the second half, Leverkusen grows into the game and increasingly makes controlled advances into the penalty area. This is often achieved by breaking through the first defensive line and injecting tempo into attacks. Midway through this phase, Roma takes a 1:0 lead "out of nowhere" with their first real chance, as Bove scores in the 63rd minute. After the goal, Roma immediately drops deeper, defending in a compact 1-5-3-2 shape in their own half. However, their defensive line does not remain static—their shifting height makes it an ongoing challenge for Leverkusen. Breaking through Roma's well-structured defense remains difficult, limiting Leverkusen's ability to dictate tempo or create surprises, while Roma constantly threatens on the counterattacks. Not until the 88th minute does Frimpong get a massive chance to equalize following a mistake by Roma goalkeeper Rui Patrício, but his shot was cleared off the line.

Overall, Roma employs every possible means to secure victory, regardless of aesthetics. They ultimately succeed, as Leverkusen struggles to generate clear scoring chances against their compact, disruptive style of play.
The second leg follows the same pattern—Leverkusen battles Roma's disciplined Italian defense, which spares no effort in shaping the game to its advantage.

After being eliminated in the Europa League semi-finals, Leverkusen's season ends with little significance; as a result, the Werkself comes close to missing out on European qualification for the following season. In his first Bundesliga season, Xabi Alonso has already accomplished a great deal: Since taking over in October, his team has progressively absorbed and internalized his game idea; he has stabilized the defense and capitalized on the players' strengths to build a dynamic and effective counterattacking system. Alonso guided Leverkusen from the relegation zone to the Europa League semi-finals. Above all, the team has developed greater maturity and clarity, despite the final game of the season against VfL Bochum suggesting otherwise. This laid the foundation for a historic season, though from the outside, it may not have seemed so at the time. Xabi Alonso , however, was already certain of what was to come: "At the end of the season, I asked some players who also had offers from other clubs to stay. I said, 'Please trust me. When you come back from the summer, we're going to have an outstanding season.'"[198] How right he was ...

198 Alonso in Robles 2024.

Excursus: Stage Spaces

"We all have to focus everything on the ball; it is the central player. Without the ball there is nothing; the ball is the mother, the source of life in football. What is the goal for? So that the ball gets in. Without the ball, nothing has any meaning."[199]

JUANMA LILLO

Jorge Valdano, 1978 World Cup Winner with Argentina, former Real Madrid coach and executive, and widely regarded as a football philosopher, is clear in his statement: "This Leverkusen was built around the ball. It is a team that masters both: space as well as possession. They have such a great sense of rhythm and so much conviction that they don't hit timid long balls. They keep passing short balls to each other with infinite patience until a gap opens."[200] A team structured around the ball, with ever-changing shapes and formations, requires a different perspective. This leads us to the concept of stage spaces, which is central in FC Barcelona's methodology and has strongly influenced on other coaches within Spain. On the one hand, it views the football game as a sequence of interdependent situations and sequences. On the other hand, it focuses on structuring a team around the ball as the central element, using key guiding principles to provide players with clear reference points for better decision-making. Moving beyond traditional formations and rigid tactical thinking, this approach fosters a fluid structure, enabling players to interact intuitively and with coordinated movements to achieve the next game objective based on shared intentions (see additional excursus).

---

199 Lillo 2011.
200 Valdano in Cáceres & Selldorf 2024.

Spacetime

In football, time is determined by space and vice versa. Space, time and opportunity are three closely related variables. One cannot be fully understood without the other. The time allotted for a player's action is reduced the closer they are to the opponent's goal. In most game situations there is little time to intervene.[201] In a sport like football, success is not about sheer speed, but rather how it is managed. Opportunity is the precise moment to intervene with the right action at the right time. Football is not about acting as fast as possible, but rather at the right moment and with the right intensity—perfect timing.

Controlling space is crucial for optimal positioning and generating new spaces. Looking at the profile of our players, it is worth thinking about which player types and attributes a coach wants in specific areas of the pitch, depending on upcoming opponents and their individual traits. Our players should also be aware of ways to buy their teammates extra time and space. Often the key to this is disguising movements and intentions.

When we watch a football match, some observers compare a game to a well-structured film: For sequences of actions to interconnect smoothly, the film's internal logic must remain intact. This is usually shaped by preceding events, which establish the foundation for the present moment and influence what happens next.

The idea of "stage spaces" follows a similar concept: every action in the game originates from what preceded it and shapes what follow. Similar to the film, a scenario is created, from which new options for action arise. What makes football unique—unlike film—is that it follows no strict script but instead resembles ongoing improvisational theater. We know the overarching theme, but neither dialogue nor moments are predetermined. Put simply, these in-game events unfold dynamically across "before," "during," and "after" phases and cannot be replicated. They are dynamic interaction spaces based on the position of the ball, and shaped by numerous contextual influences (environment, minute of play, score, emotions, ...).[202]

Long-time FC Barcelona coach Joan Vila suggests the following four criteria for assessing a game situation both in matches and in training: ball, space, teammates, opponents. He does this based on the following questions: [203]

201 Moreno 2013.
202 Peris 2022.
203 Vila 2023.

What?	The ball — what is the happening, where is is it positioned? How is it moving? Who has possession?
Where?	Space — what are the distances between the players relative to the ball?
Who?	Teammates — how and in which direction do movements occur, both in possession (dribbling, passing) and off the ball (support runs, positioning after ball recovery)? How are my teammates positioned? What is their body orientation (profile), field of vision, and the current game flow?
Why?	Opponent — how is their defensive structure set up? Do we need to adjust positioning? Can we disrupt their shape?
What for?	To score a goal! Enjoy the game, create numerical advantages, dominate possession as a team, compete more effectively, and win!

Football is not merely read; it is envisioned, shaped, and anticipated. If we are able to "read" the game, we are already reacting too late because it is over. Players must recognize—or at least intuitively sense—what is unfolding to take the initiative. Each game space has its own set of priorities where the player must identify the appropiate action (under the given circumstances). This is largely determined by the opponent's positioning.

The starting point is always the ball—it is the primary reference point. Where is the ball? Who controls it? What are our options? We seek to maintain possession with the ultimate goal of scoring. Players do not position themselves in rigid tactical lines but instead occupy dynamic spatial zones. Football is viewed as as a sequence of spatial occupations in which each phase depends on the previous one and always introduces an element of unpredictability, a fundamental characteristic of the game. Passing lines are understood as communication channels in which a pass is not merely executed but also conveys a message.

"The interactions between the players are the pass, the running path, the space, the numerical superiority. Anyone who observes them will quickly see elements that make it clear that an idea has not yet reached the desired dimension. Because to achieve this dimension, you have to know what elements make up the game. If you only look at the play and not the pass, you won't notice it. Every pass is a message." [204]

PACO SEIRUL·LO

Naturally, much of this thinking is shaped by FC Barcelona, but these criteria help us better understand the game as a whole. The concept of stage spaces aligns with this perspective. Paco Seirul·lo, who spent years working alongside Johan Cruyff and Pep Guardiola in Barcelona and later helped define and refine the methodology and working methods of La Masia, the famous youth academy of FC Barcelona, explains the concept of stage spaces as follows:

"We don't want to look at the simple and linear, but at the complex: everything is connected to everything. Nothing happens that can't happen, but everything the players do is interactions, not just action. (...) It is not an action, it is an interaction. Because when I do something to you, something changes in you, and you change something in me. (...) In football there are no plays. Everyone always talks about plays. (...) We should finally understand that football is not a sequence of plays, but a sequence of complex situations. Messi has the ball and is in a certain situation because something happened before; and while he is performing an action, things are happening around him that make it possible. (...)

We try to take the initiative as quickly as possible, not because we want to have the ball, but because we want to create a situation that is favorable for us. This is what we call 'stage space'. It is defined by the following considerations: Where is the ball? What situation is it in? Where are the opponents? How big is the distance between the ball, the opponents, and our players? Which player is currently moving where? And where does the ball go? In which direction is the game moving overall? How is it currently organized? We are talking about just one game situation that may only last a fraction of a second. As soon as the ball is moved, the players also move and a new situation arises." [205]

204 Seirul·lo quoted from Perarnau 2016.
205 Seirul·lo quoted from Perarnau 2016.

All players are always part of the game situation. How do I interact with my teammates when I have possession? How is my posture, my body positioning, and alignment? What cues am I providing to teammates (and opponents) through my stance and orientation? What is our intention? The same applies when my team has possession, but I am not directly on the ball: How can I draw defensive attention to help maintain a favorable ball situation? How can I create passing options or open space? How can I simplify the game for my teammates? It is obvious to rephrase these questions when the opponent is in possession. The key is that all players are in continuous interaction, constantly seeking to turn this into an advantage.

In the first part of the book we already looked at the different types of support and passing options, which are also relevant here.

All these questions relate to the criteria by which stage spaces can be assessed. These criteria[206] can help coaches not only in the evaluate in-game situations, but also guide their coaching during training:

→ Location (Where am I positioned? In which channel, at what hight or zone?)

→ Distances (What are our relative distances? Who is positioned near, and who is further away?)

→ Orientation (Where am I looking? What is my posture? What is our directional movement? Who is available to receive the ball, and with what intention? These considerations apply to every phase and direction of the game.)

→ Movements (What is the intention behind our movements? The primary objectives are to maintain possession and disorganize the opponent. This includes tracking the trajectories of both players and the ball.)

With regard to a player's positioning, a deeper consideration can be made of his body alignment and posture in relation to the surrounding spaces. Additionally, his situation in time and space must be examined - specifically, how rhythm and tempo shift due to player movements and ball circulation.[207]

206 Peris 2022, Damunt & Quintana 2023, Seirul·lo 2024.
207 Damunt & Quintana 2023.

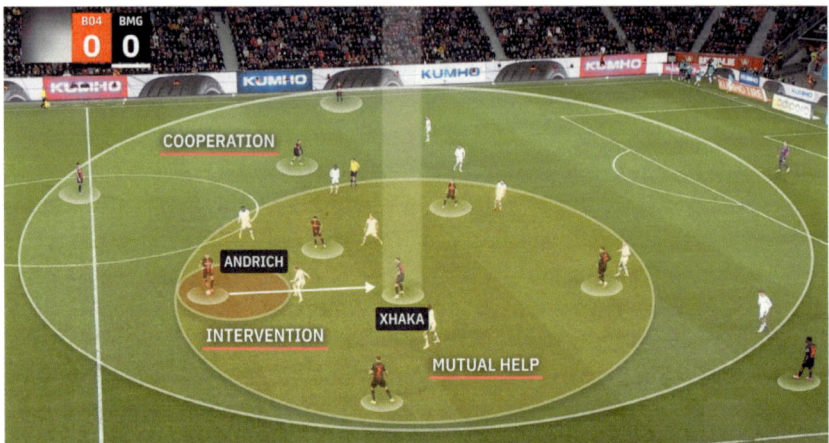

Long-time Barça coach Albert Peris compares stage spaces with a collection of pixels that together make up a particular photo.[208] The concept of stage space helps understand the organization of a team in relation to the ball within space. The ball is therefore not only a means to play but also the core and the goal of the game.[209] The concept of stage space offers a way to understand football from a different perspective, which, when applied consistently, can even replace classic game systems: Since the organization of a team is structured around the ball and not through fixed positions in a traditional sense, different roles, profiles and actions emerge among the players, who all share the ball on the basis of "a high levelof internal team communication" which remains indecipherable to the opponent.[210] It is important that everyone plays rather than dividing strictly into attackers and defenders. Positioning is rationally structured according to functional demands within the game, aiming to create one of the four key advantages (in terms of position, numerical superiority, quality, or socio-affectivity).[211]

The ball is the central reference point for the positioning of the team. So-called "contour lines" form around it, which determine the morphology of the stage spaces. This morphology emerges through an "imaginary line that connects players forming a contour relative to the ball at a specific moment in time."[212] The

208 Peris 2022.
209 Guardiola in Seirul·lo 2024.
210 Seirul·lo 2024.
211 Ibid. & Peris 2022.
212 Seirul·lo 2024.

characteristics of the players within these contour lines shape the architecture of the stage spaces and represent the qualitative elements.[213] You can think of the contour lines as being similar to those surrounding an atmospheric high pressure area or to the contours on a topographic map that indicate elevation.[214] Consequently, they represent a distinct approach to structuring teams compared to the typical approach of organizing teams in fixed positonal lines. Instead of rigid positional tasks, roles and functions shift dynamically within a network of interdependent relationships.

Within these contour lines, the position of the players serves as a communication channel and is intended to help the player in possession of the ball to assert the team's most important interest at a given moment.[215] Paco Seirul·lo speaks of the "social motor skills of the game, which are developed through internal communication."[216] Based on the distances to the ball, different interaction spaces are formed, classified into three zones based on proximity to the ball:[217]

→ (Space of) intervention (direct ball possession, accompanied by the sense of "owning" the ball")[218]
→ (space of) mutual help (possibility to receive a immediate pass or to give support with the feeling of being "close")[219]
→ (Space of) cooperation (positioned farther away, with a sense of "being distant")[220]

Since both positioning and gameplay dynamics rely on the relationships between the players and their intentions, the positioning cannot be separated from its emotional component. During the game, the players must develop a certain sense of connection in order to "feel" the game and achieve collective flow (see further explanations in the chapter on training proposals).
The *space of intervention* is formed by the players closest to the ball, who can directly influence play without requiring significant movement. The space of intervention is a compact area around the ball, typically occupied by only a few players.[221]

213 Ibid.
214 Damunt & Quintana 2023.
215 Ibid.
216 Ibid.
217 Ibid.
218 Ibid.
219 Ibid.
220 Ibid.
221 Seirul·lo 2024.

The *space of mutual help* is shared by those players who, through their positioning and (mutual) communication, offer subsequent options to the player in possession of the ball. The focus here is particularly on associative play—providing support and continuity. The *space of mutual assistance / help* is larger than the *intervention space*, and "its limit lies in the temporal-spatial adaptation in which players must communicate effectively in this intermediate level space at all moments of the game (possession and ball recovery)."[222] Players positioned along the contour lines of *mutual help* should execute trajectories that are difficult for their opponents to anticipate, deceiving them and simplifying their own game progress.[223] The concept of "deception" (*"engañar"* and "cheating" plays a major role in football. Paco Seirul·lo writes about this in his book *ADN Barca*: "The term 'tricking' covers all the movements that our pass receivers make, shifting from one side to the other in an active or an optimistic manner [*or 'activity', where the word 'trajín' can also have a more vulgar meaning, essentially aimed at causing massive harm to the other person; author's note*], but always doing something useful, in this case for others. Their goal is always to support the teammate with the ball. These are generally very short, well-timed off-ball runs, executed in the right space and at the right moment to disrupt opponents' intentions while facilitating the play for the ball possessor."[224] These players usually appear in the space of mutual assistance by creating proximity to the ball carrier from their previous space of cooperation.[225] It is precisely the switching between different "contour lines" that opens communication channels, ensuring optimal passing options for the ball holder and creating a new stage space. The teammate should conceal his intention for as long as possible and only reveal it at the last moment, so that the opponents nearby are caught off guard, but not the ball possessor.[226]

Another option is "appearing": the teammate supports the ball carrier by emerging from behind the opponent on his "blind side", while the opponent waits almost statically for the holder's next move.[227] This briefly creates a 2v1 advantage that the team in possession can exploit.

---

222 Ibid.
223 Ibid.
224 Ibid.
225 Ibid.
226 Ibid.
227 Seirul·lo 2024

A further option for impacting possession without actually touching it is blocking: this involves anticipating the opponent's path and getting in his way so that he has to make a slight detour to to the ball. This action gives the ball possessor more time to carry out his follow-up actions. Paco Seirul·lo points out the necessity "not to use the arms as a tool," as this would be a foul and therefore result in losing the ball.[228]

The players who do not occupy one of the contour lines around the ball are positioned in the *space of cooperation.* Their function is essentially to "ensure the efficiency and stability of the team in the phase in which it finds itself, by completing a global organization that they know can help them achieve their common objectives."[229] Anticipation of the next situation is particularly crucial. Martí Cifuentes emphasizes the important role of the players away from the ball:

> *"The players who bind ['fix'] opponents (although players far from the ball can also be 'correctors' [in the sense of 'balancing' the structure]) must always pose a threat to the opposing defensive line. If this is not the case, the ability to create spaces that other players can exploit is weakened. Cruyff used to tell players to try to look deep (and pass to the furthest players) when making the first pass; this is a way of breaking through the lines and, in the event of a loss of possession, usually creates a context conducive to counter-pressing. In my opinion, there is also little discussion about the interactions that can arise between players furthest from the ball. Not only does the opposing player ['Fijador' / literally: fixer] create advantages for the preceding lines, but I think it is essential to create guidelines on how they can benefit each other."[230]*

Understanding one's role in relation to this context and defining criteria of spatial phases is particularly crucial when implementing positional play. An effective structural form of a stage space is determined by the approximate occupation of two zones and three tracks, as well as their three contour lines.[231] The players should be able to maintain visual access to the ball from their position, "i.e., no player 'covers' another teammate and is at a 'functional' distance from all teammates."[232]

228 Ibid.
229 Ibid.
230 Cifuentes in Ballesteros 2020.
231 Seirul·lo 2024.
232 Ibid.

The goal is "communicative efficiency, ensuring all forms of intra-team communication with 'optimal' effort to be as 'assertive' as possible during ball ciculation
and 'sensitive' as possible during ball recovery."[233]

> *"Also to make it clear to the players that their position has a function at a*
> *certain time. When you have possession of the ball, what can you do with it to*
> *gain an advantage? If you are a close receiver [in the mutual support space],*
> *what are you trying to accomplish? Do you want to get the ball? Do you want to*
> *lure the opponent? Do you want to progress the game? Do you want to create*
> *space for a teammate? If you are a player in a remote space [cooperation]:*
> *What is your role at this moment? Are you aware that you could be a possible*
> *ball receiver at any moment? At the same time, could you also compensate*
> *through your positioning ('compensator'), forming the foundation for counter-*
> *pressing? Is it possible to adjust your position in such a way that binds oppo-*
> *nents? Could your next supporting position even place you as a goal scorer?"[234]*
> **CARLES MARTÍNEZ**

As the team structures itself around the ball in the concept of stage spaces, a
"hybrid form of organization" is created, which requires a level of improvisation
due to constantly new playing spaces and where anticipation enhances teamwork.[235] This organization eliminates any static order to ensure seamless adaptation due to the constant changes within the game. To achieve this, it is important
to foster personal creativity and enable intra-team communication during ball
possession to unsettle and surprise the opponent.
When the opponent has possession of the ball, the team's initiative and 'competitive energy' become crucial to limit the opponent's overall initiative.[236] Through
constant reorganization in possession or self-organization at the moment of
ball recovery new spaces emerge. These are shaped by the resulting relational
advantages and enable the team to be as proactive and adaptable as possible.[237]
Seirul·lo also explains why the game should not be "read": The concept of reading "assumes that there is a fixed, already written, thus static, immovable past
that is unchanging in writing; therefore, anyone could easily read it because it is
stable in time. There is no such possibility in football, where the uncertain and
immediate, once lived, is now past, does not repeat itself, and does not remain

233 Seirul·lo 2024.
234 Martinez in Ballesteros 2020.
235 Seirul·lo 2024.
236 Seirul·lo 2024.
237 Ibid.

written down to be read. For this reason, it is necessary to anticipate what will be played out while living in this fleeting present."[238]

The goal is to continiously take initiative in the game and, as a result, apply constant attacking pressure. This requires "an exceptionally structured team, which creates fluid yet structured stage spaces, where training principles manifest themselves because no one acquires this style of play simply by wearing a different jersey, but by developing it through intensive training in which spatial variability is continuously refined and understood.(...) By playing in the opponent's half, the initiative takes on a new dimension."[239]

The stage spaces are highly versatile. On the one hand, they allow for dynamic spatial arrangements by organizing various positional layers around the ball and the ball possessor. Their flexibillity also adapts the qualities and number of players. The aim is to be precise in possession and assertive in regaining the ball.[240] On the other hand, paces generate continuous, relational advantages can be generated to help maintain that the initiative and stability of the team are achieved and maintained. All of this serves the fundamental process of enabling players to exchange and communicate freely within the playing area through the ball. This grants them freedom and encourages their creativity to play fluid, intelligent football.[241]

The former coaches of Barcelona's youth academy "La Masia" Xavier Damunt and Marc Quintana refer to the type of fluid, dynamic football that results from this form of organization as the "game of spaces" or "space game" *(Juego de Ubicación)* to illustrate the difference from the classic interpretation of positional play *(Juego de Posición)*.[242] The concept of space is chosen because it is inherently more dynamic than the concept of position, which lacks an inherent sensense of movement.[243] Instead, the concept of space combines positional aspects (body position and profile in relation to the ball and teammates) and situational awareness (orientation with regard to time and space) in order to play together fluidly in different spaces and "travel together with the ball"

238 Seirul·lo 2024.
239 Ibid.
240 Seirul·lo 2024.
241 Ibid.
242 Damunt & Quintana 2023.
243 Guerrero 2020.

as a consistent further development of positional play.[244] Within these different views on positional play, as already mentioned in the debate on the "relationism game", there are many subtleties and differences in nuances. It should be noted that this style of football requires a high degree of socio-affective ("looking out for one another") and thus strong interpersonal dynamics; as well as a shared understanding of the game based on collective intentions and that these teams tipically organize themselves around the ball. Isaac Guerrero, former head of methodology at FC Barcelona, currently working at AC Venice, sees an analogy between the game and a biological cell that must be connected to the rest of the body in order to survive.[245] Conversely, a cell that remains integrated within the overall system cannot be easily damaged because it is absorbed into it, just like the player within the game.[246] The game should therefore unite all players through the ball in order to reach utimate goal – scoring. Interconectivity is an essential component of this.[247] The specific interpretation of positional or spatial play depends on the coach's precise game idea, the individual player's traits, as well as the cultural context and external circumstances of each location.

Within the "location game," Isaac Guerrero defines the "three Rs," which can be seen as a further refinement of FC Barcelona's established three "Ps" (*Posición, Possesión, Presión*): [248]

→ *Redistribución* ("Redistribution")
  ↳ Players circulate possession without the need for immediate game progress.
  ↳ This phase can be used to reorganize the team. Possession of the ball is not an end in itself; it serves to prepare for the next promising situation.
→ *Reubicación* ("Replacement" / "Repositioning" / "Reorientation")
  ↳ The players adjust their positioning and prepare for a tactical reset.
  ↳ This includes shifting positions or adjusting body posture and orientation; constantly seeking the optimal position in relation to the current game situation.
  ↳ The players' natural positional preferences are taken into account so that they can express themselves in line with their strengths.

244 Ibid.
245 Ibid.
246 Ibid.
247 Guerrero 2020.
248 Ibid.

→ *Recuperación* ("Recovery")
- ↳ At this moment, the primary goal is to immediately regain possession of the ball.
- ↳ Counter-pressing is fundamental to this interpretation of football.
- ↳ The previous positional arrangement created ideal conditions for regaining the ball as quickly as possible.

This philosophy of football helps the team express its identity. Every player is involved. The game is inherently communicative due to the constant interaction.[249] Players recognize and respond their teammates within the stage space.[250] Through this ongoing interaction, which players engage in to pursue their shared objectives, new solutions continuously emerge, and the players enter a state of flow.[251] (Further information on the topic of "flow" can be found in the Training Proposals chapter). Following on from this, Damunt and Quintana identify three further key factors for the successful implementation of the "location game":[252]

→ **Communication:** To operate effectively in tight spaces, optimal communication between the players is essential. This communication occurs through movements and the ball. Optimal communication allows players to understand each other, anticipate each other's intentions, and offer adequate solutions before the opponent does. At the same time, teams should aim to mislead and deceive opponents through deceptive communication so that their reactions remain uncertain.[253]

→ **Multidirectionality:** A characteristic of the "location game" is the lack of a permanent fixed, forward-oriented objective. The primary goal is not just to progress the game but to retain the ball and share it between all teammates. This game concept creates a fluid, multidirectional dynamic (360°). This helps the team maintain possession while destabilizing the opponent, bringing the game closer to their goal with each moment of play. The game remains multidirectional, but always with the final goal of scoring .

249 Ibid.
250 Seirul·lo 2024.
251 Guerrero 2020.
252 Damunt & Quintana 2023.
253 Peris 2022.

136

→ **Dynamic equilibrium:** Due to the fact that the "*Three Rs*" (Redistribution, Repositioning, Recovery) are in continuous practice, the team must constantly adapt to new contexts under different conditions (such as varying distances , a specific number of central players, etc.). Dynamic equilibrium refers to the team's ability to continuously adjust to the game's ever-changing flow while maintaining the core principles to achieve optimal stage spaces. The game is about finding the right symmetry to counteract the opponent's organization.

The concept of stage spaces helps identify a different organizational approach than the traditional positional structure within the game, and also incorporates many other components that aid in the implementation of this football idea. Finally, Damunt and Quintana highlight seven key principles that define the game according to this approach,[254] which are also applicable to Bayer Leverkusen's playing style:

→ Initiative
→ Ball possession
→ Ball recovery (in the sense of "counter-pressing")
→ Patience
→ Resilience
→ Submission (of the opponent)
→ New beginning (as a recurring element of the continuous "re-start" of play in possession when a new attack is initiated)

254 Damunt & Quintana 2023.

/

CHAPTER 3

Creating Champions

The team's identity is evolving for the new season, largely due to the highly successful transfer activities of Leverkusen's sporting director Simon Rolfes. In cooperation with Xabi Alonso, they assemble a team perfectly suited to the Basque coach's playing style, with each player possessing the fundamental qualities needed to execute the corresponding role on the pitch. Alonso said: "Last year we were not a possession team, we were a transition team or a counter-attacking team. (...) I'm not a fundamentalist who demands that we have to play a certain way or that this is the only way I'll ever let my team play."[255] His ideas are also shaped by his observations in his first season as a Bundesliga coach: "The rhythm of the game is very high here all the time. If you don't control the transitions, you suffer. In Spain we play more in spaces; in England, the spaces are narrowed depending on the opponent, and here, there is more space, more openness—you move from space to space. It is very complicated to dominate the opponent like this because many teams go on the offensive. Here [in Germany], the coaches are very brave when it comes to telling the players to move forward. You don't see many very defensive teams. Here, they move forward, press high, create many man-to-man situations—more than in the Premier League. There are some great teams in the Premier League that play with a 'low block' [within their own half], and they do it very well. In LaLiga, they have a different pace. The player profile is different."[256]

255 Alonso in Bienkowski 2024.
256 Alonso in Torres 2023.

At the end of the transfer window, Leverkusen acquired eight players, including Matěj Kovář, Granit Xhaka, Victor Boniface, Alejandro Grimaldo, Jonas Hofmann, Nathan Tella, and Josip Stanišić (on loan from Munich), all of whom should play an important role over the course of the season (the Brazilian Arthur is only excluded because he will miss much of the season due to injury). Already in the training camp in Saalfelden, Austria, Alonso is very optimistic: "Last season I arrived in the middle of the season and you have to adapt. Now we have time to work and build the squad the feeling that the team belongs more to you. We can still improve, but I am happy with the work the club has done on the [transfer] market."[257] At the same time, the coach stresses: "I don't want it to be Xabi's Bayer, I want it to be a team. I want the team to know how to play in all areas, to control the ball well, to be stable in defense, to be balanced, to have a good rhythm, to know how to interpret the games... Now we have time to work well and see what we feel comfortable with and what works and what doesn't."[258]

The instructions for the players and the coach's vision are clear: "I have always liked to control games, but that is not easy because the Bundesliga is 'hectic'. We want to be a dynamic team that plays attractive football and is fun for the spectators... but at the same time we want to be intense, maintain our results, and not be vulnerable defensively."[259]

The first glimpses of this style of play are already evident in the early friendly matches: Against SC Paderborn, Real Sociedad , and Olympique Marseille, a clear shift towards possession is already noticeable in many situations.
The Werkself are set to open the season against West Ham United. And the Werkself are ready to thrill their fans: Leverkusen play with infectious enthusiasm, combining fluidly while progressing forward. Hofmann scores the 1:0 with a free kick , following a counterattack (Wirtz winning the ball and quick interaction with Boniface). Their joyfull, expressive style (including heel trick) is also evident in the 2:0 after 17 minutes. There is little the opponent can do to counter Leverkusen's attacking whirlwind; full of confidence and creative fluidity, the Werkself move in sync, almost carried away by their own momentum. What is particularly striking is the frequent exploitation of the the space behind advancing opponents.

257 Alonso in Rubio 2023.
258 Alonso in Rubio (2) 2023.
259 Alonso in Rubio 2023.

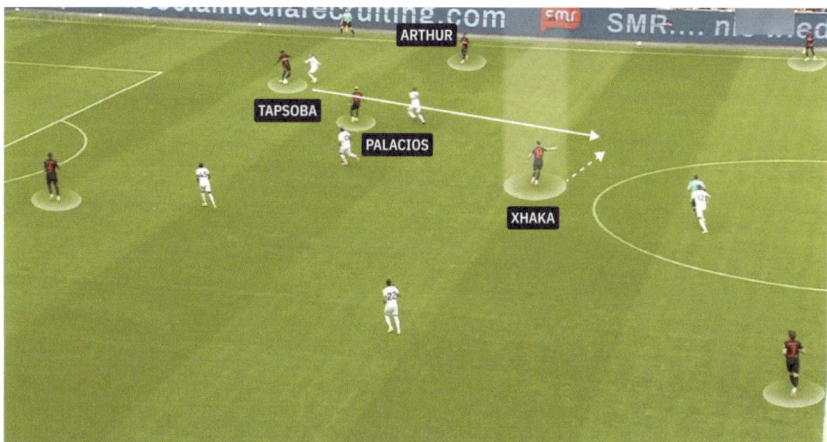

Offer behind the pressing player: Because Palacios (with bleached hair) makes a short passing offer, his movement draws opponents toward him. Tapsoba, who has the ball, recognizes this and bypasses both opponents to find Xhaka in open space.
 Xhaka then shifts his position behind the pressing players to form a new passing line (*'cambiar línea'*). West Ham's defensive shape is stretched because Leverkusen's front line maintains a deliberately wide and deep positioning. With Tapsoba's penetrating pass into the depth, the tempo shifts, and Leverkusen seamlessly combines forward.

Picture left: Leverkusen display exceptional flexibility in their own 'positioning game': The principle of occupying deeper spaces and the gaps between the opponent's defensive lines is clearly visible regardless of each player's natural position. For example, Xhaka, a player with a deep-lying playmaker profile, moves into the build-up phase as a half-back, while the left full-back Arthur slides inward into the number 8 space, as Adli simultanesously positions himself high and wide. The players adjust their positioning both in relation to the ball and the opponent, while also considering their own attributes, which their range of movement depending on the avaible space.

Picture right: Now, you can see the previously mentioned positional structure of Leverkusen's attacking players, who have effectively pinned West Ham's defensive line. Although it may appear like they are acting horizontally aligned, the players constantly adjust their positioning at different heights and form new passing lanes dynamically. Following the concept of "stage spaces", it is now clearly that the previous action determines the next one: The players closest to the ball successfully form distinct passing lanes. Although Leverkusen does not hold a numerical advantage near the ball, almost all Leverkusen players position themselves better (positional advantage) and organize their movements around the ball (see right picture). This strategic setup enables several players to "intervene" directly in the action ("small red circle"), provide immediate support to the ball carrier ("yellow circle") or at least offer the possibility of continuing the game in a more distant area ("large green circle" – cooperation). This positional organization allows Leverkusen to advance through fluid combination play, and sustain the attack until the final execution in the opponent's penalty area.

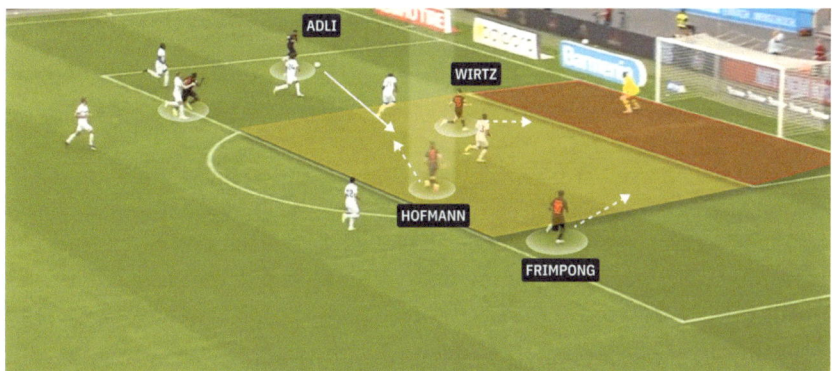

A delivery from wide areas with well-defined positional occupation: With the main intention of a low cross and finish inside the penalty area, three key attacking zones are occupied: Near post—positioned at the six-yard line to receive a flat delivery. Far post—ready to capitalize if the ball bypasses the initial target. Penalty spot—positioned against the defenders' movement, as they are oriented toward their own goal. This setup grants Hofmann, an extra split-second to execute a precise finish, who subsequently scores from this position.

A constant tactical option enabled by Victor Boniface's dynamic striker profile: Boniface, functioning not just as a target man but as a highly mobile number 9, drops deeper to receive the ball, dragging his direct opponent with him, comes towards the ball to be passed to and pulls his direct opponent with him. Jonas Hofmann perceives Boniface's movement, identifies the vacated space behind him, and attacks it with a well-timed run.

Unfortunately, at this moment, Xhaka does not share Hofmann's (and possibly Boniface's) intent to exploit the open space in depth and instead redirects play to the opposite side. One of the biggest developments of Xabi Alonso's team is the growing alignment of shared intentions and structured cooperation among players in their respective roles.

Towards the end of the first half, Bayer momentarily eased their intensity—demonstrating their ability to control the game even without possession. Bayer continues to dominate in the second half. Victor Boniface gets two chances to score after well-timed deep passes, finding himself one-on-one with goalkeeper. On the second opportunity, Boniface is fouled, leading to a penalty, which Robert Andrich converts to seal a 4:0 victory.

Perfect Start, 19.08.2023

Compared to last year, the Werkself faced no difficulties in the first round of the DFB-Pokal against Hamburg-based team Teutonia Ottensen, securing a dominant 8:0 victory. This already highlights the newly developed strength in offensive set-pieces, an area where Robert Andrich offers some interesting insights. He explains to *kicker*: "It's about us scoring set-piece goals, then we get a little treat from the coaches."[260] Looking at the seasons progression and the distribution of goals, this incentive seems to have paid off.

The match against RB Leipzig felt like like a perfect advertisement for Bundesliga: fast, dynamic, and aggressive. In particular, players receiving the ball in a closed stance are repeatedly sprinted amplifying the game's relentless tempo. The pace of play from both teams is exceptionally high, making it a thrilling contest from start to finish.

260 Andrich quoted in Kicker online.

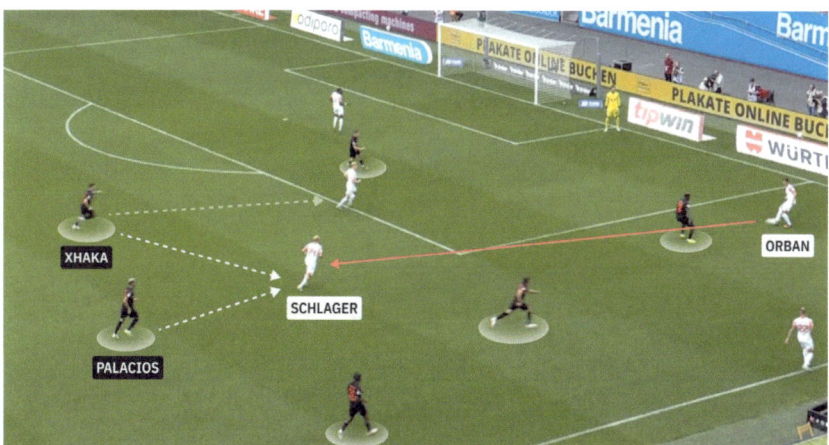

Leverkusen transitions into an aggressive high press. On the one hand, they establish access to their next opponent, but on the other hand, it becomes evident how brilliantly Xhaka and Palacios anticipate Orban's pass to Schlager, immediately closing him down in his restricted position, thereby forcing a turnover. Xhaka also maintains coverage on a second opponent but adjusts his moving pattern depending on Orban's pass direction and ultimately secures possession.

Kossounou delivers a phenomenal pass to Hofmann, bypassing seven opponents in a single move. The pass is delivered with a subtle curve over the foot, making it exceptionally difficult for defenders to track while immediately shifting play diagonally. The pass to Hofmann on the turn signals a drastic tempo shift and initiates Leverkusen's direct attack into depth.

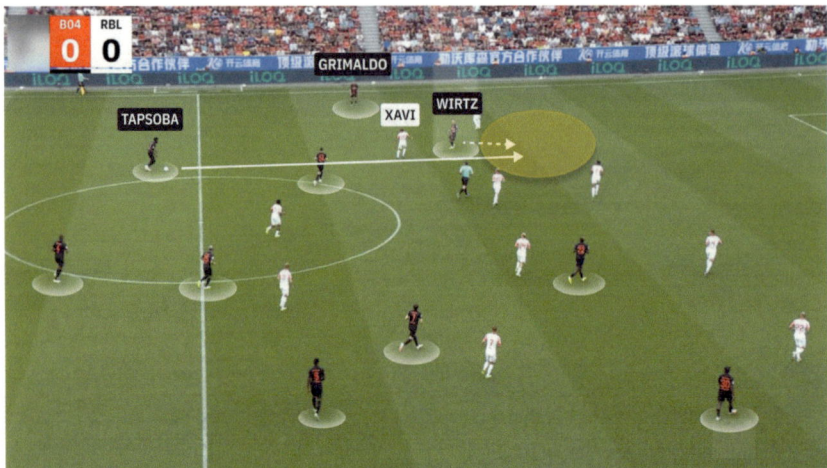

Leverkusen maintain their typical structure, with multiple players positioned between the lines or behind the opposing midfield. With the pass played to Tapsoba, who finds himself time and space, Wirtz moves into the gap between the central defender and full-back. At the exact moment the opposing full-back shifts attention to Grimaldo, Wirtz makes a backward run into open space, positioning himself to receive the ball in the gap. The vertical pass signals a sudden change in tempo, immediately launching an attack on RB Leipzig's defensive line and goal.

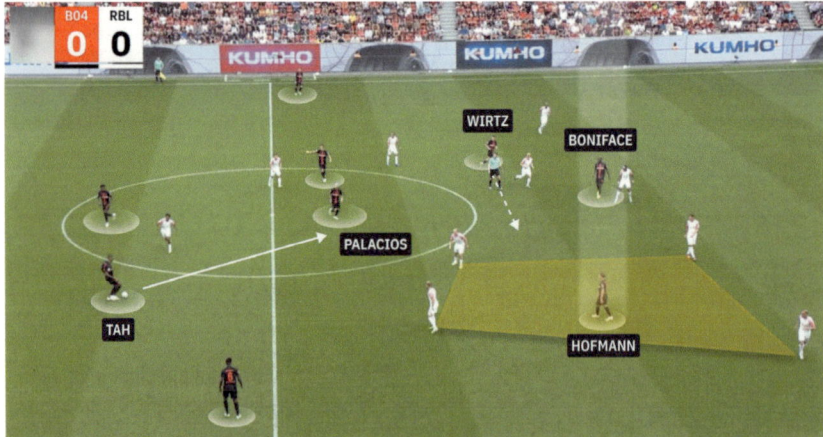

Leverkusen initate play with Tah in possession at the start of the play. Regarding the Werkself's positioning, we see multiple options to facilitate ball progression and maintain continuity. This includes passing options in close proximity, minimizing the risk of losing possession. Additionally, Hofmann's positioning in the *'cuadrado'*, deserves to be specially mentioned. In Spanish, *'cuadrado'* refers to the space formed between the lines, defined by the positioning of the wide midfielder, central midfielder, center-back,

and full-back (see also introductory chapter). A fundamental requirement for this is that opponents are pinned down through positional occupation, as seen here, with Boniface positioned centrally as a striker and Frimpong as a winger.
In this scene, Palacios (positioned behind the first pressing line) receives the ball and can progress play, combining the existing advantages (in Spanish, 'encadenar'). Wirtz makes a diagonal run and closes in on the ball, ensuring he receives the pass while moving. Since all defenders focus solely on the ball, and fail to track his movement, he receives possession with a dynamic advantage, allowing him to immediately continue the attack together with Hofmann.

As the game progresses, Leverkusen gradually takes control through sustained ball possession and executes fluid combinations. However, it is a high turnover that leads to the opening goal: Wirtz plays a precise pass to Victor Boniface, who controls the ball but fails to convert. He maintains possession with a dribble to the outside and finally finds Frimpong with a flat pass close to the goal, who only has to score.(24'). The 2:0 follows after a header by Tah following a corner (35'). The flexibility in positioning in Leverkusen's game is also striking: Xhaka drops out from the center, while Grimaldo reacts immediately to the movement and takes over Xhaka's position in the midfield. The two remain in this arrangement for quite some time, which suggests that it is a clearly communicated principle for the Leverkusen team that the positions should be occupied according to the moment of the game, field height, opponent pressure and ball position. However, the functional roles and tasks within this system can certainly be fluidly swapped. Grimaldo deliberately positions himself behind the pressing player in order to receive the ball while staying out of his opponent's immediate field of vision. At the same time, he adjusts his height strategically to ensure that his first touch immediately takes him past his nearest opponent.
Before half-time, Dani Olmo heads in a corner kick from the right to make it 2:1. In the second half, Leverkusen achieves extreme control of the game and demonstrates excellent positional play in possession. They dictate the game's rhythm (shifting between slow and fast tempo) almost at will and effectively neutralize their opponent's attempts to develop play.

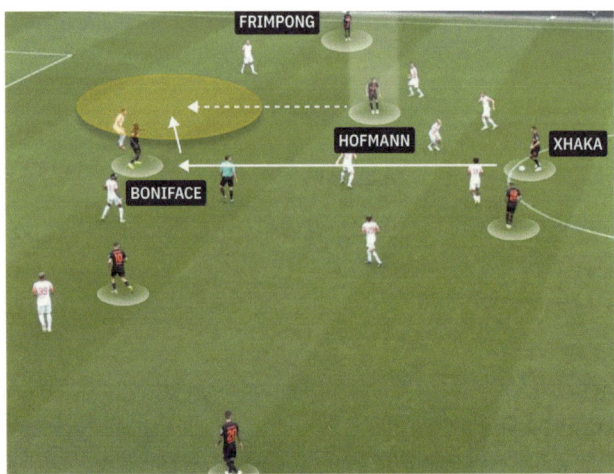

A typical "play to the third man" combined with an attack on the space between the center-back and full-back. Xhaka, in possession of the ball, finds Boniface positioned close to the center-back, effectively pinning him down. Hofmann again occupies the "square" or the space between the lines but is not in an optimal position for Xhaka to pass to from his current angle. By positioning Boniface near the ball-side center-back and Frimpong in a wide position, the space for Hofmann is opening, into which Boniface places the ball. These movements and interactions frequently appear in the early stages of the season.

In the end, it is a counterattack that decides the game: After winning the ball in midfield, Kossounou plays the ball down the right to Frimpong, who crosses with his first touch and allows Wirtz to make it 3:1 with a lob. Leipzig, again after a set piece (free kick from midfield), scored to make it 3:2 – but in the end Leverkusen held on to secure the first three points of the season.

In the Flow, 26.08.2023 & 02.09.2023

The away game against Borussia Mönchengladbach that is not only the next difficult opponent, but also a reunion with former coach Gerardo Seoane. However, the Werkself show little sentimentality, delivering a performance full of authority and class. In the process, the Werkself managed to attack the opponent's penalty area in a variety of ways, creating good, high-caliber scoring chances, many of which were blocked by selfless Gladbach defenders. Leverkusen operates at a high tempo, executing rapid, high-density passing sequences.

Gladbach with ten players in their own penalty area, without exerting pressure on the ball or gaining optimal access to the opponents. The referee's space is always free – Wirtz gladly takes cue of it and is found by Xhaka with a hidden pass. In this scene, the observer first expects a lobbed pass into the box to the onrushing Grimaldo, but instead Wirtz surprisingly receives the ball and can initiate an attack together with Boniface centrally into the box.

Hofmann is positioned between the lines ("in the square") and lures the central defender out. He sees from Wirtz's movement that the opposing central defender is stepping out - Wirtz immediately notices the space and attacks it with a run. Leverkusen consistently identifies opposing running movements, also because the positioning of players between the lines naturally facilitates attacks on the space or backs behind the opponents. A key to this movement and the space being created is the position of Frimpong, who provides a certain width and thus ties up the opposing full-back.

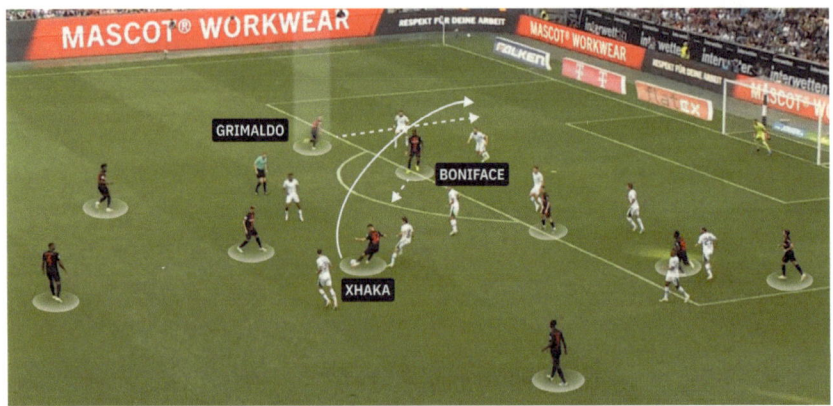

Another counter movement opens the space for Leverkusen to make it 1:0: Xhaka lobs the ball into the penalty area to the onrushing Grimaldo, who can head the ball into the center. There, Boniface (also with a header) prevails and scores 1:0. What has been particularly impressive throughout the season is the hunger and variability in attacking the opponent's box - preferably with flat combinations from foot to foot or high balls towards the edge of the six-yard box.

Leverkusen goes into the break with a well-deserved 2:0 lead. The Werkself repeatedly find the full-backs in the interface between the opposing central defenders and full-backs, thus ensuring positional advantages. A special duo stands out on the right side between half-back, Kossounou and Frimpong, who initiate a particularly large number of attacks. Gladbach have great difficulty closing the gaps in their back four - and this does not change in the second half, which ends with a comfortable 3:0 victory for the Werkself, who show extreme ease in their combinations.

In the next home game against newly promoted Darmstadt 98, the Werkself marches on unfazed and remains in consistent "forward mode". While Boniface made it 1:0 after a counter-attack following a very unfortunate collision between two Darmstadt players, Leverkusen managed to play their own game, unimpressed by the equalizer in the meantime, and consistently played for the next goal. Nevertheless, Darmstadt's 1:1 equalizer after a set piece (played overlong and crossed in front of goal again) is worth mentioning; Leverkusen will concede more goals in an almost identical manner.

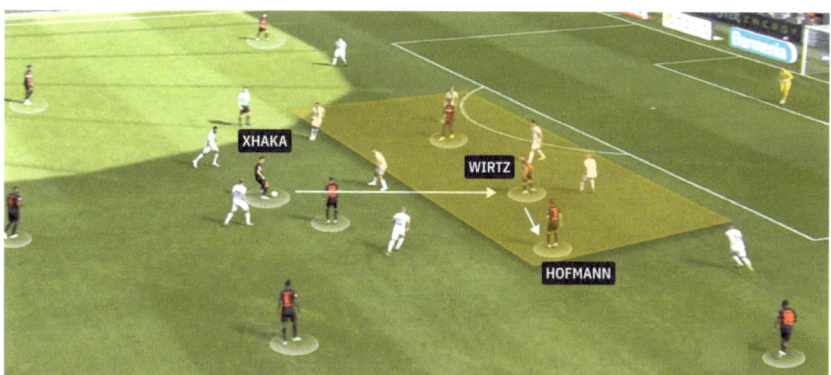

Leverkusen is with three players centrally in front of the central defenders in a positional advantage: Although it is an equal numerical situation, no Darmstadt player has access to the opponent. Wirtz and Hofmann are positioned close to each other, which allows for quick passing and makes it even more difficult for Darmstadt to react or attack. Leverkusen consistently attacks the space in front of the defense through good positioning. In this situation, the opponent's only option is to react, which inevitably results inconstantly being "late".

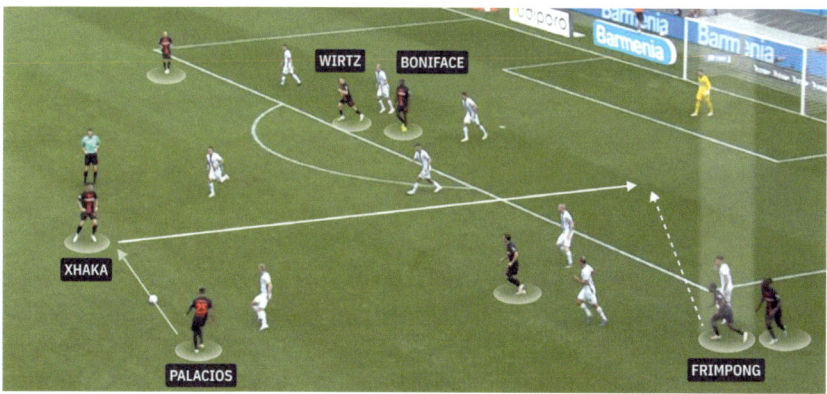

A cross pass is followed by a pass into space: Palacios finds Xhaka, who passes seamlessly into the gap to Frimpong, who is sprinting into the box. Frimpong attacks the back of the defenders diagonally and has a free shot from seven meters diagonally out front of the goal. The resulting gap is also caused by the position of Boniface and Wirtz, who pin down the central defenders in the center.

Hofmann moves out of the right half-space, luring out both the right center-back and the right No. 6, drawing their focus. This opens the space that Kossounou can immediately exploit and he receives it via a pass from Tah.

The Werkself came out flying after the break: Frimpong broke through on the right and came into the penalty area, from where he placed the ball perfectly behind the defence towards the penalty spot. Palacios is there, and his shot is deflected twice and hits the bottom right corner (49'). A perfect pass between the full-back and center-back from Wirtz to Boniface finally makes it 3:1 (61').

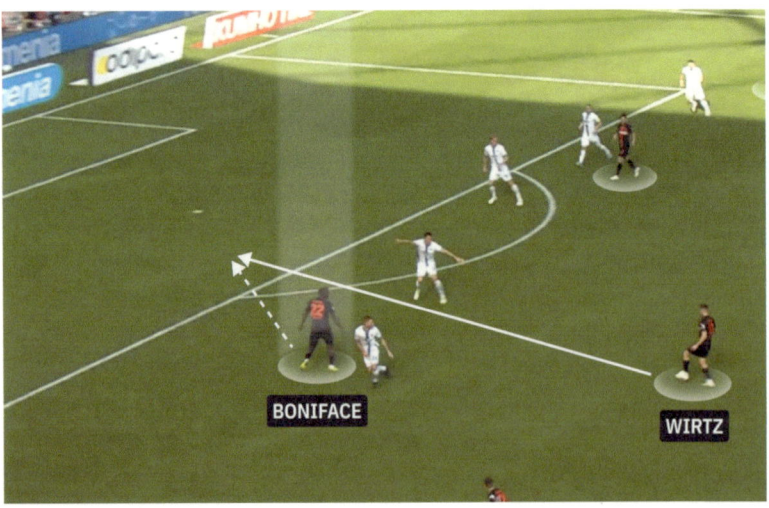

Picture bottom left: Wirtz receives the ball in the space directly in front of the penalty box and with his second touch plays it perfectly into the gap and the run of Victor Boniface, who scores to make it 3:1 against Darmstadt. What is particularly remarkable about this scene is Boniface's position: behind the opposing full-back, who reacts (or has to react) to Grimaldo's run; at the same time, he is positioned to the side of the center-back – opening the gap for himself. Another example of the positional advantage that comes into play here: Because "we" are better positioned, we threaten the goal/the opponent and create a dangerous goal-scoring situation.
Especially in the second half, Boniface repeatedly looks for the space on the left between the full-back and the center-back.

As the game progresses, Leverkusen continues to play consistently for the next goal without slowing down. In the end the score is 5:1 for the Werkself. Overall, Leverkusen feels very comfortable playing through the opposing block despite having a lot of opponents.

How good are "we" really? 15.09.2023

After a dream start to the season, Bayer 04 will face a crucial duel on the fourth matchday: away against record champions Bayern Munich. Xabi Alonso initially sticks with the 1-3-4-3 organisation, whereby the arrangement of the front row can be interpreted as 2-1 with Boniface as a clear No. 9. After about 20 minutes, the Basque decides to make some adjustments out of possession, which leads to more moments with four players in the back line. Instead, Frimpong holds the first pressing line longer and is very focused on Bayern's full-back Davies. Bayern starts with momentum and a strong pressing, managing to double the ball carrier. At the same time, Munich repeatedly initiated attacks and dangerous counter-attacks, which eventually resulted in something tangible: After a corner kick extension, Harry Kane is on the far post and heads the ball in to make it 0:1. Especially in the early stages of the game, Bayern presses aggressively – Leverkusen struggles to break free and maintain prolonged possession.

Goretzka tries to pass the ball through to Kane. In this scene you can see very clearly how Tapsoba acts in a direct duel with Kane: He recognizes early on Kane's intention to run between Tah and himself, blocks his path and thus prevents timely start into the box. This delay gives Hofmann even more time to put pressure on Goretzka, who has the ball, so that the impending danger is thwarted.

You can see the quality, development and a certain maturity in Leverkusen's game: Whereas in the past the team might have "collapsed" following an early goal against Bayern in Munich and conceded further goals, they now remain clear-headed and stick to their plan. The team remains calm when in possession of the ball and consistently looks for its strengths. After 20 minutes, this becomes increasingly successful and the team finds their combinations. It was precisely during this phase that Grimaldo scored the beautiful equaliser with a free kick (24'). Already in the first half, a tight, intense game is developing, in which the momentum constantly swings back and forth. Towards the end of the first half, Bayern once again gains the upper hand and has very good scoring opportunities.

In the second half, Bayern tries even more clearly to block the two No. 6s in the build-up (Xhaka & Palacios) with Kane and Müller. Leverkusen responds to this by having Grimaldo drop back as the "third" No. 6 and thus become available to play. The space he has cleared is immediately occupied by Palacios, who is making a deep run. In this way, Leverkusen progresses - in principle in stages - to the next level.

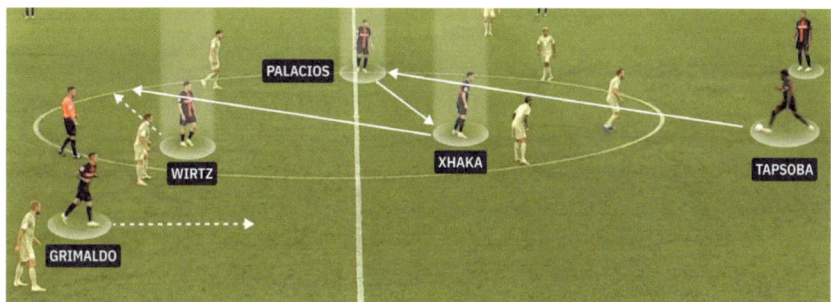

Leverkusen occupies the center with four players who are positioned either behind the first pressing line or in the gaps, in order to move directly and easily to a higher level. Leverkusen makes their way forward almost positioned like a staircase and outplay seven opponents with three passes through the center (like visible in the image section). The passes through the center are synonymous with a change of pace, as the opponent is immediately attacked "in the flow." This passing sequence recurs frequently and again with the Werkself, who repeatedly tries to move forward through the center with quick passes.

In the 70th minute of the game, Bayern's *xG* value is 2.27 – Leverkusen's is 0.48 – also an expression of the fact that Bayern has good scoring opportunities and ultimately fails to capitalise on them. As a result, however, Leverkusen again has a few chances to score (Wirtz with Boniface, Boniface himself), which shows in the open game that each of the two top teams is capable of scoring a goal at any time. At first it seems as if Bayern has the final say: Goretzka scores in the 86th minute to make it 2:1. But then Leverkusen counters once again with a late goal. Leverkusen is pressing, but unable to finish. The referee then calls a foul after a tackle between Davies and Hofmann in the Bayern penalty area - Palacios converts the penalty in the 94th minute to equalize. A top match in which the Munich team finishes with a 2:2 draw due to insufficient utilization of opportunities, and the Leverkusen team with their own luck.

Like Clockwork – 21.09.2023 – 24.09.2023 – 30.09.2023

The game against Bayern was a first self-test for the Werkself – and they passed it. In the following games, Bayer flies from result to result, even if each individual result is based on a tireless, perfectionist approach and by no means comes "by itself". In the Europa League, the Swedish champions from Häcken visit, and Leverkusen beats them 4:0. It is already noticeable here that Alonso trusts Matěj Kovář in goal in the cup competitions and allows him playing time, while also regularly substituting other players. But the rotation (which happens less frequently at the beginning of the season than later on) does not harm the flow of the game or the players' desire to combine with each other: Wirtz scores after a through pass from Boniface, who has dropped back slightly from his position; Adli makes it 2:0 when he runs in from the left wing with outstanding speed and timing and converts a deep cross from Xhaka. Boniface and Hofmann "put the lid on it" in the second half.

The next game is against the brave newcomer from Heidenheim. But even if the Werkself has some trouble against the team of the Brenz region, at least at times, the qualitative difference between the individual players is very clear.

The 1:0 for Leverkusen: Palacios recognizes that Boniface is controlling his direct opponent and has a 1v1 situation with his back to the opponent in the penalty area. Boniface physically dominates his opponent and uses his body technique (and thus his qualitative advantage) turn past his opponent and score the 1:0.

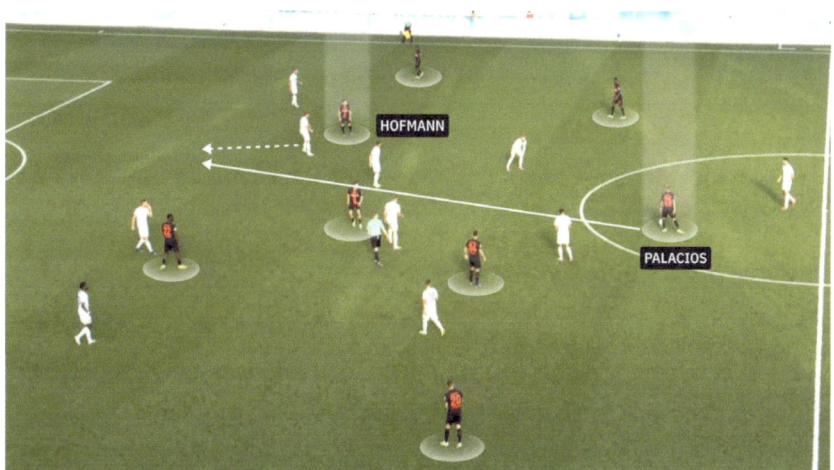

Palacios with his second stroke of genius against Heidenheim: While the Argentinian has his body profile (and thus his posture) oriented more towards the outside, both he and Hofmann perceive the space behind the backline against a very static opponent (no pressure on the ball). At this moment, both share the same intention to attack this space, with Palacios additionally deceiving the opponent with his body position and the deep pass catching the opponent unprepared. Hofmann safely converts the opportunity to score 2:1.

In the end, Leverkusen secures an unchallenged 4:1 victory, in which constantly attacking the opposition's backs and coordinated runs into depth were key to success.

In the following game, Mainz 05 manages to heavily compact the center, which results in a lot of ball possession for Leverkusen's center backs. In this game, the Werkself is also lucky: With the first real attack, Leverkusen takes a 1:0 lead. A pass from Frimpong is cleared by a Mainz player into his own goal (18'). Until then, Leverkusen struggles to get into the final third against a hard-working Mainz. The Werkself try to control the game through possession of the ball and thus minimizes the danger of possible counterattacks from Mainz. Therefore, the ball is mainly moved in a confined space with players very close to each other, without necessarily wanting to gain ground or create a goal-scoring opportunity – the main aim is to control the game. In this context, the high quality and secu-rity of Leverkusen's passing game become clear once again: Despite high levels of aggressiveness in duels and Mainz's great attention, Xhaka and Co. manage to combine their way through and stay in possession of the ball. Technical details are also crucial: Xhaka plays the ball directly to Wirtz's leading foot as he moves behind the opponent, allowing him to turn in one fluid movement and continue the play forward. This technical superiority is a key factor in consistently evading Mainz's combat-oriented game. This also includes appropriate balance and good transition behavior after losing the ball.

Leverkusen in the transition moment after losing the ball: A total of five players drop back to cover the spaces behind while Palacios slows down the opponent and directs them straight towards one side so that the game is not changed into the counterattack. Another special detail: Nearly all the players in Leverkusen's back line are looking towards the player with the ball and trying to anticipate his intentions. As a result, Hofmann is already changing his course and slowing down slightly. A second later, thanks to his good anticipation, he manages to intercept the pass and start the counterattack.

Picture bottom left: All ten Leverkusen field players are in the Mainz half. You can see the narrow distances and the open passing lines, which allow a pass to a teammate at any time. Tapsoba recognizes that Wirtz and Boniface are only partially marked on the last line and even then would have a 1v1 with opponents in behind, which in the case of Boniface already led to a goal against Heidenheim from a similar situation. Tapsoba plays the ball deep to Boniface, who is fouled. Grimaldo scores a great goal from the following free kick to make it 2:0 for Leverkusen.

When Hofmann scores to make it 3:0 after a counterattack (perfect interpretation of the advantage by the referee), (65'), the game is finally decided. Overall, it could be seen a more pragmatic side to Leverkusen in this game, which also shows how much respect Leverkusen has for Mainz. It's about maximum game control through ball possession – which ultimately works out thanks to the course of the game, and Leverkusen's highly efficient finishing.

Start to dream – 08.10.2023

The Werkself also remained unscratched in their second group match in the Europa League and managed to win 2:1 after taking a quick 2:0 lead despite the unfamiliar artificial turf in Molde (Norway). Even the players who have not yet received much playing time show that they can be relied on.

A game that, in Xabi Alonso's memory, was a point from which he should "dream" a little more was the derby against 1. FC Köln and, in particular Jonas Hofmann's 1:0 goal: "Because it wasn't Jonas' goal, it was a total team play. They [Cologne] put us under a lot of pressure. (...) We built up bit by bit and lured their pressing. And as soon as we reached the space behind their No. 6s, we accelerated the game and attacked with many players in the penalty area. Boniface played the ball wide, and after a cross from Grimaldo, Wirtz's back pass gave Jonas the space to score. That was a perfect summary of our ambitions, how we want to play. We had a good change of pace between the 'stability moment' and the 'acceleration moment' and then a ruthless finish."[261] For a coach, this collective moment is almost equal to the joy you get from playing, says Alonso, adding: "When you're on the sidelines watching, you still think, 'I wish I could do what they're doing!' As any kid can tell you, football is about playing."[262] In any case, the Werkself are on the right track in trying to implement the ideas and instructions of their coach.

261 Alonso in Robles 2024.
262 Ibid.

Bayer plays continuously with close spacing, well connected and at an extremely high pace. What is striking is the tight positioning other and the many changes of pace, to then consistently exploit the speed advantage when the majority of the opponents have already been outplayed, and to use the momentum to get into the box and score. In doing so, inside runs or quick one-twos (play & go) are continually sought. It shows the typical Leverkusen game with a certain verticality of passing lines behind the opponent or in the gaps between defenders.

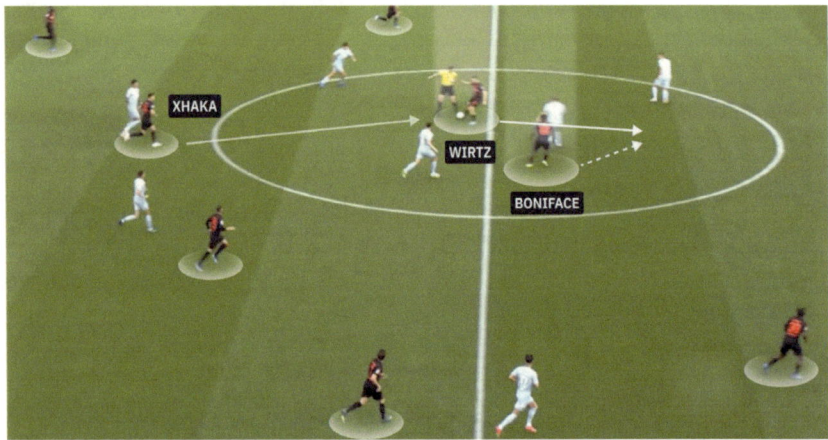

True to the motto: "If you are positioned with the referee, you are always free." Leverkusen finds Xhaka diagonally forward in the build-up, who can continue the play through the center (via the center circle). Wirtz and Boniface are positioned close together and perfectly synchronized: Wirtz plays the ball with one touch behind the standing leg into the space to Boniface, who moves exactly behind the opponent and can accelerate the game further forward. The first change of pace was already triggered with the pass from Xhaka, who now, with the progress of the game via Wirtz and Boniface, ensures that Leverkusen is able to go at maximum speed to take advantage of the many outplayed opponents and attack Cologne's goal.

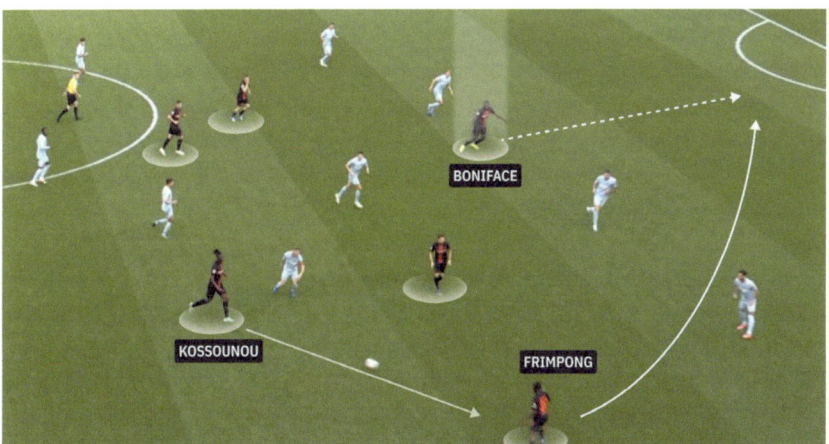

Boniface is well positioned between the two central defenders and out of their reach. At the same time, there is no pressure on the player with the ball from the defending team. Kossounou finds the free Frimpong, who has the space and time to cross into the open space behind the opposing back four, into which Boniface can run freely. Boniface's closest opponent/center-back is in a worse position (because he is behind him) and can only challenge him for the ball with great difficulty.

Directly after the opening goal: Leverkusen pushes Cologne to one side and puts the ball carrier under extreme pressure. Here you can see once again the guiding and forcing to one side, to then win back the ball in direct duels with a situational man orientation (or in space, but oriented towards the man).

Even the 2:0 (32') by Frimpong is a "typical" Leverkusen goal: Prepared by Grimaldo, who sends the ball low to the far post, so that Frimpong, as an inverted
and advancing winger, only has to tap it in. This was preceded by an attack by
Leverkusen, in which an attempt to clear the ball accidentally deflected into
the path of Grimaldo – who moved into the penalty box with a quick step and
crossed.

In the second half, Leverkusen controlled the game through possession at thight
spacing and effective counter-pressing, and repeatedly created scoring opportunities through counter-attacks or well-worked moments.

All ten Leverkusen outfield players are visible, recognizable in their slightly shifted,
asymmetrical positioning to the right. Particularly noteworthy are the positions of Wirtz
and Hofmann behind their opponents (between the lines, or "in the square"), as well
as the feint of Xhaka, who signals a straight pass to Wirtz through his body posture,
but plays the ball diagonally to Hofmann, who can pass the ball directly to the onrushing Wirtz with his first touch. Leverkusen's two deep players, Boniface and Frimpong,
maintain their advanced positions and manage to tie up four opponents in the opposing
backline through their positioning. In this way, they ensure that the space "between the
lines" remains expansive. This scene creates a very good scoring opportunity for Leverkusen.

An attack after a shift in play to the right side with a typical "play and go" by
Jonas Hofmann (in a duo with Frimpong) is finally the action that brings the 3:0
and thus the preliminary decision. Boniface only needed to tap in the low cross
(67').

Restart – 1.10.2023 - 26.10.2023

Even after the international break, which meant a long journey to the USA for the German national players, Leverkusen's game continues as usual: Leverkusen starts in Wolfsburg in a dominant manner, even if the game remains open in the early stages. That changes suddenly when Leverkusen's first notable action results in the 1:0 lead (13'): After a long ball, Boniface dribbles into the penalty area and attracts the attention of all defenders. Frimpong is alone at the second post and receives the ball with a lob, nudging it over the line.

Leverkusen's game is neither dogmatic or rigid which is also evident in the way the game opens: It does not always have to be opened briefly, for example if a 1v1 situation can be created on the last line or if the second ball can be secured by moving up quickly. At the same time, Stanišić, who plays as a half-back, repeatedly shows timed actions on the right side together with Frimpong, which also puts him in the situation of playing like a winger at times.

Concept of "foot and space": Frimpong has now started to the highest point and is ready to attack the depth or the space behind the Wolfsburg defense line. Boniface looks at the ball and therefore not only waits for the deep pass, but can also be played directly into his feet without losing any momentum. This concept is special because in these situations players often only make deep runs and want to be played through the space or the interface, which, due to the difficulty of this pass, is then often unsuccessful. However, the deep runs of Frimpong and his counterpart on the other side cause the backline to drop and Boniface can receive the ball from Tapsoba at his feet and still remain fast. At the same time, Tapsoba's pass takes five opponents out of the game and creates a 3v3 situation just 45 meters from the goal.

After Leverkusen took the lead, Wolfsburg came into the game a little more, without posing any real threat. This changed when a second ball after a corner led to equalize (41'). From the beginning of the second half, Leverkusen dominated and controlled the game through possession without creating any clear-cut and compelling scoring opportunities. However, this is not necessary in this case—the constant threat posed by Boniface in a few actions, for example, is enough to understand that a goal for the Werkself seems inevitable. It remains a game of the wingers: Grimaldo scores after a cross from Frimpong to make it 2:1 (62'). Especially notable: After successful counter-pressing in the attacking third Frimpong, who receives the ball between the central defender and full-back, cuts into the penalty area and advance to the byline. He passes the ball back, where Wirtz initially misses, but finally Grimaldo is there and scores. Although Leverkusen controls the game and tries to see out the remaining time, Wolfsburg still has a great opportunity to equalize due to Wind. Hrádecký holds on to the victory.

In the third Europa League match against Qarabag, the Werkself played as one and literally overwhelmed their opponents. Consequently, Wirtz scored the 1:0 after just four minutes.

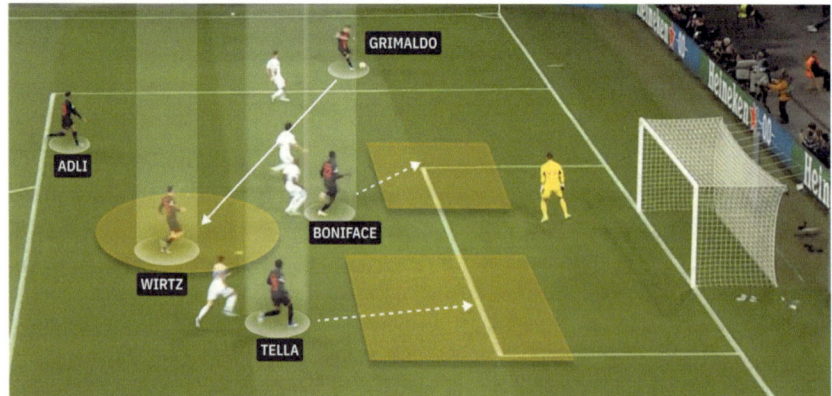

Leverkusen took the lead through Wirtz in the fourth minute of the game: Grimaldo lays his pass perfectly back to the penalty spot. The space for Wirtz also increases because Boniface consistently runs into his target area at the first post and drags the defenders with him. We can also see that the target area at the second post is also occupied by the winger furthest from the ball (usually Frimpong; in this game, Tella).

Out of nowhere, Qarabag then receives a penalty due to a mistake in the build-up, which is directly converted to equalize the score at 1:1. Leverkusen maintains the high tempo of the game and particularly looks for the flanks, whose passes result in clear-cut goal chances. The Werkself repeatedly create positional advantages on the right flank, in particular through Kossounou, as he does not interpret his role like a typical full-back, but instead acts more like a half-back in Leverkusen's model of play when in possession and pushes forward extremely aggressively, as he did when Grimaldo made it 2:1.

Leverkusen's positioning in possession of the ball in the middle third: The access of the pressing players is made extremely difficult because Leverkusen is 5v3 (and therefore in the majority) in this area. Against an attacker, two center-backs are enough to create a numerical advantage, which allows Kossounou to move up as a half-back and create a 2-3 structure. The Leverkusen players are also positioned in the interfaces – next to the opponents – which further makes it difficult for them to gain direct access. Also particularly noteworthy is the positioning of Boniface, who repeatedly alternates with Wirtz on the last line. Boniface is positioned alongside the center-back on the same axis as Wirtz, which complicates access and clear assignment to Wirtz. Through his position, Boniface also ties down the opponent, allowing Grimaldo and Wirtz to be free between the lines behind the opponents. Adli is broadly positioned in this situation, which suits his dynamism. Basically, he also acts in an interplay with Grimaldo, which leads to a permanent "appearance" and""disappearance" of the Leverkusen players and puts extreme demands on the opponent due to the extremely high mobility and constant alternation between spaces and positioning.

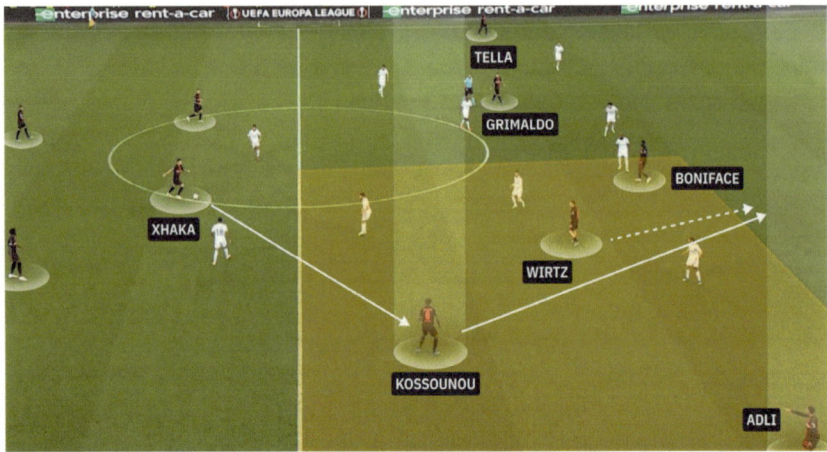

The 2:1 for Leverkusen: Again, Kossounou is positioned higher as a half-back and is directly in an interface outside the opponent's access. At the same time, together with Adli, who has moved to the right side, Wirtz, who is positioned between the lines or next to the opponent's No. 6, and Boniface, who is positioned alongside the center back, Kossounou ensures positional superiority in the right half-space (the opponent has four players, just like Leverkusen - but without having any access or influence over them). Basically, you can clearly see the intentions in this game of Leverkusen: In the build-up, the central defenders, together with the 6s create a 4v3 majority. Grimaldo and Wirtz, acting as 8s and 10s respectively, are positioned next to the opposing 6s – slightly behind them, thus attracting attention and creating an assignment problem for the opponent, which bears fruit in particular through the high-moving half-back (in this case Kossounou). The wingers Adli and Tella provide width in the game and condition the position of the opposing full-backs. Boniface ties up the center-back closest to the ball through his position and thus isolates the left-back, who cannot attack Kossounou and subsequently has to decide between defending Adli and Wirtz. Wirtz dribbles into the penalty area and finds the onrushing Grimaldo with his cut-back, who scores to make it 2:1.

A short time later, Boniface scores a great goal from the edge of the box after Andrich wins the ball. It is noticeable that the striker repeatedly drops back, deliberately seeks positional rotations with his teammates and interprets his position very fluidly. As a result, Leverkusen controls the game, moves the ball well and combines. This repeatedly led to good scoring chances and, as a result, goals: Grimaldo scored a second goal (54') after a fine combination in the right half-space. The 5:1 goal was then (somewhat unusually) scored by central defender Tapsoba, who ran forward on a counterattack and pushed the loose ball over the line after a Boniface shot.

Golden Autumn, 29.10.203 - 01.11.2023 - 04.11.2023

Leverkusen's winning streak continues into November. Against SC Freiburg, Boniface continues to show his flexibility as a striker, capable of linking up play and creating space, so that it can be exploited by deep runs from Wirtz, Hofmann and— in this game— especially Palacios. Freiburg defended disciplinedly, without initiating any particularly noteworthy attacking moves themselves. This is also due to Leverkusen's ability to make the game predictable while the opponent is in possession.

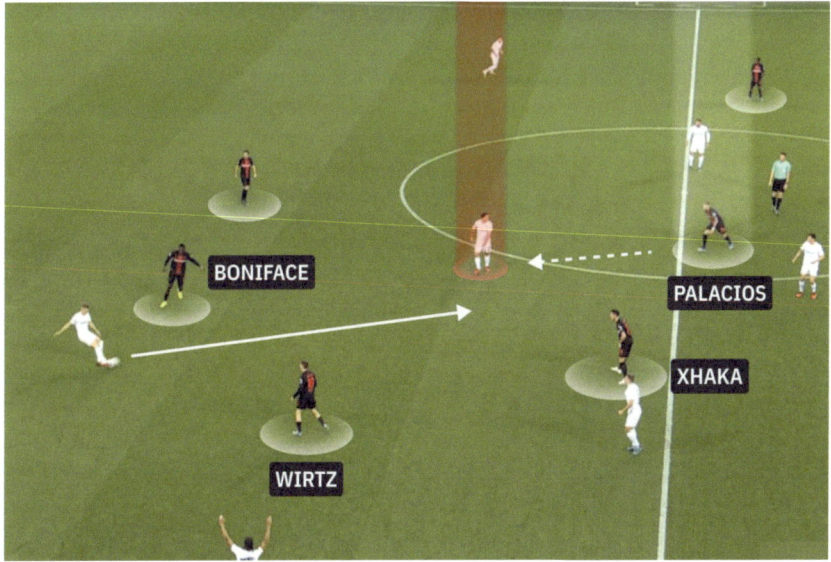

Leverkusen manages to make the opponent's game predictable when pressing: Boniface and Wirtz guide their opponent in such a way that only the pass to the middle appears open and attractive. Palacios controls three opponents from one position and is already in motion to defend the pass to the opponent's No. 6 and win the ball. In this situation, Palacios manages to stop the game's progress and force a back pass.

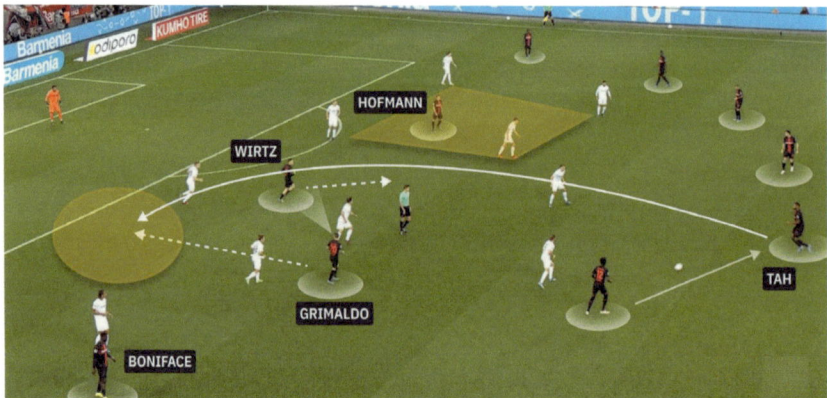

Leverkusen's positioning is almost like handball: the players stand diagonally next to each other in an arc and try to find passing options between the lines. Hofmann is already "in the square" (between the lines). Boniface drops to the left wing again, while Wirtz moves into his position. Now Wirtz moves once more from the front line into the space between the lines. Grimaldo sees the opening gap and attacks it with a perfectly timed deep run. Tah has the same intention and sends the ball to Grimaldo in the box.

Witz's goal for 1:0 after a magical dribble and an absolutely outstanding move in the 36th minute that opens up the game for Leverkusen, who had previously struggled to create clear scoring opportunities.

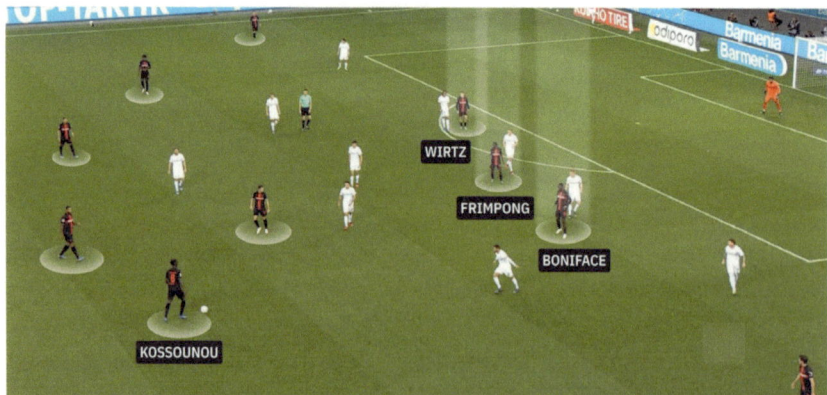

Even in the second half, Leverkusen's positioning is almost like handball: The players stand diagonally next to each other in an arc and try to find passing options between the lines. Compared to the first half, however, the players now intentionally stand closer to their opponents (Freiburg's formation resembles a 5-man backline in this situation). This creates three 1v1 situations in the box where the attackers have their backs to goal.

What is also interesting is the profile of players that are brought into this situation: Boni-face has already shown his quality in this area in other games; Frimpong swaps position (and role in this moment) with Hofmann. Like Wirtz, he is agile, mobile, and well-balanced with a low center of gravity. All three are extremely difficult to control in 1v1 so close to opponent own goal and, "to make matters worse," they can also interact with each other and with onrushing teammates. In this situation, Kossounou finds Frimpong, who manages to dribble into the penalty area but is then unable to get the ball to his team-mate.

In the second half, Leverkusen again controlled the game through possession, without creating any clear scoring opportunities themselves. It is finally a coun-terattack in the 60th minute, in which Wirtz decisively advances the game before the ball comes to Hofmann in the penalty box, who finishes. The shot bounces off the post hits the unfortunate goalkeeper's back, and deflects into the net.The 2:0 is the preliminary decision in a tight game. As a result, Leverkusen controls the game through possession and creates good scoring opportunities, especi-ally through counterattacks. Seemingly out of nowhere – after a free-kick cross near their own right baseline – Freiburg pulls one back through Gulde's header (70'). It feels like it is Freiburg's first real chance to of the match. In the remai-ning time, Leverkusen also manages to create scoring opportunities of their own, but there is always danger from Freiburg : Freiburg threatens mainly through set pieces and second-ball situations. In the end, the score remains 2:1 for Lever-kusen.

Leverkusen also overcome the hurdle of Sandhausen in the Cup, initially living up to their role as favourites before the game briefly threatened to tip over. At this stage of the season, Leverkusen is already showing a tendency to score late goals: Hložek and Adli secure a comfortable 5:2 victory in the final ten minutes of the game. A key aspect of this game is Leverkusen's frequent use of cros-ses towards the two central strikers (Hložek and Adli) while the game remained level. After Leverkusen takes the lead, Adli shifts to the left wing and seals the victory with a brace.

In a game with a high effective playing time against 1899 Hoffenheim, both teams once again display lively football, with Leverkusen reinforcing their repu-tation for attractive play. Following an elaborate Hoffenheim kick-off sequence that takes them into Leverkusen's box, Wirtz gets the game's first scoring oppor-tunity after just 30 seconds. The Werkself take the lead in the 9th minute after a well-executed combination between Boniface and Wirtz. The second goal is also special: In first-half stoppage time, Jonas Hofmann takes a corner. As his teammates clear space at the edge of the box, Grimaldo storms forward and fires a stunning shot into the top corner, making it 2:0.

A corner variation makes it 2:0 through Grimaldo: the back remains completely free. At the moment of the corner, every Leverkusen player uses their body and arms to block a Hoffenheim player, creating a clear path for Grimaldo, who storms in from the back and sinks the ball into the left corner of the goal.

At the beginning of the second half, Hoffenheim starts a little stronger and keeps getting chances to score. The 2:1 is nevertheless curious: After an errant pass from Hrádecky outside the penalty area, Hoffenheim scores from nearly 35 meters (56'). And then it all happens very quickly: In the 58th minute, a long-range shot strikes the post - Weghorst reacts first and suddenly within two minuets, it's 2:2. Leverkusen fights its way back into the game, which now sways back and forth without any clear opportunities every minute. In the 70th minute, two of the day's standout players once again demonstrate their brilliance: Boniface holds the ball exceptionally well in the penalty box before finding Grimaldo at the edge of the area, who once again finishes with his left foot into the corner, making it 3:2.

The last 20 minutes are exciting, but lacking in chances: Leverkusen seeks to preserve the lead with controlled possession and disciplined defending, preventing Hoffenheim from creating further chances. This shows that Leverkusen is now a team that is no longer solely reliant on ball possession but can also defend with focus and stability for extended periods, allowing the opponent to hold possession in non-threatening areas. Looking at Leverkusen's tactical approach, multiple facets emerge - possession based play and disciplined defending - each taking precedence at different moments within a match. Instead, Leverkusen creates two good counter-attack opportunities and wins 3:2.

Consistently "stay in", 12.11.2023

After a gritty win in the rain-soacking Azerbaijan against Qarabag in the Europa League, the Werkself face a Union Berlin team that has had a turbulent season but can still cause problems for opponents with its direct, combative game. Leverkusen starts stronger, pushes Union into their own half and plays their own game. The many diagonal shifts are noticeable, with Frimpong often being sought out to pick up the pace. But the Werkself's exceptional ball security and combination play soon yield results: after a structured attack and effective counter-pressing, it is Grimaldo (23') with a fantastic long-range shot from the just outside the left edge of the penalty box that makes Bayer celebrate.

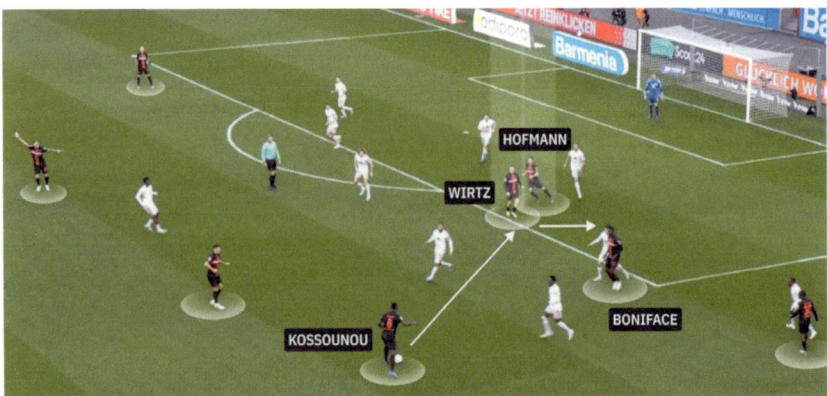

Wirtz and Hoffmann are in the same space, close to Union's central defender. This creates an assignment dilemma, because two occupying the same space and then continue to interact. In Spanish, the concept of overloading or encircling an opponent or defender ('*rodear*') is similar. Although Boniface doesn't fully anticipate Wirtz's idea, Leverkusen remains optimally positioned to immediately regain the ball again in the event of a counter-pressing situation after losing possession.

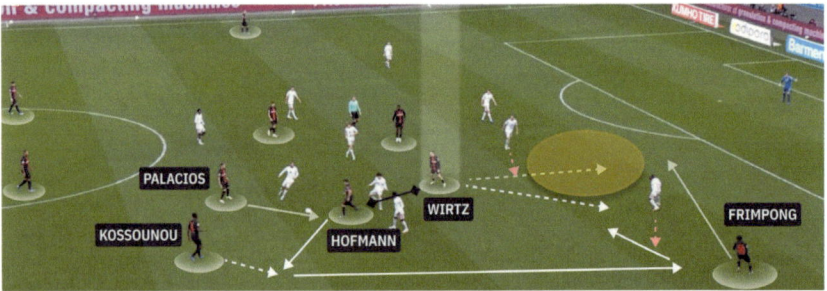

Leverkusen connects in a triangle: Palacios passes to Hofmann, who lays it off to Kossounou, who in turn finds Frimpong on the outside. What is special about the positioning is that Wirtz and Hofmann are on the same axis and Hofmann has an opponent closely marking him from behind. By passing to Hofmann, his opponent is drawn out and momentarily destabilized. This allows Wirtz, who is positioned just behind this opponent, to immediately exploit the space in depth and attack. He also tries time his run perfectly with the pass to Frimpong, as the gap between the center-back and the full-back has opened up further. Union reacts sharply in this situation, which is why a direct breakthrough is not possible. Leverkusen instead recycles possession to probe for the next opportunity towards the goal.

As was the case against Hoffenheim, a corner gave Leverkusen a crucial chance and almost made the game-deciding goal (Kossounou, 57'). Up to this point, Union had failed to become dangerous even inside the opponent's penalty area. This is also due to Leverkusen's exceptionally attentive defensive performance.

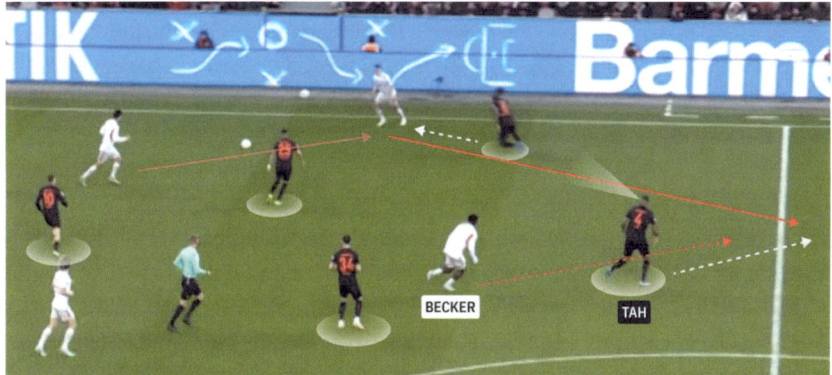

Small detail highlighting the exceptionalskills of Leverkusen's defenders, which allow them to defend extremely high and far away from their own goal: Bayer has again direc-ted the opponent towards the outside and tried to recover the ball. In this situation, Tah – as the second-to-last player – perceives both his direct opponent Becker (who he needs to mark) and the sourrounding situation. This allows him to anticipate the intenti-ons of the ball carrier and anticipate Becker's trajectory. In fact, he keeps his eyes on the ball almost constantly, but simultaneously adapts his trajectory to his closest opponent in order to maintain control.

Leverkusen remains dangerous and score again after a corner through Tah (73'). Nathan Tella seals the victory 4:0 after a counterattack in the 84th minute. Leverkusen remains top of the Bundesliga.

Anger, 25.11.2023 - 30.11.2023 - 03.12.2023

In the game against SV Werder Bremen, Andrich fills in as a central defender in place of Tah and takes on this role very well. The Berlin native is very atten-tive and manages to anticipate deep balls behind him, proving a stable factor in the back three. Bayer starts with a lot of possession and good positioning. The 1:0 in the 9th minute, however, came as a bit of a surprise, when, following a cross from Hofmann (after a Leverkusen corner), Werder defender Olivier Deman scored a very unfortunate own goal. As a result, Bayer remains dominant and controlls the game, but struggles to create clear-cut goalscoring opportunities. This changes after a second ball following a corner when Hofmann finds Hincapié, who turns, runs from the half-left position into the penalty area and crosses the ball. Frimpong appears at the second post and scores to give his team a 2:0 lead at half-time (42'). In the second half, Leverkusen continues to control the game. There are always phases in which Leverkusen drops into a deep midfield press, defend and simply close off spaces, preventing Werder in particular from progressing and allowing them to win the ball easily without too much effort. In the 75th minute, Leverkusen finally wins the ball back in counter-pressing on the left wing. Substitute Adli plays the ball to Grimaldo, who dribbles diagonally into the penalty box. While everyone is waiting for a cutback pass, the Spaniard scores high into the near corner to make it 3:0. The basis for Leverkusen's very stable play is mainly the defense with the two central players Palacios and Xhaka and the back three, which performs very reliably in various constellations (in this game even with Andrich). The players repeatedly block the ball, especially in the central area in front of the penalty area, and manage to stay compact, while at the same time the players behind them carefully control and defend the options in the box.

Even in the Swedish snowstorm of Häcken in the Europa League, Bayer remained ice cold: Boniface scored the opening goal in the first quarter of an hour after a combination on the right between Frimpong and Stanišić. And the final goal also came from the right: After good counter-pressing by Stanišić and a subsequent cross ball, Schick, the other center forward, scored to make it 2:0 (74').

The next top match in the Bundesliga is against Borussia Dortmund. It starts with an early setback: With the first real attack of the game, BVB takes the lead 1:0 through Ryerson after five minutes. Before that, Leverkusen had defended tightly and closely, but had not gained full control, and Füllkrug had also held up the ball very well in the penalty area. As a result, Leverkusen gradually oranizes itself, grows stronger minute by minute, and is increasingly taking control of the game, even if Dortmund remains an unpleasant opponent to play against and engages the Werkself in many duels. Many small fouls repeatedly interrupt Leverkusen's flow of play.

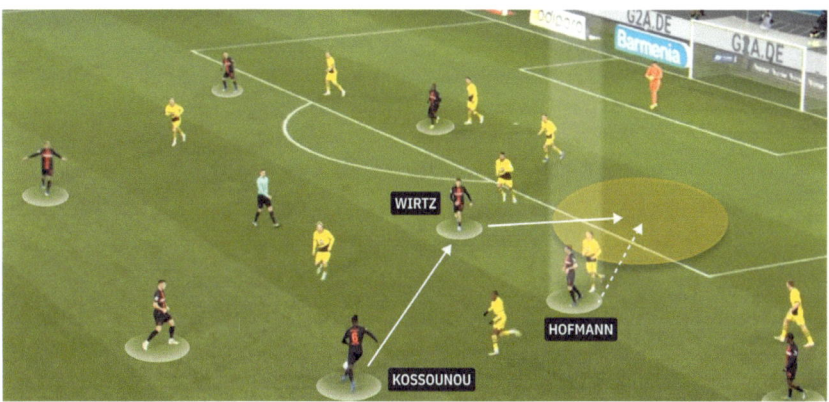

Another example of shared intentions: Hofmann pulls his direct opponent out of the backline with his run. Wirtz positions himself diagonally to Kossounou, who is in possession of the ball, and passes the ball directly to Hofmann into the space he has created. Hofmann and Wirtz both recognize the free space and the same opportunities within it. As a result, Dortmund can only clear the ball with great difficulty.

Towards the end of the first half, Leverkusen repeatedly attempts to position at least two players close to the defensive line. In addition to Boniface, who takes on this role mainly in the left half-space, Hofmann and Frimpong take turns to tying up opponents and pull the opposing No. 6 or full-back out of position. As was the case against Union Berlin, two players often position themselves close to each other in the interface between full-back and centre-back. Due to strong positional awareness and increasingly effective position findings, Leverkusen gradually creates dangerous situations in the opponent's penalty area. Frimpong even joins the attack alongside Boniface at times to create a 1v1 against Dortmund's central defenders.

At the beginning of the second half, Leverkusen gains confidence. More positional changes, more rotations and more trust in intuition help the team regain its flow. The Werkself constantly attack the interfaces with runs and repeatedly take shots from distance, which then lead to corners. It is a whirlwind of position changes (Frimpong suddenly appears on the left, Grimaldo on the right), opposing movements, deep runs, and constant movement into gaps, with no pauses - only interrupted by the occasional long, predictable ball from Dortmund, which is not less dangerous for that reason.

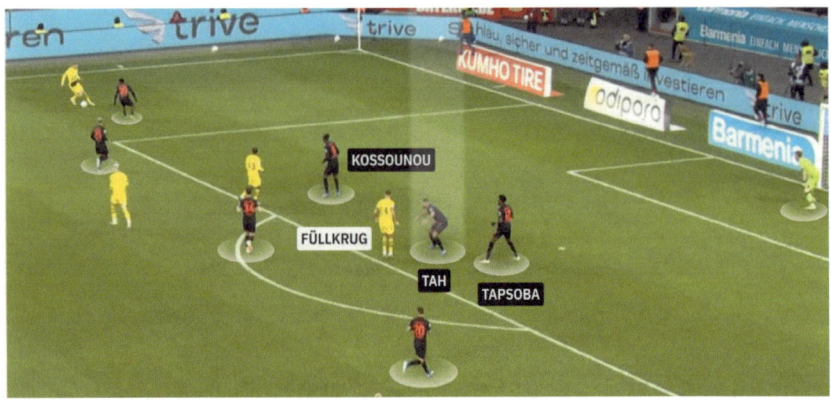

Focusing on 1v1 defending in the box: With Füllkrug's slight feint, Tah immediately lowers his center of gravity and adjusts himself towards his opponent. He has a peripheral view of the ball, but at the same time he is now on his front foot and prepared and flexible to accommodate any run the striker makes. Kossounou is positioned further forward and has his direct opponent in sight. Tapsoba checks his positioning and looks to see whether he needs to take on an opponent or whether he can remain in the space to defend.

A particularly well-executed move brings the equalizer: Kossounou wins the ball and dribbles into the opponent's half. He deceives the opponents with his posture and plays a disguised pass to the perfectly positioned Schick in the box, who crosses – Boniface is there – 1:1 (79'). In the last ten minutes, Dortmund briefly tried to become more active, but only Leverkusen had a few opportunities, even if they were not clear-cut enough. The score remains 1:1.

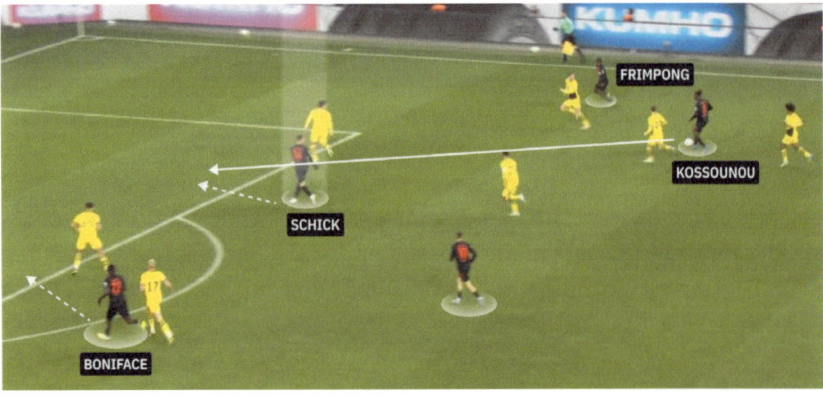

Picture bottom left: The long-awaited 1:1 against Dortmund: Kossounou dribbles deep into the opponent's half after winning the ball near midfield. Two of Alonso's ideas go hand in hand: on the one hand, to maintain possession for as long as possible after winning it and to pick up the pace himself, and on the other hand, to disguise his own intentions rather than revealing them. The body orientation of all Dortmund players shows that everyone is expecting a pass to Frimpong. However, Kossounou suprises them by playing a disguised diagonal ball into the box to Schick, who only has to square it to the onrushing Boniface: goal and 1:1!

After the game, Xabi Alonso is still visibly angry. It is not just the result, which the otherwise composed Basque certainly feels was harsh but knows how to analize rartionally that dampens his mood, but also the statement by Dortmund coach Edin Terzić, who said after the game, with an eye to the approaching Africa Cup of Nations in January and February 2024: "There is still so much to come for us and for Leverkusen. I think Leverkusen has a very exciting phase ahead of them in January with the Africa Cup of Nations. We all know that."[263] Leverkusen could lose five players (including Kossounou, Tapsoba and Boniface), but the prediction of a difficult phase irritates Alonso deeply. He and his staff have already developed contingency plans in the background to compensate for the losses with a broad and qualitative high-quality squad. Half a year later, ahead for the rematch, the frustration is long gone. But at this point, nobody yet suspects that the Werkself will already be German champions...

Top match, 06.12.2023 – 10.12.2023

November is just over — and in Paderborn it's still "Movember" time: mustaches are flourishing everywhere. This global initiative, originally launched in Australia, encourages men from worldwide to grow a ""mustache" every November (mustache + November = "Movember") to raise the money for prostate and testicular cancer prevention, research, and treatment. And the Paderborn team is visibly in this cause...

263 Terzic cited in Welt online 19.04.2024.

Paderborn defends compactly and effectively closes the center in their in a 1-4-2-3-1 formation, aiming to deny Leverkusen's central midfielders access to the game. Leverkusen's players adjust immediately by positioning themselves higher and circulating the ball around the block via the half-lane. Overall, the Werkself execute a fluid interpretation of their typical 1-3-4-3, in which Adli stretches the width on the left flank, while Grimaldo enjoys full positional freedom, drifting appart into the middle and sometimes even to the right. This positional movement opens the gaps allowing several opponents to be bypassed with a pass through the center. Leverkusen dictates play through possession, stays relentless, dynamic, and vertically aggressive, while excelling in counter-pressing, shutting down Paderborn entirely before they can transition into counterattacks. The Werkself take the lead after a perfectly timed cross from Stanišić, who found Boniface in a direct 1v1 in the penalty area for the 1:0. In the 28th minute Palacios doubles the lead with a long-range strike after a pass from Frimpong, making it 2:0.

After scoring the goal, Bayer shifts focus to ball retention and controlled the tempo: they alternate between slower passages and explosive tempo changes, depending on available space. The only downside: Wirtz had to leave the pitch injured at the end of the first half.

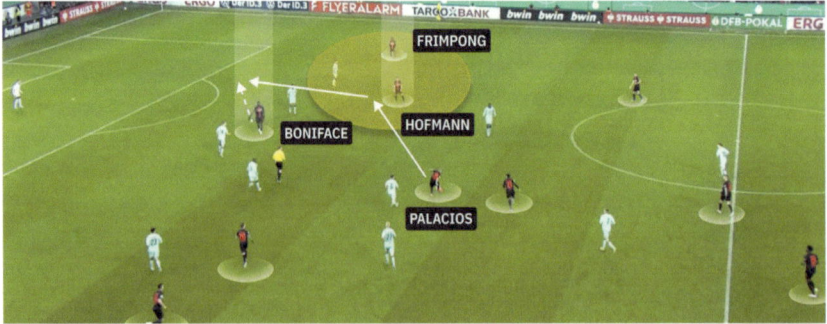

Leverkusen draws Paderborn over by overloading the left side with passes and number of players, and is then switching the game. We see that in the highlighted zone, Leverkusen creates a 2v1 situation with Frimpong and Hofmann against the opposing full-back. Palacios plays to Hofmann, who positions himself in an interface beyond the opponents' access. Hofmann delivers the ball directly into Boniface's path, who times his run well into a 1v1 situation with the goalkeeper. However, Paderborn's goalkeeper reacts quickly and denies the goal at the very last moment.

Leverkusen maintains dominance in the second half. Paderborn struggles to create box entries, let alone attempts on goal. In a somewhat fortunate way, Paderborn pulls one back to 2:1: After a well-worked move down on Leverkusen's right side and a flat pass, that Tapsoba struggles to clearin a duel with Paderborn's Grimaldo, the ball ricochets from Kinsombi to Klaas, who reacts instantly and fires. Goalkeeper Kovář hesitates, caught between assisting the injured Grimaldo and staying focused, which allows the shot to find the net (83'). Leverkusen regains stability and stays focused defensively before taking back control through possession and capitalizing with another direct attacking move: Frimpong assists Schick, who slots home for 3:1 (87').

After reaching the DFB-Cup quarter-finals, the Werkself face the Bundesliga high-flyers Stuttgart a few days later. Like Leverkusen, their football is dynamic, entertaining, and highly effective, earning them a top-three spot in the Bundesliga. On December 10, 2023, the league leaders and the third-place clash.
In the "high-intensity match" (*kicker*) with notably high, effective playing time, the Swabians came out flying in their own stadium and had numerous clear-cut scoring opportunities in the first ten minutes. Bayer has rarely been under such sustained pressure this season .
It remains an intense, fairly even game, through Stuttgart carves out scoring opportunities. After 28 minutes, Stuttgart boasts an xG-value approaching 2 (Leverkusen sits at 0.3), while the score stays level at 0:0.

Leverkusen sets up in a 4-4-2 mid-block shape when out of possession, aiming to manage the overloaded Stuttgart flanks, while maintaining offensive flexibility. Thanks to the squad's profiles, Leverkusen can fluidly shift between different structures based on the game situation and pressing intensity.

Leverkusen's savior mentality: Hrádecký saves a free kick. The final cross and subsequent goal-bound efforts from Stuttgart were all parried by defenders positioned on the line. With fearless commitment, Leverkusen's defenders put their bodies on the line, blocking every attempt with maximum effort to deny Stuttgart a goal.

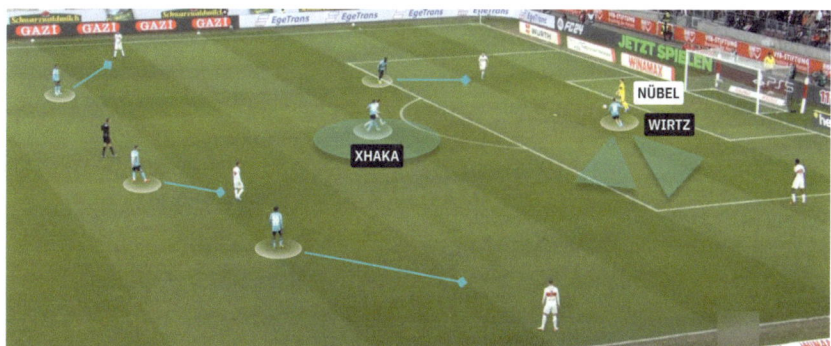

Leverkusen presses high in a (4-)3-3 shape in the final third. Wirtz closes down Stuttgart goalkeeper Nübel in such a way that his cover shadow prevents passes to the left center-back or full-back. Xhaka marks his opponent tightly in midfield; the rest of the team is staggered to apply immediate pressure upon ball movement. Nübel's only option remains the long ball, which Leverkusen wins back instantly through an aerial challenge.

All outfield players compressed into a tight space. Leverkusen moves as a compact unit with the ball ('*viajar juntos*'). Xhaka drops deeper and draws the opponent toward him. Palacios exploits the resulting gap, attacks the space behind him, and is fed by a pass from Wirtz near the penalty area. Adli and Grimaldo pin their markers, complicating Stuttgart's man-marking approach (multiple players positioned tightly around the ball ensuring options for progression or a second-phase attack).

Leverkusen spends more time defending, appearing composed but unable to contain all of Stuttgart's rapid attacks. One of these swift attacks pays off as Führich finishes at the far post making it 1:0. Leverkusen attempts to control possession, but the lead energizes Stuttgart, who move it around with even more confidence. At halftime, the *expected goals (xG)* score is 3.32 to 0.61 – and in reality it is 1:0 for Stuttgart.

The second half begins with the roles switched, and Leverkusen is immediately on the front foot: In the 47th minute, Wirtz equalizes to 1:1 after a direct combination between Xhaka and Boniface.

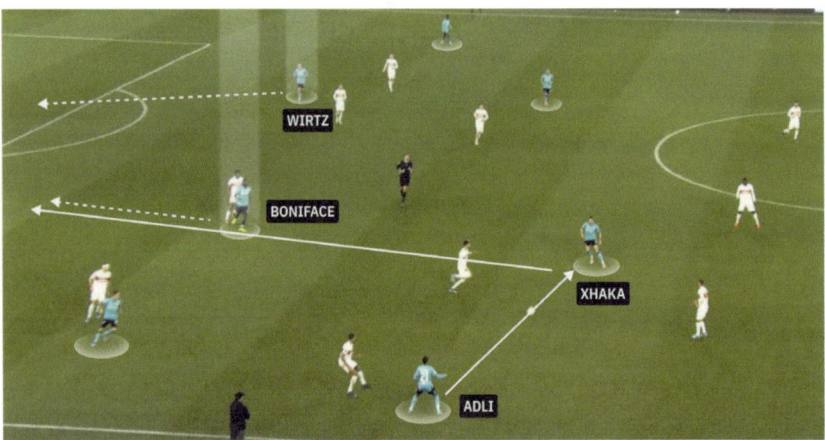

Leverkusen's equalizer: Xhaka receives a switch of play from Adli, and follows up with an immediate vertical pass: Xhaka plays the ball in behind to Boniface, who is positioned 1v1 with the center-back, using his strength to shield the ball and drive forward. Boniface then lays it off for Wirtz, who benefits from his initial offside position (when Xhaka plays the ball), giving him a movement advantage as he bursts in behind and finishes unchallenged.

Leverkusen remains full of intensity, and shortly afterwards Xhaka hits the post. Overall, Leverkusen grows in confidence, asserting themselves with greater authority. But Stuttgart remains dangerous, continuing to probe in attack. It remains a tight, high-quality game, serving as a fantastic showcase for the Bundesliga. Both teams create further chances, with Leverkusen pushing hard in the closing stages, but the score remains 1:1.

Prepared for the winter break, 14.12.2023 - 17.12.2023 - 20.12.2023

There are still demanding weeks ahead for the Werkself, but squad rotation, managed effectively by the coach, ensures that all players get game time. Notably, Bayer's style has become so distinctive that it appears independent of the personnel on the pitch - regardless of who plays, the team consistently execute the same clear tactical ideas.

In the final match of the group stage of the Europa League, Leverkusen demonstrates from the outset that, despite already securing qualification, they are taking the match seriously, determined to finish the group with maximum points. This makes coach Xabi Alonso particularly happy, who appeals to the "natural drive" to "always want to win" ahead of the match against Molde FK. "(…) This is very important. That this naturally comes from us, regardless of whether it is a friendly match or a final."[264] Alonso clearly emphasizes how important this culture is to him. He wants his players to "raise awareness (…) that every training session is important" and therefore also every game. "That's professional football. The one who relaxes will be punished as soon as he does so. Hopefully we are not that stupid," said the Basque, whose team has obviously heard the words of their coach.[265] Already in the 6th minute, Schick finishes off a counterattack from just under 16 meters to make it 1:0. A short time later, Tapsoba scores from a corner variation from the left to make it 2:0 (22'). And the Werkself don't stop: Three minutes later, Molde deflects a pass from Tella into the net to make it 3:0 (25'). After this preliminary decision, Leverkusen controls the game, albeit with a desire to score goals, but not as compelling as before. Hložek (60' & 70') extends the score with double scoring: first after a nice change of pace and a great turn by Mbamba in the build-up, and shortly afterwards again after a corner. Molde pulls one back 15 minutes before the end to make the final score 5:1.

In the second last game of the calendar year, there will be a reunion with Eintracht Frankfurt. We remember: Almost a year earlier, Xabi Alonso and his team had suffered a "system crash" against this opponent. Only one year later, the teams meet again under completely different circumstances. The Werkself welcome the guests from Frankfurt as undefeated league leaders, while Eintracht experiences a season with some ups and downs, seeming to look for the same stability as the Werkself.

---

264 Alonso quoted by kicker online from December 14, 2023.
265 Ibid.

Frankfurt attempts to start with a lot of pressure, but as so often this season, Leverkusen absorbs the initial pressure with a solid defense and quickly takes control of the game themselves. The Werkself demonstrate exceptional efficiency: Boniface scores with the first clear chance after a speed dribble from just under 15 meters flat into the right corner to make it 1:0 (14'). As a result, it remains a tight game in which Frankfurt defends with concentration, although not always with maximum access to the opponent. Leverkusen struggles to find their usual flow in their passing game and gathers multiple players around the ball in order to combine with each other. In addition, the holding midfielders repeatedly drop to the wing or even get into the opening positions in the back three to facilitate ball progression. Nevertheless, when in possession of the ball, Leverkusen fails to find their way into the "usual" spaces to become dangerous. In the second half, Leverkusen pushes higher and dictates the game from then on: Through many high ball recoveries, Bayer immediately creates chances to score and finally makes it 2:0 through Frimpong, who taps a rebound from a Boniface shot over the line (51'). Shortly afterwards the decision: Leverkusen draws Frankfurt toward the wing and creates a 1v1 situation for Boniface on the halfway line. Hrádecký plays over the pressing line, and Bayer picks up the pace. Boniface manages to lay the ball off to Wirtz, who sprints the 50 meters at full speed and successfully slots home to make it 3:0 (57').

A numbers game: In the frame, you can see ten Leverkusen players (including goalkeeper) – and nine Frankfurt players. Leverkusen positions so many players close to the ball that they completely drag their opponents out of their structure. Boniface (not pictured) stands near the center line in a 1v1 against his opponent. Hrádecký spots this and plays over the Frankfurt block with a lofted pass, sending Boniface into a 1v1, where he manages to keep the ball and lays it off for the sprinting Wirtz. He slots home to make the final score 3:0. Fun fact: Frimpong arrives in the penalty area at the same time as Wirtz.

As a result, Leverkusen remains very focused, constantly creates chances to score (through counterattacks or via possession – attacking the opponent's back) and even strikes the post twice. In the end, it remains a well-deserved 3:0 victory.

In the last game of 2023, VfL Bochum visits the BayArena. Bochum starts well and boldly, repeatedly exploitng the interface between Leverkusen's defense and their fast attackers, who pose the home team challenges. It feels as if the Werkself is already self-preparing for January: Stanišić and Hincapié start, as does Patrik Schick. Alonso chooses to leave out Tapsoba, Kossounou and Boniface, who are expected to be at the Africa Cup of Nations in January, at least at the beginning of the game. Leverkusen looks prepared for their absence and stuns Bochum early: With the first good opportunity, in which Schick benefits from a huge defensive lapse by Bochum's defense, he wins a penalty. Schick cooly converts to make it 1:0 (30'). From this moment on, Bochum's resistance fades: in the very next attack, Schick shakes off his marker, latches on to Frimpong's pass, and scores to bury it 2:0. The Werkself finds its rhythm, dazzles with quick combinations, and generates chance after chance. There is no sign of Bochum's early confidence anymore. In first-half injury time, Schick completes his hat-trick with the 3:0. Blessed are those who have such strikers in their squad. Substitute Boniface also demonstrates his killerinstinct in the second half: Perfectly assisted by Xhaka and Wirtz, the Nigerian fires home to make it 4:0 (69'). In the final minutes, while the crowd's wave sweeps through the BayArena, Andrich once again slots into the center in the back three. It becomes increasingly evident how Leverkusen plans to handle the challenges of the Africa Cup of Nations and the associated absences in central defense and attack. The Werkself looks ready.

"Bayer Football", 13.01.2024 - 20.01.2024

After the Werkself's warm-up match against AC Venice, in which Adam Hložek stood out with a brace, and Andrich assumed the central role in the defense, FC Augsburg hosts the Werkself, and with a new coach to boot: Jess Thorup from Denmark aims to revitalize the Augsburg team. This seems to work in the first game. In the early stages, Leverkusen has a surprisingly difficult time on an uneven pitch against an aggressive and very well-prepared opponent. The Augsburg team always succeeds positioning themselves smartly and capitalizing from their direct play. Leverkusen fails to create any clear chances, but earns corner kicks, though none lead to a breakthrough. As the game progresses, a familiar pattern from this season emerges: Leverkusen takes more and more control through possession and composure. The Werkself strikes the post with efforts from Grimaldo (long-range shot) and Andrich (header from a corner) and creates good chances overall.

In the second half, Leverkusen remains dominant, with extreme calmness on the ball and consistently pushing forward to threaten the Augsburg's goal, which leads to good opportunities (including Schick with a header), even if they are still not crowned with success.

Leverkusen demonstrates its clear development in this game: The Werkself sticks to its approach without ever losing patience or resorting to forced intensity (and thus possibly changing its approach completely). Instead, Bayer steadily utilizes possession to advance forward and apply pressure on the opponent's goal. This eventually pays off in the 94th minute: Palacios converts a cross from Grimaldo to score, the long-awaited winning goal, 1:0. A second step towards "Laterkusen" has been taken and Bayer clinches the symbolic title of Winter Champion.

The second half of the season kicks off against RB Leipzig and is just as fast-paced as the first leg. Leipzig gets off to the perfect start: In an intense opening phase, Xavi Simons puts Leipzig ahead 1:0 after seven minutes following a fine attack down the right-hand side of Leverkusen's defense. In the first 15 minutes, Leipzig consistently builds momentum and carves out promising chances. The Saxons remain dangerous throughout the entire half with their direct attacking approach and continuously test Leverkusen with their speed.

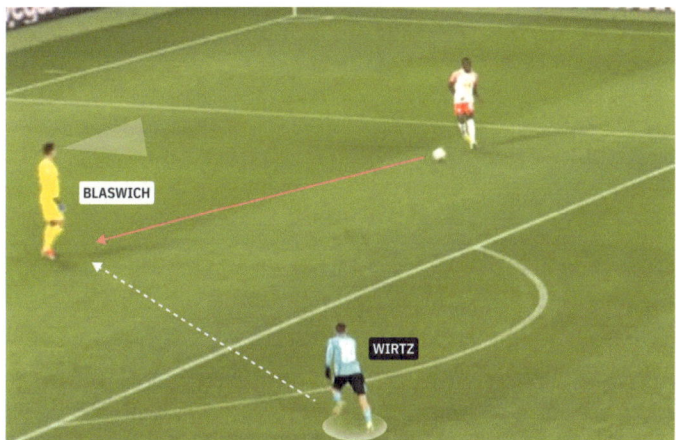

Details in the pressing: Wirtz attacks RB goalkeeper Blaswich from his "blind side", approaching from an angle where the goalkeeper only registers his run at the last moment. Wirtz also starts his action in sync with the pass recipient's touch, so that he arrives simultaneously with the ball and thus generate immediate pressure.

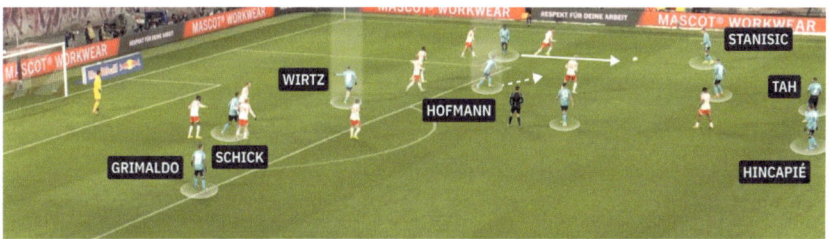

Leverkusen positions itself close together in the attacking third. Tah and Hincapié provide a very high level of protection, and at the same time serve as passing options for Stanišić to give the game continuity.
Hofmann and Wirtz execute opposite runs, leaving Wirtz alone in the penalty box behind the defensive line. Schick occupies three opponents in the center, creating space for Grimaldo on the far side.
Positioning intentions: Always position for the back of the defender; manipulating the opponent's attention and field of vision (e.g., by own viewing direction), and having multiple accessible passing lines (communication channels) to the ball.

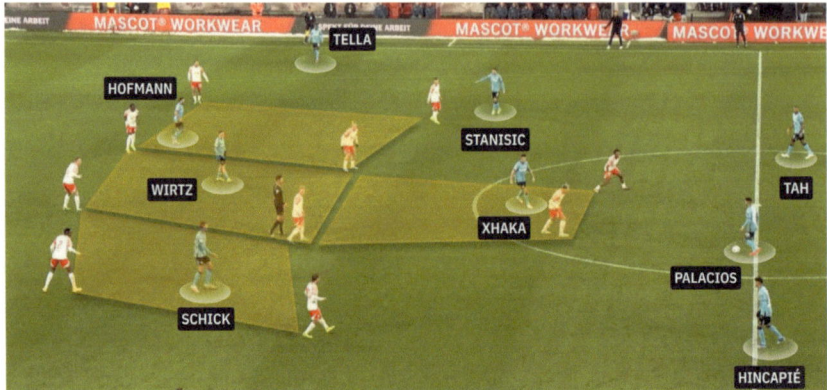

Leverkusen's positioning for their fluent positioning game: Palacios (in possession) drops into the back three with Tah and Hincapié in the build-up. Xhaka is positioned directly behind the strikers, staying just inside their cover shadow and offering an immediate passing option should they press the ball carrier. Staniśić is positioned half-right on the same vertical line as the outside midfielder, which pins him back and prevents him from stepping out, allowing Tah to receive the ball on the move with more space. Tella and Grimaldo maintain width positioning themselves just behind the outside midfielders, so that the full-backs always have to keep an eye on them both. In the center, Hofmann, Wirtz and Schick form in shape in a "square" and stay primarily behind the midfield line, making it difficult for the center-backs to track them tightly without leaving a large hole in the defence. These three players constantly adjust their positioning and are not fixed to specific spots. The same applies to the other players, although a higher degree of positional fluidity will develop further over the course of the season and will be adapted based on the game context.

Leverkusen gradually getting into the game, but without generating any clear scoring chances. At half-time, Xabi Alonso lashes out in the dressing room: "I don't give a damn how the game ends. But now we are playing Bayer football."[266] And his team listens to him: The Werkself becomes more flexible, which yields an instant effect: Grimaldo moves inwards, while Wirtz shifts over to the left and dribbles towards the opponent. Grimaldo now runs back to the wing and receives the ball via Hofmann on the flank, which he whips into the box. Tella is alone on the second post and scores the 1:1. Many goals this season have come from this exact pattern, and there will be plenty more.

266 Alonso quoted in Welt-Online from 19.04.2024.

Already in the early stages of the second half, noticeable adjustments to the structure of Xabi Alonso's team can be seen: Palacios takes deeper positions in the build-up; more players make themselves available at shorter distances. Wirtz always finds moments to rotate alongside Grimaldo or add numbers to the wing, consistently generating danger.

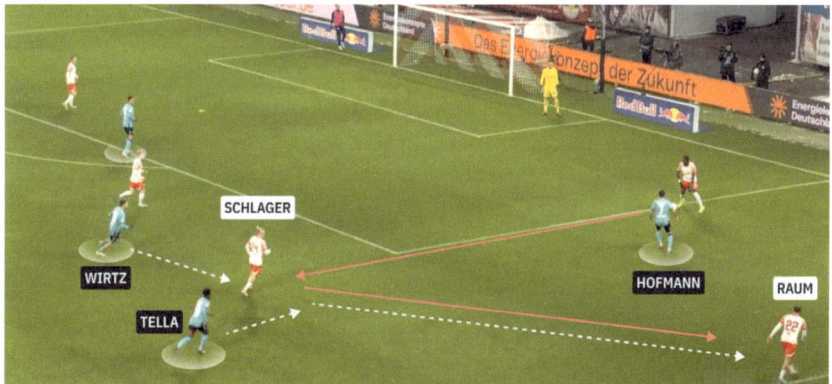

Hofmann runs at the opposing central defender in such a way that he cuts off the passing lane to the full-back (No. 22, Raum). The opposing No. 6 positions himself in a side-on (closed) body position and signals his intended pass by turning his head and eyeing his target. Tella anticipates this perfectly: He continues his run towards Schlager just long enough that Schlager feels he is under heavy pressure. As soon as Schlager touches the ball (and redirects it wide with his first touch), Tella immediately shifts his run to the wing and presses Raum at full speed. Raum opts for a backpass, but misplaces it slightly, allowing Wirtz to intercept and win a free kick for Leverkusen.
The similarity of this scene to Leverkusen's pressing sequences in the first leg is impressive.

Just as it seemed Leverkusen's second goal was only a matter of time, Leipzig struck: The "Red Bulls" anticipated a short corner routine and countered Leverkusen with textbook precision: Openda scored to make it 2:1 (56'). Less than ten minutes later, Leverkusen responded once more: Tah converted another corner to make it 2:2. Especially Wirtz's involvement, demonstrating a recurring pattern we've seen in previous matches, stood out.

Creating advantages at corners: As in the reverse fixture against Bochum, the goalkeeper is impeded by the positioning of a Leverkusen player and prevented from coming off his line. It is important that the Leverkusen player does not colide with the goalkeeper, but simply positions himself so the goalkeeper cannot move freely or build momentum and certainly cannot attack the ball effectively. Tah scores at the back post.

Few months later against RB Leipzig, a player impairs the goalkeeper with his positioning. Here it is Andrich who stands where Bochum goalkeeper Riemann advance (without it being a foul). Schick wins his matchup with an outstanding header and scores 3:0 for Leverkusen.

In the second half, the Werkself succed in creating greater stability, ball control and thus dominance, particularly through better link-up play between Grimaldo and Wirtz, as well as through closer distances and multi-layered positioning. Leverkusen keeps up the press, but the goal does not come immediately. It is once again a reward of their relentless approach and their set-piece strength that brings victory to Leverkusen: In the 91st minute, after a corner kick from Grimaldo, Hincapié rushes in at the far post and bundles the ball home for the winning goal, 3:2. These Leverkusen players never seem to give up – and above all, they are almost impossible to beat.

945 passes, 27.01.2024

After six points against Augsburg and Leipzig in 2024 and extending the unbeaten streak, Xabi Alonso is optimistic in his *Sky* interview before the match against Borussia Mönchengladbach: "We want to enjoy ourselves on the pitch and be competitive." Surprisingly for outsiders, Kovář is the chosen goalkeeper for this match. Alonso said: "Both goalkeepers are at a top level and there is good competition. Kovář should be prepared for the cup match." On the personnel decision to put Amiri in the starting eleven (who leaves Leverkusen for Mainz a few days later): "Amiri has a good connection with Granit, with Flo. He is totally ready."[267] With regard to the concepts explored earlier in this book, as well as the idea of "cooperation" [in complex systems] Xabi Alonso's way of expressing himself on this topic is of course particularly noteworthy, since when choosing personnel in midfield he addressed how connections, i.e. "networking" play a crucial role and are particularly important in Leverkusen's game. Another interesting statistic ahead of the game: Granit Xhaka is league leading with seven second-to-last passes.

Leverkusen displays maximum fludity, joy in playing, dominance and control right from the start. Playing forward and pressing, the Werkself repeatedly create top-class scoring opportunities, but fail to convert them throughout the entire game. It becomes the ongoing story of this game that Leverkusen struggle to win against an extremely deep-lying Gladbach team, even linking-up well in the penalty area. All statistical values clearly underline their superiority: Leverkusen's *expected goals (xG)* value is 2.64; a total of 945 passes with 92% pass completion rate led to 28 shots on goal for the Werkself.[268] Xabi Alonso remains self-critical after the game: "We were very dominant, but the last shot and the last pass were not good enough. (...) The victory would certainly have been deserved, but that is up to us. (...) Gladbach stood very compact with many players, very deep. We should have been more clinical. But that happens, and we have to learn from it."[269]

---

267 Personal transcript from SKY TV broadcast from January 27, 2024.
268 Statistics according to bundesliga.de
269 Alonso quoted by Kicker online from January 27, 2024.

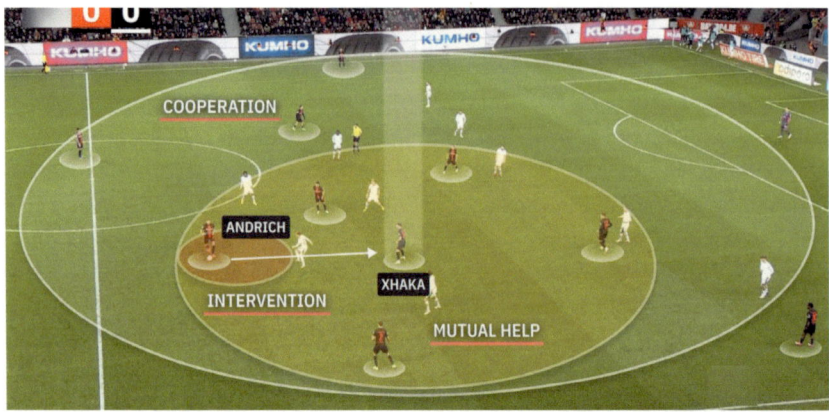

This ball movement shows another elementary concept of Xabi Alonso's central mid-fielders in Leverkusen's positional play. Xhaka in particular repeatedly runs backwards and positions himself between two opponents while remaining behind the pressing line to available for a pass. The player who is behind the pressing player always shows up, as often a small movement is enough to become a passable player (*"Quien salta abre puerta" – "He who goes up opens the door"*). At the same time, we see how Andrich conceals his intention to play centrally through his posture (*'perfil'*), and the direction of his gaze, faking an outside pass instead. Aspects like these can already be emphasized in Rondos and *"Juegos de posición"* (positional play exercises). This game situation is also ideal to illustrate the concept of stage spaces (see the excursus before this chapter).

In recent years, most teams have tended to search for the red-marked area with a switching ball from this position. Xabi Alonso's Leverkusen now capitalize on the momentum of the defenders (partly caused by Leverkusen own central attackers) to play a "straight" diagonal ball into the yellow zone to Grimaldo, who arrives in space with enough space-time to finish with his first two touches.

While Leverkusen lacked finishing precision against Borussia Mönchengladbach, this is no longer the case against their next opponent, Darmstadt. Also new to the team is winter newcomer signing Borja Iglesias, who immediately starts as the central striker. In the opening minutes, Leverkusen dominates possession as usual but takes a more structured, positional approach. The intention of generating direct goal threats through deep runs and long passes over Darmstadt's compact block can be seen repeatedly. Many small fouls by Darmstadt disrupt the flow of the game, even though Leverkusen appear well-prepared and consistently seek for a quick continuation of play. As the game unfolds, Leverkusen completely dominates the game and pushes Darmstadt deep into their own half. However, Darmstadt stays courageous in their vertical approach, repeatedly attempting to find their strikers with long balls and move forward at pace with intent. In some situations, they manage to challenge Leverkusen, creating shots on goal and winning set pieces.

Hincapié's back pass is "answered" with a direct attacking ball from Xhaka. Special: Xhaka and Wirtz share the same attacking intention for space in the box. Wirtz's posture indicates his imminent run into open space before Xhaka even receives the ball. At the same time, Xhaka's head movement reveals that he scans the game context again before receiving the ball and registers Wirtz's movement into the gap. The space becomes even more accessible as Iglesias shifts closer to Darmstadt's central defender, tying him up and preventing him from stepping forward. Once again, Leverkusen manipulates the opponent's attention (all eyes are on the ball), so that Wirtz - diagonally from behind his opponent - makes his run from the blind spot, making it nearly impossible to defend or anticipate.

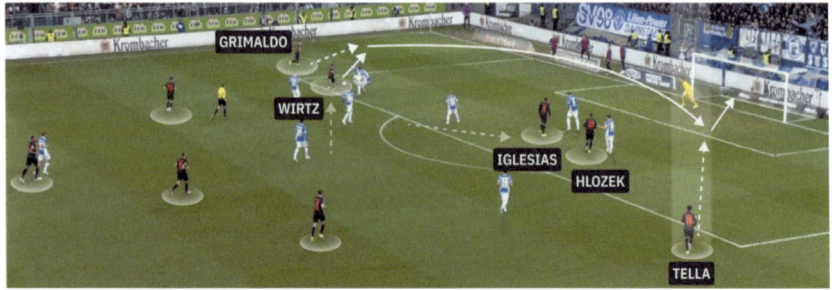

The lead for the Werkself: Borja Iglesias creates space in the penalty area, allowing Wirtz to make a diagonal run and receive Xhaka's pass. Wirtz then lays the ball off to Grimaldo, who delivers a precise cross to the far post with his second touch. Inside the box, both Iglesias and Hložek are tightly marked, but the far post remains completely open. Tella, using his pace and keen sens of positioning, attacks this free space and heads the ball into the net for the 1:0. To maximize this space, Iglesias and Hložek deliberately pull towards the near post, drawing defenders with them and freeing up Tella's area at the back post. A textbook Leverkusen goal this season.

Leverkusen remain unfazed by disruptions and keep pressing forward relentessly. This persistence pays off when Tella finishes at the far post following a brilliant cross from Grimaldo (33'). Yet again, an advancing winger converts from a cross. Leverkusen maintain their intensity, repeatedly exposing gaps in the Darmstadt defense, though they fail to add another goal before halftime. Bayer frequently exploits diagonal passing lanes to shift the attack into different areas. A clear pattern emerges: diagonal shifts from the left half-space, typically around the halfway line, aim to position Tella in a scoring role. This strategy pays off early in the second half when Tella, set up by a clever Wirtz initiative, scores a superb goal in the 52nd minute make it 2:0. Leverkusen then controls the game and even gets opportunities – nothing is left in danger.

Peak, 06.02.2024 - 10.02.2024

February presents a demanding stretch for Xabi Alonso and his team: In a "week of truth", VfB Stuttgart, one of the strongest teams this season, is waiting in the quarter-finals of the DFB Cup, a match that could already be described as a potential final. Only four days later, Bayern Munich comes to Leverkusen, for a crucial top-of-the-table clash in the title race.

The cup match at the BayArena starts with a very aggressive approach and strong man-orientation by VfB Stuttgart, who deliver a courageous performance, challenging the Werkself to the maximum. Even when in possession of the ball, the Swabians show why they are the surprise team in German football. Stuttgart have shown proactive, dynamic football throughout the season, which in its basic approach is not so different from Leverkusen's style. Nevertheless, certain nuances set them apart, such as their strong opponent orientation in defense: While the Stuttgart players prioritize their individual duels, the Leverkusen defenders, while assigned to their nearest (direct) opponents, often position themselves between opponents instead of marking tightly. This allows them to have the best possible access to their opponents, while ensuring quick support for teammates when necessary. At the same time, Leverkusen's play seems slightly more intuitive and (from the outside) is driven more by a natural instinct for occupying the right spaces to maximize effectiveness.

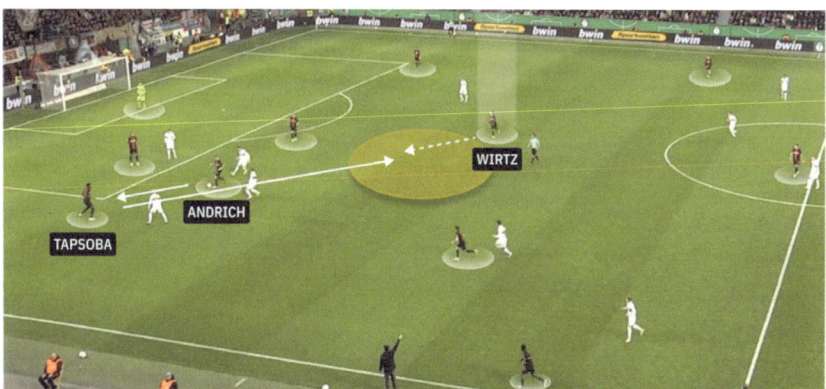

Concept: Repeating the pass ('*repetir pase*'). Andrich receives the ball and keeps coming closer to Tapsoba. He looks over his shoulder several times, both to see the expanding space behind him, and to recognize that this space can be used by Wirtz. Therefore, Andrich delays his back pass to Tapsoba until the last moment so that the space for Wirtz is as large as possible. Tapsoba plays the ball past the Stuttgart players without any problems and finds Wirtz, who can turn with plenty of space and accelerate the game forward.

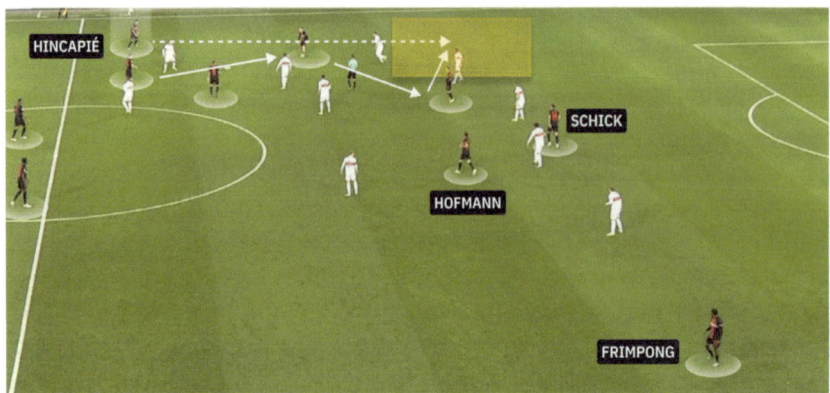

Leverkusen uses Stuttgart's man-oriented defensive style and lures the opponents completely out of position. This example shows once again the magical attraction and attention of the ball, which ensures that all eyes are on the ball and no opponent notices the deep run of Hincapié, who is attacking the depth behind the opponents. The Stuttgart players step towards their closest opponents, but in this scene they are always just too late, so that Hincapié receives the ball in depth and can cross without problem. Additionally, you can see Frimpong's isolated position, who is always hoping for quick switches to accelerate the game and into 1v1 situations. Also interesting are the positions of Schick and Hofmann, who are both close to Stuttgart's left center-back and almost "surround" him, which could make marking difficult for the defender.

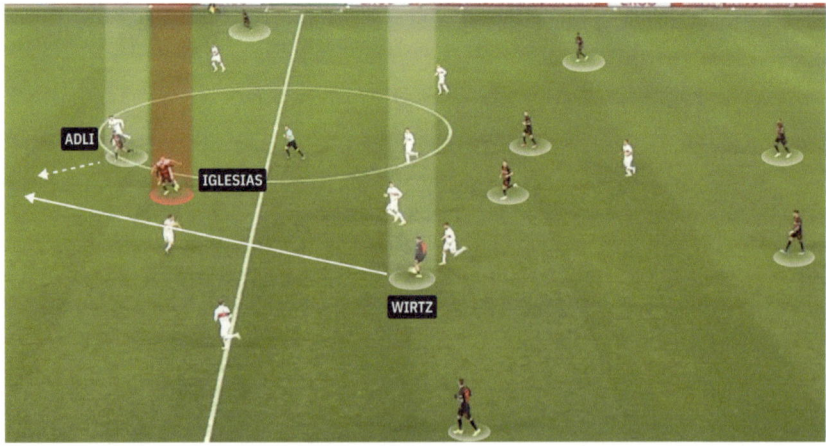

Picture bottom left: Wirtz with an outstanding pass in behind to Adli, who attacks the space and subsequently scores the 2:2 equalizer. In this scene, you can see several interesting aspects of individual and group tactics: Borja Iglesias, who was substituted a minute earlier, blocks his opponent and thus ensures that Adli can go into a 1v1 sprint battle and exploit his speed. At the same time, you can see that the Stuttgart player in the passing lane is trying to close the passing option to the wing and thus opens the inner path for Wirtz's pass. This suggests Wirtz concealed his intentions the best he could and apparently indicated a pass to the outside through his gaze and/or posture. (Concept in Spanish: *'falsear intenciones'*).

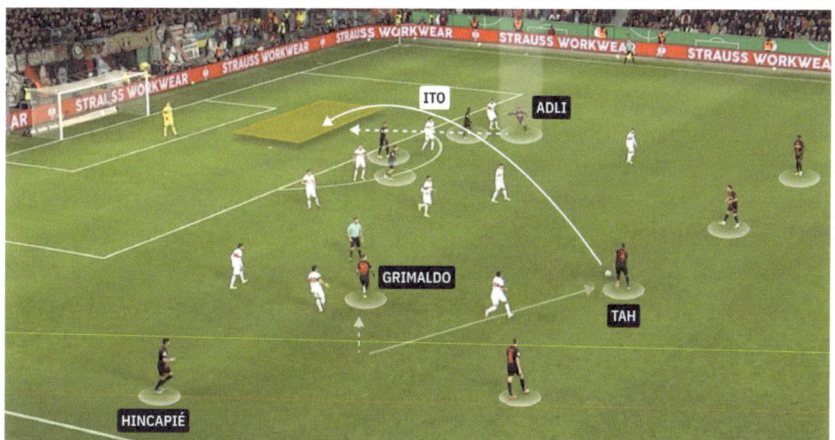

In an attack down the left, Grimaldo misses Hincapié, who is running behind, and therefore secures the ball with a pass "around the back" to Tah and is immediately ready to play again. Together with Adli, Tah takes advantage of the moment to attack the space behind Stuttgart's back five with a chip / cross. This is another example of the shared intentions by which the Leverkusen players play, perceiving the game based on the same opportunities and aligning their joint actions accordingly. Adli occupies the interface between full-back and centre-back. Stuttgart's Ito, who anticipates well, takes on the duel with Adli, but has to clear the ball for a corner, from which Tah will score the 3:2 winning goal.

In the end, Leverkusen managed to win a thrilling cup match against one of the biggest opponents and one of the best teams of the season just before the end, after falling behind twice. Once again a corner helps. Xabi Alonso honestly admits after the game: "Sometimes we win with structure, with control. Today we won with our hearts."[270]

270 Alonso quoted in Spiegel online on February 7, 2024.

The top match against FC Bayern a few days later was accompanied by great media fanfare. There is wild speculation that Xabi Alonso could succeed Thomas Tuchel in Munich. And in other respects, too, this match is tantamount to a preliminary decision in the championship winning race between Bayern and Bayer. Alonso himself gives an insight into his thoughts at the time: "Ok, we have come a long way and we are doing well, but it is still Bayern Munich... We are only two points ahead."[271]

In the run-up to the match there was also talk of a potential formation shift. It is pointless to discuss whether a 1-4-4-2 (as reported by *Sky*) or 1-4-2-3-1 (in the media coverage) was actually played or whether certain roles and tasks of players in the defensive phase of the game were simply modified; the Werkself had already shown in previous games that they were able to master different structures and concepts adapted to the respective defensive height. When in possession of the ball, the players' roles look unchanged: Due to the profile of the agile strikers Wirtz, Adli and Tella (with Wirtz preferring to operate from the center), it is clear that the focus is on speed and mobility and not on a clear target player.

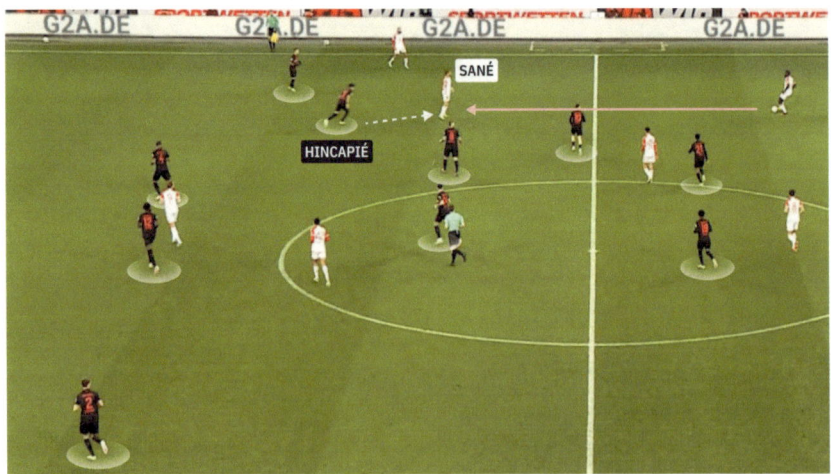

Leverkusen blocks the center in a compact manner (interestingly similar to AS Roma in the game against Leverkusen in the Europa League a year earlier). The five-man defensive line moves forward to defend the space between the lines. In particular, players in a tight receiving position (like Hincapié against Sané here) are singled out and defended in advance. The direct backpasses are also followed up, putting further pressure on the ball to keep the space tight.

271 Alonso quoted in Robles 2024.

Dier wants to hit a long ball to the left wing for Bayern Munich. Full-back Stanišić recognises this early on, can pick up his opponent's running movement and thus defend the space. At the same time, another interesting detail can be seen in Leverkusen's back line: all players stand with their feet staggered (which means they are prepared to start in both directions) and their body profile is aligned either to the ball or in response to the intentions (direction of view / posture) of the ball possessor.

Defending in space, but man-oriented: Leverkusen's defensive block with close distances to each other (approx. 15 m), densely staggered and at the same time at a good height (approx. 25 m in front of their own goal), which makes it difficult for the opponent to attack their backs. The defensive unit remains active and actively defends all movements close to the ball and between the lines through clear responsibilities in the respective playing area (Hincapié on the move forward). The player closest to the ball (in this case Wirtz) applies pressure and tries not to be overcome.

At the beginning of the game, Bayern Munich is present and looks for direct duels. As a result, Leverkusen respond with a slightly different build-up: If they pressed high and it is almost 1v1 on the last line, they play the long ball. Leverkusen is well prepared both for Bayern's changed formation (1-3-4-2-1) and for the aggressive start. As often this season, Leverkusen remain calm and manage to repeatedly create their own actions through variable possession play.

The 1-4-2-3-1 system "circulated" by the media can be seen here: Hincapié, the left central defender of the back three, pushes high and wide and takes on the role of a full-back in possession. This role differs only minimally from his usual role in possession of the ball, where the half-backs also repeatedly take part in offensive actions in the opponent's half and sometimes act very offensively alongside their wide partner. The key to this flexibility are Grimaldo's characteristics, who can act both as a winger and as a central player and can play with his strengths in both areas. This is why you can state that with Grimaldo it feels like having "two more players." His flexibility allows for a different position in the centre or the half-lane, depending on the game situation, sometimes requiring his dribbling skills and sometimes his passing to be emphasized. The basic organisation in possession of the ball has only changed minimally for Leverkusen: many players remain positioned close to the ball, trying to attack the spaces between the opponent's defensive lines and play in them.

It also shows the maturity of the team in this game, as they withstand extended phases of opposition possession. The facets of their own game model do not just consist of one game moment, but go hand in hand with all game moments. It is clear to see that Leverkusen knows what to do even when the opponent has the ball, and with mixture of short and long passes consistently finds the right space for passing. This ensures that the balance within the game gradually tilts in their favor and Leverkusen finally wins the top game 3:0 thanks to three goals from full-backs/wingers.

Xabi Alonso remembers this special match afterwards: "We wanted to control the game without the ball and wait for our counterattack moments – which is not usually our approach, but it worked. At halftime, when we were 1:0 up, the most important thing I saw was that I looked around the dressing room and nobody was interested in just standing deep and defending the 1:0 lead. Everyone wanted to score more goals. There was no fear.
If we didn't have this collective attitude, who knows what would have happened? If we had retreated and defended, who knows? Maybe a 1:1 draw (…) But we don't have that. We stayed disciplined and attacked when we had our chances and in the end we won 3:0. We passed the test."[272] Alonso also refers to the *"collective attitude"* that the team has already internalized. This does not just mean pulling together; it also means thinking and feeling the same way about football and interpreting the game using the same shared reference points.

272 Alonso in Robles 2024.

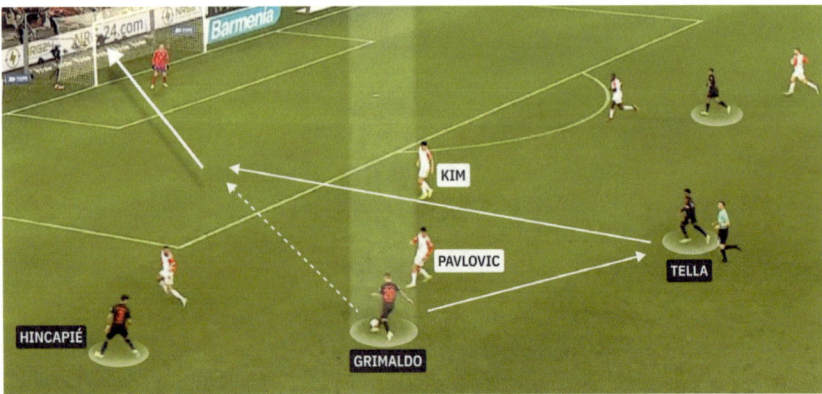

Leverkusen initiates a quick counterattack. Grimaldo, once again tracked by Hincapié, dribbles toward his opponent Pavlović. Nothing in his posture suggests a pass to Tella ("play and go" – one-two). However, Tella's one-two is slightly delayed. Tella delays the second touch in behind in order to find Grimaldo with precise timing. The slight delay forces Kim, the center-back, to step out toward the ball carrier. This further opens the gap for Grimaldo as Pavlović does not track him properly. Tella draws another opponent before slipping the ball to Grimaldo inside the penalty box, where he finishes brilliantly into the top-left corner.

After a quickly taken corner that Leverkusen recycles around the back, the Werkself attacks down the right wing with tight spacing. The overload in the wing creates a 4v3 advantage. The close spacing enables quick passing exchanges, making it harder for the opponent to intervene. Leverkusen consistently seeks numerical superiority near the ball, which also leads to positional advantages, especially on the wing.

Grimaldo himself describes the situation before his goal as follows: "I waited until Piero [Hincapié] ran past me so that the full-back was busy with him. Then I knew there would be room in the central lane. It's about reading the spaces and seeing where they are. I'm good at that. I knew the one-two would work and if I continued to move inside, the passing line would open. Nathan [Tella]'s pass was great. Then I was able to put the ball past [Bayern goalkeeper Manuel] Neuer, which is not easy because he is a great goalkeeper. It was an important goal, because at 2:0 felt more relaxed."[273]

After the game, the press went crazy. Whole of Germany was impressed. Above all, the overall phenomenon of Alonso is celebrated, who, thanks to his team's fearless style of play, is still unbeaten in first place in the Bundesliga and gene-rously shares this success with his entire team. This is also evident in a comment from the BILD newspaper, which states in the well-known category "Post from Wagner": "There is this scene that reveals everything about you. Your players danced and sang about their triumph over Bayern in front of the fans [in the *Nordkurve*]. But the *Nordkurve* did not want the players. The *Nordkurve* was cal-ling for you. Alonso, Alonso.
You stood alone in the coaching box, then turned around and waved your coa-ching staff over. The physios, the video specialists, the goalkeeping coaches. Together you then went to the Nordkurve. (...) This also shows your tactics. Your players always play close to each other, six meters apart. Your players have to help each other. Only a coach who has won everything as a player can think like that. Alone you are nothing."[274] It is Xabi Alonso's entire approach – not only the tactical finesse, the style of play with all its details, but also the consistent living of his own, deeply ingrained values that impress almost all of German football public. In fact, the commentary simply sums up how the game model must align with the team's values: "Your players always play close to each other (...) Your players have to help each other." It is therefore also clear that a holistic, con-sistently pursued game idea emerges in all facets, since only such coherence in a coach's work can endure over the long term of a season, admits the countless challenges of each individual game.

273 Grimaldo quoted by Corrigan 2024.
274 BILD online from February 11, 2024.

Work, 17.02.2024

Less than a week after the emotional moments of the DFB Cup quarter-final and the top match in the championship, the Werkself must mentally flip the switch: The next away game is in Heidenheim. And the Werkself would do well not to underestimate the promoted team, who will continue to impress this season.

Leverkusen starts with very sharp passing in order to keep the pace of the game high against the physically aggressive Heidenheim team. At times, Leverkusen looks for high balls forward, especially in the opening stage, in order to overcome the pressing and exploit how the last line is often defended in a 1v1. Heidenheim manages to prevent Leverkusen from creating clear chances and keeps the game intense with tackles, even though they struggle with the dynamics of the Werkself's game. They once again proved their stamina and scored in injury time of the first half through Frimpong after a beautiful combination between Tah, Wirtz, and Adli to make it 1:0 (45+2).

In the second half, Heidenheim tried to take more of the initiative, but only had a few scoring opportunities. Bayer is defensively stable and confident in this phase and gradually takes control of the difficult match. In the 81st minute the preliminary decision came with Adli making it 2:0. Wirtz is again found between the lines who dribble towards the backline – this time Adli breaks away well from behind and gets alone in front of the goalkeeper. However, Heidenheim does not give up and scores in the 86th minute following a wide free kick with a header to make it 2:1 – but no more scoring chances follow, so the three points deservedly go to the Werkself.

The (decisive) 2:0 for Leverkusen: Xhaka plays centrally through to Wirtz, who is able to turn and dribble onto the backline again. Wirtz feints a run to the right with his posture; likewise, Adli briefly feints to claim the ball in the run before cutting into the defender's back. Wirtz plays the ball against the movement of the defenders to Adli, who is alone in front of the goalkeeper and and scores for 2:0.

Overcoming resistance, 23.02.2024

The game against Mainz 05 begins with a shock – for the Mainz team, who are down 0:1 from the 3rd minute, and the Werkself's medical department, who got worried about the scorer: Granit Xhaka had shot from outside the penalty area and scored, but now grabs his harmstring. It takes a few seconds until everything turns into relief, and the way the goal was celebrated could be classified as a playful joke (and as evidence of the excellent atmosphere within the team). Under the new head coach Bo Henriksen, Mainz engage the Werkself in many duels and show a particular intensity. It turns out to be a game with a noticeably short effective playing time (just under 65 minutes).

Bayer Leverkusen's center kick: From the beginning, one side (here the left) is overloaded, so that the opponent has to expect a long ball. This leads to Mainz immediately adjusting to this move, retreating and preparing to defend against it. This allows Bayer Leverkusen to build up play from the start in a controlled, calm manner and, above all, without immediate pressing by the opponent. In this case, Kossounou changes Leverkusen's attacking axis with his pass to Tapsoba, so that the numerical advantage and proximity created on the left can still be used – not for the long ball, but to combine with each other down the left flank and half-track.

And Mainz responds immediately: A set-peice variation results in the equalizer in the 8th minute. What follows is an intense, physical game in which Mainz makes it very difficult for Leverkusen to advance. At the same time, the 05ers repeatedly create danger from set pieces. Until halftime, Leverkusen has few clear chances, while Mainz manages to slow down and complicate Leverkusen's game through physicality and aggressive duels. This hectic rhythm continues throughout the game in the second half.

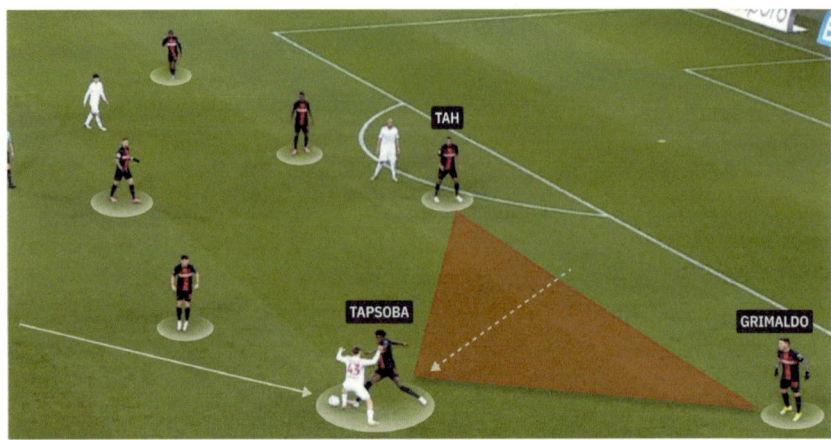

Tapsoba stands out from the five-man defense and defends up front. The so-called "defensive triangle" is created together with Tah and Grimaldo. What is special about Tapsoba's move is the timing: he reaches his opponent at the same time as the ball and immediately limits his avaible options. The defensive timing of starting and arriving at the same time as the pass is essential and we can observe it in all parts of Bayer Leverkusen's team this season.

Tapsoba and Xhaka with the concept of the "repeated pass". Xhaka plays the ball back to attract the opponent and increase the space between the lines. Hofmann changes the passing line (and axis) and runs across the opponent's back. This not only changes the assignment for Mainz, also creates difficulties in marking, as Hofmann now appears in a similar space to Adli, but the nearby central defender is occupied by him. Leverkusen positions itself on three different levels (floors) close to each other. Tapsoba plays a very sharp pass, which Hofmann takes in stride and continues the attack on the right side. Leverkusen repeatedly demonstrates the ability to find forward passing options in tight spaces.

In the second half, the Werkself manages to free themselves more and more and literally besieges the Mainz goal. The result is repeated attacks into the penalty area and quick ball recovery due to Leverkusen's good structure and close distances. However, the goal comes from a long-range shot: Andrich takes a courageous shot – the ball slips through for the decisive 2:1 winner. When a Mainz player receives a red card ten minutes before the end, the game is finally decided. After the game, Alonso pays respect to his opponent: "It was a very intense game. Mainz came with a very good energy that we had to respect. We were prepared for it, but it wasn't easy."[275] His team may not have played at their best, but "you can't always play brilliantly."[276] In any case, the team continues to grow, having managed to overcome Mainz's tough resistance and score three important points.

Luck attracts, 03.03.2024 - 07.03.2024 - 10.03.2024 - 15.03.2024 - 17.03.2024

Many are hoping for a fiery match in the derby against their relegation-threatened neighbors from Cologne. The guests from Leverkusen start as sharply and dynamically as possible and immediately set an extremely high pace. Leverkusen's superiority is already clear in the first ten minutes. Cologne only manages to get in front of Leverkusen's goal once, through a well-played counterattack - but it immediately becomes a goal threat. After 15 minutes, the dynamic of the game changes fundamentally when Thielmann is sent off with a red card for a foul on Xhaka.

275 Alonso quoted in The athletic online from 23.02.2024.
276 Ibid.

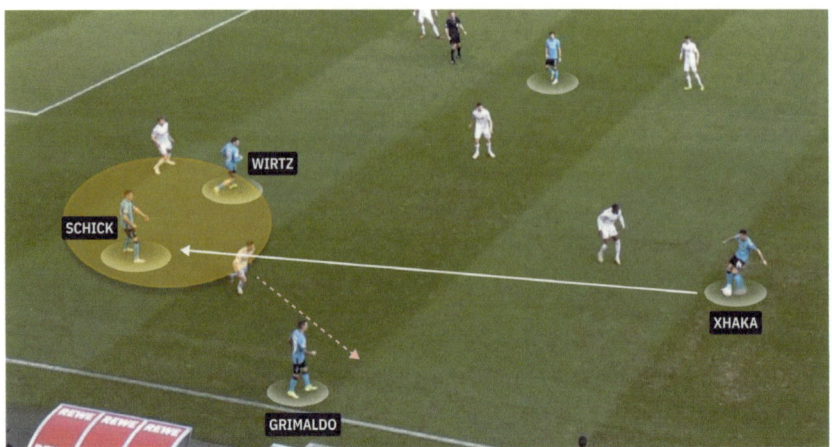

Xhaka is very good at hiding his intentions. Through his posture and alignment, he feints a pass to Grimaldo, but the ball actually goes to Schick. The Cologne full-back reacts to Xhaka's non-verbal, deceptive communication and covers Grimaldo. The passing lane to Schick opens and a 2v1 is created together with Wirtz against the Cologne central defender.

Leverkusen intensifies the pressure gradually, even if they struggle to find the final touch. This changes in the 37th minute, when the pressure from Leverkusen becomes overwhelming. Cologne keeper Schwäbe parries a shot from Wirtz after a great combination with Grimaldo. A short time later, however, he is powerless: A Grimaldo cross from the left sails into the penalty area, Frimpong starts from behind his opponent, beats everyone to it and scores to make it 1:0 in the Rhine derby. The basic scenario remains unchanged, even though FC creates another header chance from Alidou shortly before half-time after a nice combination on the right.

The Cologne side remained lively in the second half: Adamyan hits the post in the 51st minute. As a result, Leverkusen calms the game down by keeping possession and controls the match without allowing any direct shots on goal. They force Cologne to defend extremely deep and don't allow them to touch the ball. Instead, they attack selectively when space opens up to score the second, presumably decisive goal. Grimaldo finally delivers in the 72nd minute after a nice combination on the left side.

Leverkusen with the decisive 2:0: Hincapié finds Grimaldo on the left touchline. Wirtz and Adli are positioned near the corner of the penalty box and interact brilliantly through their trajectories: Wirtz positions himself behind the opponent and offers a simple pass to Grimaldo, who also has two additional passing options close to the ball with Xhaka and the option to play back back to Hincapié. Adli immediately occupies the space created by Wirtz. With a bit of luck, Adli receives the ball from Wirtz and is able to advance further into the penalty area. Grimaldo follows on his pass, consistently drives into the penalty area and receives the ball at the left corner of the box, calmly slotting it home to seal the 2:0 victory. Wirtz and Adli also have space because striker Borja Iglesias stays in the center and ties up his opponent.

In the last 15 minutes, Leverkusen combine at will with a numerical advantage, pass the ball around effortlessly and even create occasional chances to extend the lead. A comfortable derby victory for the Werkself, also thanks to the early red card.

Things were not so easy for Leverkusen when they met their group opponents Qarabag in the round of 16 in the Europa League: Driven by a frenetic crowd, Qarabag countered the Werkself with brutal dynamism and efficiency and brought Leverkusen to the brink of their first defeat of the season. At half-time, the hosts from Azerbaijan lead 2:0. But in the second half, Leverkusen comes back into the game: A very attentive Florian Wirtz capitalizes on a back pass from the opponent to lob the ball spectacularly into the net for 2:1. In the rainy Azerbaijan, Leverkusen has to wait until stoppage time until they finally are rewarded for its pressing attacking efforts. Previously, the Werkself had not displayed the clarity and flow they have had in previous games. The 92nd minute is already ticking away, when Andrich swings in another cross. And this time Schick rises high and heads in the equalizer with a header. The cheering is limitless – and Leverkusen escapes from the first leg of the round of 16 with just a black eye and a good starting position for the return leg.

In the "factory-duel" against VfL Wolfsburg, Leverkusen once again underlines that they are playing in their own league this season. No sign of tiredness from the Europa League match that was rescued only at the last minute. Instead, Leverkusen displays a very high pace of play right from the start. It quickly becomes clear that the Werkself completely dominates their opponents from Wolfsburg and dictates the tone in terms of pressing and their own game approach.

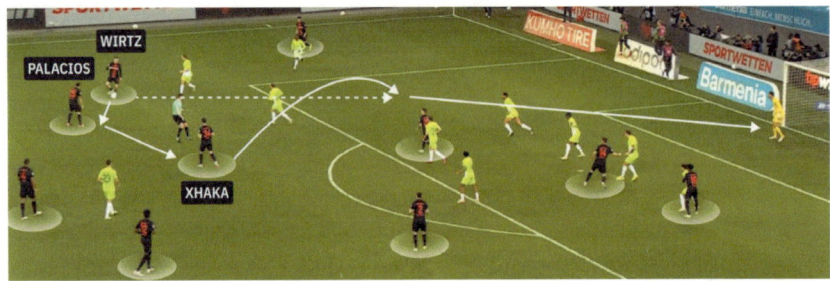

'*Pared doblada*' – a delayed one-two, in this case with three players: Wirtz plays to Palacios and starts a deep run. Palacios delays the game briefly with his second touch and draws opponents and their focus; then he passes to Xhaka, who chips the ball directly into Florian Wirtz's path with his left foot. The young German hits the ball against the post – an outstanding scoring opportunity.

Wolfsburg repeatedly attempts to counterattack, but without much success – in the first 30 minutes, Leverkusen in particular creates top-class scoring opportunities (including Wirtz hitting the post). In the 28th minute, the game finally tilts in Leverkusen's favor, again due to a red card: Wolfsburg defender Moritz Jenz receives a second yellow and is sent off for repeated fouls. This means he joins the long list of red cards that VfL Wolfsburg has had to endure this season. What happens next had been coming for some time: A wonderfully played 1:0 by Tella, in which not only a winger who has moved in scores again, but Grimaldo particularly shines with an outstanding first touch pass. In general, Grimaldo once again interprets the game in a new dimension today: In Leverkusen's classic 1-3-4-3, he acts almost like a false nine, while Wirtz moves into the center and Hincapié (actually a half-back in the back three) shifts wide in possession, making the overall organization look like a back four.

In the second half, Leverkusen used a lot of shifts of play to pull the opponent apart and controlled the game at times in the handball team style, without threatening the goal or any final consequence. This changes again towards the end:

After Adli plays the ball back to Xhaka and he signals a shift in play via Palacios, Wirtz starts from the half-left position exactly into the interface between the full-back and the centre-back. Palacios finds the German international with a perfectly timed diagonal pass and he shows all his class when he scores the final goal to make it 2:0.

After the narrow and fortunate first leg in Azerbaijan, the Werkself is warned: Qarabag is by no means the opponent from the group stage that can be defeated effortlessly anymore. Accordingly, the Werkself tries to control the game from the start in the return leg and immediately put their own stamp on it. This only works partially, and the longer the score is 0:0, the more nervous the game becomes. The number of scoring opportunities, which Leverkusen had in abundance in the early stages, decreases. The score remains 0:0 at halftime. And the second half turns out to be a tough one...

It starts with a shocking moment: In the 58th minute, Qarabag comes forward on one of their rare forays, creates a numerical advantage on their right side, crosses and scores with a header to take a 1:0 lead. In the 67th minute, things get even worse for the Werkself: Qarabag intercepted a counterattack, outplays Leverkusen, again on the right, and scored to make it 2:0. Now, as in the first leg, Leverkusen needs to score at least two goals to even reach extra time. A mammoth task considering the start and course of the second half so far. But the mentality of Xabi Alonso's team is characterized by one thing above all: Never give up and always play to the end! And so the madness takes its course against only ten players, as the left-back of Qarabag is sent off with a straight red by referee Anthony Taylor after a harsh tactical foul.

From then on, Leverkusen laid siege to their opponents' penalty area and is able to score a quick goal through Frimpong to make it 1:2 (72'), who was able to convert a cross from the left at the second post. Bayer now has a clear advantage and chances every minute – but the ball just won't go into the goal. The minutes tick by and injury time begins. The 93rd minute is already running, when another consistent attack by Leverkusen on the left, carried out with the necessary patience, ends with a flat cross from Grimaldo. Schick is there at the first post - and with a long lunge, he puts the ball over the line from just under five meters to equalize. The BayArena is roaring. Leverkusen strikes again in injury time. But the game is not over yet. The six minutes of added time has already elapsed when Palacios regains the ball with a sensational sliding tackle in counter-pressing. Leverkusen looks for the last chance, passes the ball back and forth in the penalty area several times until finally Palacios crosses the ball from the left half to the second post - and Schick is there again. The Czech scores with a header to make it 3:2 – and everything explodes in pure ecstasy! Leverkusen pulls the game around completely in injury time. At this point, the myth of "Laterkusen" is born.

Xabi stays! 17.03.2024 - 30.03.2024

After the excitement of the Europa League, the Werkself remain ambitious. SC Freiburg is an opponent that has already been difficult to crack in the first half of the season. But Leverkusen gets off to a dream start: In the second minute, the Werkself manages to pick up the pace from their own throw-in in the middle of their own half, brutally attacks the ball deep and, after a combination from Grimaldo to Wirtz, scores the 1:0.

Particularly in the early stages, Leverkusen often try to establish an equal number against the last line, which in turn is very man-oriented and therefore easily thrown into disarray by this maneuver. Werkself 's compact center repeatedly draws overloads from Grimaldo, who moves inside from the wing with the intention of being an additional option at the back of the opponent.

However, after ten minutes and with Freiburg's first chance to score, Doan delivers an absolute dream goal (one-two with Höler) to equalize at 1:1 and put the score back to the beginning. Leverkusen then tries to control the game as usual through possession, but Freiburg acted courageously and also tries to set accents in the game. As a result, clear scoring chances were lacking and the second real opportunity gave Leverkusen a 2:1 lead through Hložek (40'). The young, talented Czech, who has often shown his skills (especially in preparation phase) but has yet to fully display them iun the Bundesliga, takes advantage of a rebound after a good move down the left side, initiated by Wirtz, who is once again hard to stop. In the end, so many Leverkusen oplayers flood the penalty area until the ball inevitably finds the net.

In the second half, Leverkusen initially manages to control the game better. An unbelievable goal arrives in the 53rd minute by Patrik Schick: The Czech takes a cross from Frimpong directly – the ball bounces from the left inside post to the right inside post – and into the net to make it 3:1. The shooter doesn't mind – he's just riding the wave after the magical Europa League night.

The rest of the game seems to be a typical Leverkusen game: controlled possession – playing forward when there is enough space and attacking the depth, the box and the goal. But today's opponent is Freiburg – and they can also play at a very high level. The Breisgau team demonstrates this once again with their second goal in the 79th minute, when a beautiful possession sequence is played diagonally from the left into the penalty area and ends into a follow-up goal. But the Werkself were too strong for Freiburg that afternoon. Leverkusen had several more chances to increase the score (Wirtz hits the post, among others), and then is briefly put under pressure after a corner in the final action, but the ball flies over the goal.

The next game against 1899 Hoffenheim begins with good news even before kick-off: Xabi Alonso will definitely remain Leverkusen coach in the coming season: "My job is not over here yet," said the Basque. "I made this important decision and took everything together. I am convinced that it is the right decision. This is my first full season as a coach. I still have a lot to prove and a lot of experience to gain. At the moment I am in a situation where I feel very stable and happy. This is the right place for me to develop as a coach."[277] In view of Alonso's previous career decisions, this is the only consistent and logical decision; even though the temptation must have been huge due to other interesting open coaching positions (such as Bayern Munich, Liverpool FC or potentially Real Madrid). Xabi remains true to his style and his path - taking a development step by step that he considers "healthy" and organic, until he feels prepared for the next step.

The players, who greeted the good news with applause, show a tight game with a lot of possession but few scoring opportunities. Hoffenheim tries to make some incisive attacks, but is unable to score against an attentively defending Leverkusen. The Werkself holds firm until exactly the 33rd minute – then Hoffenheim scored with the first good opportunity to make it 1:0 (Beier). Leverkusen becomes more assertive, but were still lucky that Hoffenheim did not score a second goal with their next high-quality chance. Leverkusen goes into the break 1:0 down.

In the second half, the game takes place entirely in one half: Leverkusen presses and presses and consistently creates scoring opportunities, corners and free kicks in dangerous zones. Despite several close calls (including a shot on the crossbar by Borja Iglesias), it takes until the 88th minute, when Robert Andrich converts a corner that was flicked on and fires a volley from just under eleven

277 Alonso quoted by The athletic online from 30.03.2024.

meters. The Werkself's goal celebration makes it clear that the team wants more and is pushing for a second goal in the short time remaining. The Werkself keeps up the high rhythm of the game and lays siege to the Hoffenheim goal. In the 91st minute, as so often in recent weeks, it is Patrik Schick who meets Frimpong's cross and slots home for the emotional 2:1 winning goal. It is the self-fulfilling prophecy and the belief of the players that makes this incredible mentality possible. The Werkself has already scored 22 goals after the 80th minute – this team seems invincible and never gives up. Jonas Hofmann tries to explain the secret of "Laterkusen": "We pull together and don't start sending long balls out of the back line. We keep playing our game and feel like we're just waiting for someone to fly in. We have already done that a few times, it gives us energy."[278]

Leverkusen tends to play with a direct relationship to the opponent, particularly in the attacking third and near the ball. Even in the last line of defense, a 1v1 setup is established as Hincapié advances to take on the next opponent. When the opposing goalkeeper is in possession of the ball, this approach generally allows for high pressure on the ball and at the same time enables the defenders away from the ball to anticipate the potential pass well in advance and therefore defend more easily.

278 Hofmann quoted in Kicker online on April 1, 2024.

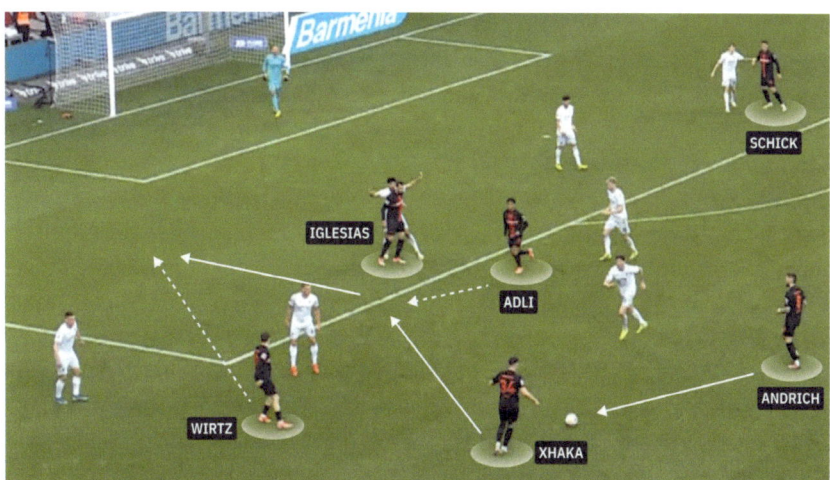

Leverkusen plays in the box: Andrich's cross is followed by a perfectly timed deep ball from Xhaka to Adli, who moves well between the different positional axes. Iglesias ties up his opponent, who is therefore unable to defend, and at the same time is a passing option to pose a goal threat in a 1v1 hold-up situation inside or just outside the box - similar to Boniface in other games before. Wirtz immediately recognizes the situation, sprints deep over the edge of the penalty box into the penalty area and receives the ball from Adli. Due to the momentum in this situation, Wirtz can advance to the edge of the six-yard box and serves the incoming Schick close to goal. His shot is blocked for a corner.

A pinch of Mourinho, 06.04.2024 - 11.04.2024

The Werkself also easily overcomes the semi-final hurdle in the DFB Cup against Fortuna Düsseldorf and thus maintains all title chances. And the trip to Berlin is even quicker for Bayer: Leverkusen will face Union in the capital on the Saturday after the semi-final.

The Werkself remain true to themselves, control the game and try to outmaneuver the Union's defensive block again and again. Until the end of the first half, Leverkusen's game remained controlled and pleasing, with Union merely attempting to capitalize on chaotic moments (particularly through counterattacks and subsequent set pieces). At the end of the first half, however, events at the *Alte Försterei* (Stadium of Union Berlin) take a dramatic turn: First, Tella dribbles into Robin Gosens, who has already been booked, in a 1v1 and can only be stopped by a foul – Robin Gosens receives his second yellow card and is sent off. At the end of injury time, the ball is suddenly in the net: In a scramble inside the penalty area scene, defender Kossounou pushes the ball over the line. After a lengthy review by the video assistant, the goal is disallowed. Instead, a penalty is given for handball. Wirtz confidently converts this to make it 1:0 at halftime.

In the second half, Leverkusen initially pushes for the second goal, but without success. The Werkself consistently defends every attempt by Union and controlled the game with a numerical advantage, securing another three points.

In the quarter-finals of the Europa League, there will be another reunion with an old foe: West Ham United will visit the BayArena - similar to the opening game of the season just eight months earlier. But this team is no longer in last season's form: Coach David Moyes has shaped the London side into a stubborn team and sets up deep defensively, defending their box in Leverkusen with eleven players. Leverkusen, which according to the broadcasting TV station lines up in a 1-4-2-3-1 formation, actually displays the usual position structure in a 1-3-4-3, with Grimaldo and Frimpong as wingers and Wirtz as a "free spirit" in the front area. Adli drifts inside, allowing Grimaldo to have central playmaking moments. Schick is the clear striker.

Leverkusen dominates the game from the start and seems prepared in several facets: Several West Ham players are on yellow cards, facing a suspension in the second leg if booked again, are put in tight situations where they have no choice but to foul. So Leverkusen quickly forces West Ham's key player Paquetá into yellow card, knowing that his temperament puts him at constant risk of a yellow-red card from now on and likely means he'll certainly miss the second leg. As in the case of Robin Gosens, who had already been booked in Berlin, the Werkself shows here too that their coach has learned not only from Pep Guardiola, but also from José Mourinho mastering the art of tactical advantage. Leverkusen links up in close spaces and pushes the opponent deep into their own half, so that the game at times resemble handball . At the end of the game, Leverkusen registers 78 touches in the opponent's penalty area - the highest number since recording began for the 2016-17 Europa League season.[279] Other parameters also underline the strong performance of the Werkself: 33 shots on goal (with eleven shots on target) set more Europa League records and illustrate the team's total superiority. Bayer concedes just a single shot on goal and once again dominates possession impressively: For the fifth time this season, Leverkusen achieves a pass rate of over 90%.[280]

Despite this dominance, Bayer cannot score a goal. Adli positions himself a little wider to pull the opposing five-man defense apart and create more space. West Ham sits extremely deep, defending with all outfield players in and around the penalty area with the clear idea of parking the bus. But it is not without reason that Leverkusen is known as "mentality monsters" this season. The massive pressure eventually breaks through: substitute Hofmann scores in the 89th minute. Almost on cue, it's yet another late goal - and once again from a corner. And it happens again: Boniface, who came on as a substitute together with Hofmann, scores the decisive 2:0 with a header from another corner at the beginning of injury time. A well-deserved victory in which Leverkusen once again manages to convert dominance into goals late in the game, and at the same time demonstrates its maturity and development compared to last year.

---

279 see *kicker* online from 12.04.2024.
280 Ibid.

German Champion, 14.04.2024

Before the home game against Bremen, Alonso once again rotates his squad. It remains impressive how naturally each player adapts to different roles, such as Hincapié playing a left winger in this game, immediately integraining into the team dynamic and executing the game plan according to his abilities. The game idea is clear and and firmly in place.

It was destined to be a historic, sunny day in the BayArena – and the Werkself left no doubt that they were ready to be crowned German champions in this home game. In the 22nd minute, Hofmann goes down in the penalty area. After a review from the VAR, Leverkusen earns a penalty, which Boniface calmly converts in the 25th minute against a resilient Bremen to make it 1:0. This score holds until halftime.

The second half features a masterclass from substitute Florian Wirtz. As a result of his substitution, Boniface shifts on the left side, from where the Nigerian promptly assits Xhaka for the 2:0 (60'). It is a typical Xhaka goal this season: a long-range shot from outside the box, aimed precisely into the corner. Everyone in the stadium feels the dream becoming reality. Something historic is unfolding—*Leverkusen is about to become German champions!* And it is far from an ordinary game. But it has everything a title-clinching match should: After a fantastic combination through the center, Wirtz scores an absolute dream goal from almost 25 meters to make it 3:0 (69th). In the 84th minute, a counterattack goal by Wirtz finally sends the stadium into a frenzy: Fans begin storming the pitch, forcing security to intervene and restore order so the match can be completed properly. When Wirtz then completes his hat-trick in the 90th minute and makes it 5:0, Referee Harm Osmers blows the final whistle while making his way off the field: Leverkusen is German football champion for the first time in Bundesliga history!

After weeks and months of concentration, all players are just soaking in the moment and finally allow themselves to embrace pure joy. The special emotions shared by fans, staff, and players alike are palpable, even to those watching from afar.

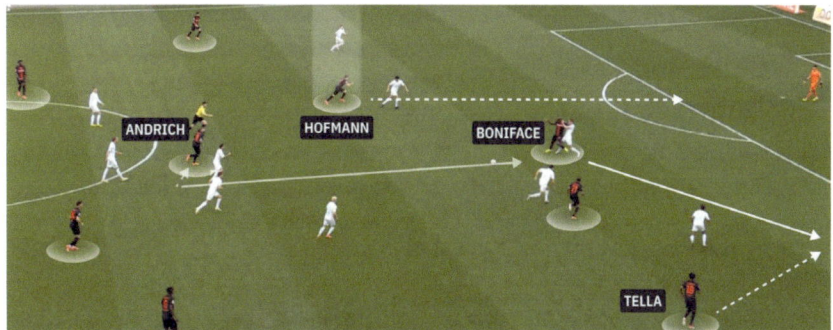

Andrich plays a deep pass to Boniface, who uses his body and position to hold off his direct opponent and secure the ball. The outplayed players immediately start to drop deeper: Tella receives the ball from Boniface and delivers into the penalty area, where Hofmann goes down under a challenge. A penalty follows for Leverkusen after a review from the VAR.

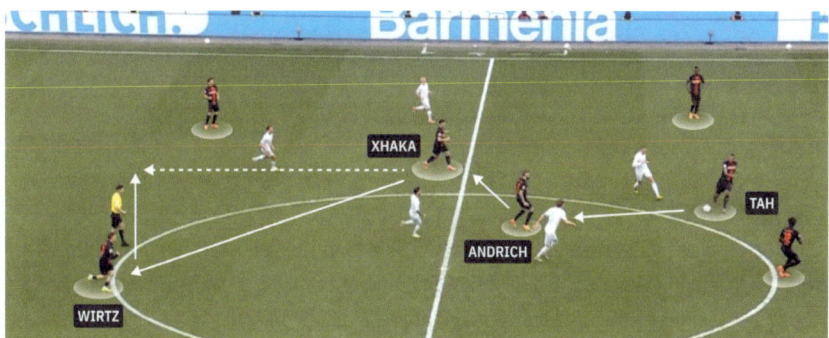

Leverkusen progresses thorugh tight spaces in a staircase-like passing sequence through the center: Tah plays a disguised pass to Andrich, who immediately lays it off to Xhaka, who in turn plays an penetrative diagonal pass to Wirtz. He notices that he is under pressure and executes the ball directly back to Xhaka, who immediately presents another passing option. This passing pattern recurs frequently in Leverkusen's game.

And even at the moment of his greatest triumph - both for the club and his young coaching career - Xabi Alonso does not think about himself, but describes this moment at the press conference after the game as follows: "Finally saying that Bayer Leverkusen are German champions is a great honour for me. Not only this team, but also the coaches and sports directors of the past have fought for this title. Therefore, it is a consequence of the top work of the past years. Christoph Daum, Klaus Toppmöller, Roger Schmidt – and many more. I want to share the success with many people in this club."[281]

The culture that Xabi Alonso has shaped at Bayer becomes clear throughout these moments. In an interview with *DAZN*, Jonas Hofmann reveals the group's own desire to sit down after "bad" training sessions, close the door and have a heated discussion. Granit Xhaka had already said in January about Alonso's high expectations: "We see it every day – he runs almost more than we do in training. He gives us this hunger that he has, this feeling of wanting to win. And of course we try to give that back to him."[282] Goalkeeper Lukáš Hrádecký also emphasizes the quality of their training: "We have a different training culture, you can see that every day. (...) As I said: We have a different level of training with the players who came in the summer, that's the secret. Cabin life is a good mix of challenge and fun. The mutual respect in the dressing room has never been as high as it is now. Somehow we all got a feeling that it's about higher goals and that we have to earn them."[283] The foundation for successful work was certainly laid in training and the everyday routine. The Spanish coach Rubén de la Barrera (currently working in Portugal), who visited Alonso in Leverkusen, later raved about the coach's obsession with spatial and temporal control. He points out: "How he masters the different rhythms of the game. His training sessions are incredible, always with maximum intensity, with a lot of content and meaning. In the same game, they are able to master and adapt to all rhythms."[284]
But it is not only training that gives the players orientation. Hrádecký also clearly highlights Alonso's leadership skills as an essential factor when he says: "He makes no distinction whether it is Granit Xhaka, Hrádecký, Frimpong or one of the young players. If he doesn't like something, he says so. Then he can also be loud."[285]

281 Alonso quoted by *kicker* from 14.04.2024.
282 Xhaka quoted by Spox Online, 24.01.2024.
283 Hrádecký quoted in SZ Online, 09.02.2024
284 de la Barrera, in Blaya, 2023.
285 Hrádecký quoted in SZ Online, 09.02.2024.

Alejandro Grimaldo adds: "Xabi is very demanding, but with respect. If you play a bad pass in training, he says: 'Come on, come on, you can't make that mistake'. He sets these demands, but at the same time he encourages you when you do well. (...) This is something that motivates you and I love it. I have experience and I'm relaxed about it [being corrected]. I like to see how he encourages the younger players too. I wish I have had a coach like him when I was 20 years old."[286]

Captain Granit Xhaka stresses that the consistency demanded by the coach also includes more responsibility: "He wants the players to take responsibility, he wants us to address it when we see that one or two players are not performing as well in training in order to keep the level as high as it is at the moment. We are in the locker room. We see things. He is not there all the time. So it's up to us to sort things out."[287] However, this is not just about responsibility off the pitch. Courage is also important on the pitch: "Courage can be defined in different ways. (...) [It] says a lot about players who, when the mood is bad, take control of the game and try to assume responsibility for the team."[288]

The team composition of the current season, which is repeatedly praised by the players, also helps. Captain Xhaka: "Fortunately, we have great personalities, even among the younger players. The mentality is great. The boys listen, they want to learn something and implement it immediately on the pitch."[289] Central defender Jonathan Tah, who has already spent many years at Bayer 04, unintentionally talks about almost the same attributes that are writ large in San Sebastián when he says: "We are very close, very familiar and have a good age structure in the team: some are very young, some are very experienced with many games under their belts. This mix makes the whole thing special. We also have a lot of different nationalities in the team, which I think is really nice. Because it simply works well and harmonizes. Because everyone respects each other and ultimately pursues a common goal: to be successful. This feels good right now."[290]

286 Grimaldo quoted in The Athletic Online, 02.03.2024.
287 Xhaka quoted in The Athletic Online, 19.12.2023.
288 Alonso quoted in The Athletic Online, 02.04.2024.
289 Xhaka quoted in The Athletic Online, 19.12.2023.
290 Tah, quoted in Behnisch, 2024.

Leverkusen's success is, not surprisingly, a mixture of many factors that work well together and create decisive synergies. Similar to what was already explained in the section on the game model, one (the leadership) influences the other (the style of play) within the implementation of the game idea. As Xabi Alonso said when he was introduced, the personal connection to the players came first and then the content. A way of working that has borne fruit, driven by an ambition that should not be satisfied with just winning the German championship this season.

Survival in London, 18.04.2024

After celebrating their historic triumph in the Bundesliga, Bayer Leverkusen travels to London as the new German champions. And West Ham showes a completely different side in the return match: the "Hammers" try to turn the deficit around with pressure and a lot of intensity right from the start. Defender Kossounou has a terrible day, receives an early yellow card and is substituted in the first half. West Ham consistently creates a hectic atmosphere: Not only the English team takes the lead 1:0 after just 13 minutes, but in the 30th minute a Leverkusen assistant coach even receives a red card after a verbal altercation with the English bench. The Werkself struggle to settle and return to the dressing room with a one-goal deficit.

Frimpong and Boniface are substituted during the break and from then on the game takes on a different, more balanced face. Leverkusen gains more composure, controls possession better near the ball, and finds passing options more deliberately, taking control of the game from then on.

It remains a tight game, even though Leverkusen is now clearly in the match and no longer has to worry about qualification like they did in the first half. Several counter-attack opportunities are initially missed, but it is finally Frimpong who scores the deserved equalizer in the 89th minute. The Dutchman's goal is already the 27th goal in the last ten minutes of the game – 13 of which were scored by the Werkself in injury time – a particularly impressive statistic that also underlines the winning mentality of this team. "We knew what was coming, but we didn't deal with it well," Xabi Alonso analyzed the game afterwards, "we lost the ball easily. We were lucky not to concede the second goal. (...) That was the best thing about the first half. It was a good lesson for us." The decision to make a substitution before half-time was not an easy one for him either: "Of course it was not an easy decision. But Odi had a yellow card, we had some problems. Sometimes you have to act. (...) It's not the prettiest solution either, but I talked to him. I think he understood it. It was about the well-being of the team.

A bad day can happen to anyone."[291]
Once again, the quality of the squad and the positive influence that the substitutes can immediately have on the game are evident: "By having Jerry [Frimpong] and Grimaldo higher up, we created more space in the midfield and developed the game better there. "It felt like we haven't had any contact with the ball before," said managing director Simon Rolfes about the successful move.[292] Like last year, Bayer Leverkusen has again qualified for the semi-finals of the Europa League. As in the previous year, AS Roma awaits them there. But the Werkself is still challenged in the Bundesliga...

Invincible, 21.04.2024 - 27.04.2024

As the new German champions, the Werkself goes into the duel with Borussia Dortmund, who had already caused problems for Leverkusen in the first leg with their very pragmatic, functional style of play. As always this season, the new German champions start with initiative and the aim of actively shaping the game through ball possession. The Werkself manages to dominate possession against BVB's solid defense, but fail to create many clear-cut scoring opportunities. With regard to Xabi Alonso's personnel selection, the changed roles of Grimaldo (who had already appeared in the center in previous games) and Stanišić are particularly noteworthy. Stanišić in particular allows for several options in his playing style due to his versatility as a player and can unsettle the opposition with his various positional options. On the one hand, he can act as a typical full-back and allow Frimpong to move into the center as a striker. On the other hand, he can - if the situation demands - act as in the back three (which he actually does when the opponent has the ball). And he can also move inside and occupy the right half space (like an attacking 8). Needless to say, all these options are designed to create numerical superiority in the respective space. All this provides additional fluidity in Xabi Alonso's system and takes the team to a new level of quality.

291 Alonso quoted by *kicker* online from April 19, 2024.
292 Rolfes quoted in *kicker* online on April 19, 2024.

Leverkusen with the next stage of development in terms of the functional roles and combinations of their players: In the game against BVB, the Werkself opt to play without a striker and instead start with Frimpong, Hofmann and Tella on the front line. Frimpong and Tella operate particularly wide and ensure space in the centre, which the nominal wingers Grimaldo and Stanišić take up as the new No. 8s. In this situation, Andrich drops back to form a back three with Tah and Tapsoba. Hincapié takes on the role of a full-back (which gives Tella the chance to move inside from the left) and Frimpong is responsible maintaining width on the right. The advantage of this positioning is that Grimaldo and Stanišić, coming from wide into central areas, are rarely picked up by their opponents or only noticed very late (usually when they receive the ball).

The Werkself gains superiority in possession – but Dortmund has the one clear chance to score. Hrádecký saves the clean sheet for his team at the end of the first half and at the beginning of the second half.

The second half also remains a game with few chances , with Leverkusen holding a slight advantage. Nevertheless, it is once again Dortmund who creates more clarity: After a long throw-in and the ensuring cross, Füllkrug is free in the six-yard box: The German international has no trouble volleying the ball into the net (81'). When Leverkusen pushes hard but fails to create any clear chances and injury time begins, even the biggest optimists start to believe that today might be the day when the Werkself finally suffer their first defeat in ages. But Bayer 04 sees it differently: With the last action in the 97th minute, following a corner from the left by Wirtz, Stanišić rises highest at the near post and flicks the ball into the net to make it 1:1. It remains the same – even as German champions, Leverkusen remains unbeaten.

The next top game is just as tough: VfB Stuttgart, the team having a similarly outstanding season to Leverkusen, visits the BayArena and, after the cup game, are now making their third attempt this season to inflict the Werkself's first defeat. Up to this point, the new German champions have only conceded 20 goals and kept 15 clean sheets. The team's passing accuracy stands at a pass rate of 93%.

As expected, VfB start the match courageously with the aim of imposing their own game. So Stuttgart are the first to create a chance. For Leverkusen, the absence of Xhaka is noticeable (yellow card suspension). The intense, tightly contested top game may be poor in clear-cut opportunities, but despite the championship being decided, it remains very exciting. The score is 0:0 at half-time.

The second half barely begins before the score is already 0:1: After a beautiful long ball down Leverkusen's left defensive side, Stuttgart gets a free shot. The first attempt hits the post – but the rebound lands at the feet of Führich, who is following up – and the young international scores (once again against Leverkusen) to give Stuttgart the lead.

Leverkusen attempt to break free by controlling possession and dictating play; however, Stuttgart are the ones who strike again: Undav scores to make it 2:0 in the 57th minute. Today, Leverkusen's game lacks maximum sharpness, persistence, in short: the key attributes that previously allowed them to beat almost any team.

Almost out of nowhere, Adli manages to make it 2:1: After Hincapié dribbles down the left wing and lays the ball back to Grimaldo on the edge of the box, he finds Adli, who flicks it forward and then slots it into the bottom right corner. From now on, the game turns into a fast-paced battle, in which Stuttgart goalkeeper Nübel delivers a standout performance. But Stuttgart stays active and looks for a decisive third goal. The result is a thrilling end-to-end contest that has less of the "control" that Xabi Alonso demands, but serves as the best advertisement for the Bundesliga. And this game also delivers its most dramatic moment in the final action: the five minutes of stoppage time are already up, when there comes another free kick for the Werkself not far from the left edge of the penalty box. Wirtz steps up to the ball and hits it into the penalty area. The ball takes a slight deflection, falling short - but Andrich reacts quickest to make it 2:2. An incredible final twist in this game!

Robert Andrich in general: A synonym for the development of Bayer Leverkusen under Xabi Alonso and a phenomenon for many. In 2018, the current international and European Championship player was still playing in the second division. A player who has thrived under his coach and demonstrated remarkable progress, but at the same time possesses exceptional skills when it comes to adapting to the next, higher level. His former coach Rüdiger Rehm, who trained Andrich at

Wehen Wiesbaden, recalled in the sports magazine *kicker*: "There were no real limits for him because he already had many important skills back then. But of course he has worked incredibly hard on himself. If a player is still playing in the third divison at the age of 22 or 23, then you can assume that he will not necessarily become a national player (...) Nobody who was there in Wiesbaden at the time would have said that Rob would have a good chance of being a important player of the national team at EURO 2024." Everything was hard-earned with diligence and adaptability. Not much has changed for Rehm: "I actually see him playing the same way as he did back then, but he is now playing at an absolutely top level. [He is] strong in tackles, always available to pass to, technically good, he coaches on the pitch, stays positive."[293] And this season he has added an impressive accuracy, having scored a total of six goals in the Bundesliga.

Successful revenge, 02.05.2024 – 05.05.2024 – 09.05.2024

In the semi-finals of the Europa League, Leverkusen faces their opponents from last year: AS Roma may have seen their coach José Mourinho leave, but the team remains a formidable force. It is the maximum stress test for Leverkusen in the atmospheric Olympic Stadium in Rome.
Xabi Alonso has again chosen a 1-3-4-3 as his base formation, but with slightly more defensive profiles than last time. In addition, the Werkself operates without a clear striker, but with very fluid players up front who repeatedly push into spaces and can variably rotate and emerge within deeper areas. Frimpong in particular frequently pops up in the box.
The Werkself defend with focus, even if world-class striker Romelu Lukaku remained a constant threat throughout, as his shot to the crossbar in the 21st minute showed. Nevertheless, the Werkself stay fully locked in, determined to avoid another elimination by Roma. This determination leads to Wirtz scoring the 1:0: Grimaldo pounces on a back pass that was too short and found Wirtz in the penalty area. He slots it home to give Leverkusen the lead (28'). Overall, it is a very mature performance from Leverkusen, showing grit, resilience, and composure - all attributes that applied to their opponents last season.

---

293 Rehm quoted by *kicker* online, 01.04.2024.

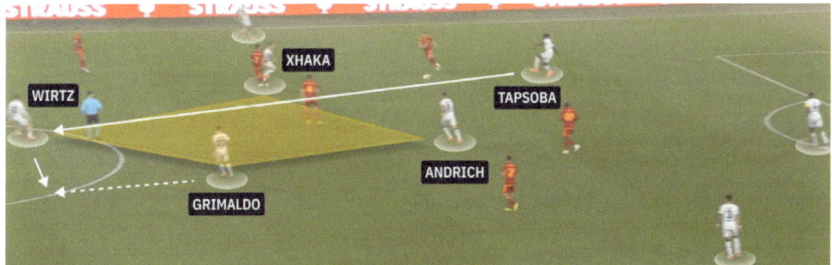

The mobile square in the center: Grimaldo once again interprets his position more centrally and repeatedly creates a square (or in this case: a diamond) together with Xhaka, Andrich and Wirtz to create more passing options in the center and especially behind the back of the opponent. Tapsoba bypasses six opponents with his pass. Wirtz lays the ball off for Grimaldo, who immediately ensures the tempo of the game situation.

An individual look at the duel between Lukaku and Tah: The Roma striker is inherently difficult to defend against, as he combines immense physical strength to protect the ball and explosive pace on the break. Tah anticipates the deep pass early. Just before the pass is made, he nudges Lukaku slightly, so that he loses his timing for the deep run. This happens at a moment when all referees and players are focused on the ball. This action, executed just outside the penalty area, is only a detail, but it gives Tah a decisive advantage in intercepting the through ball.

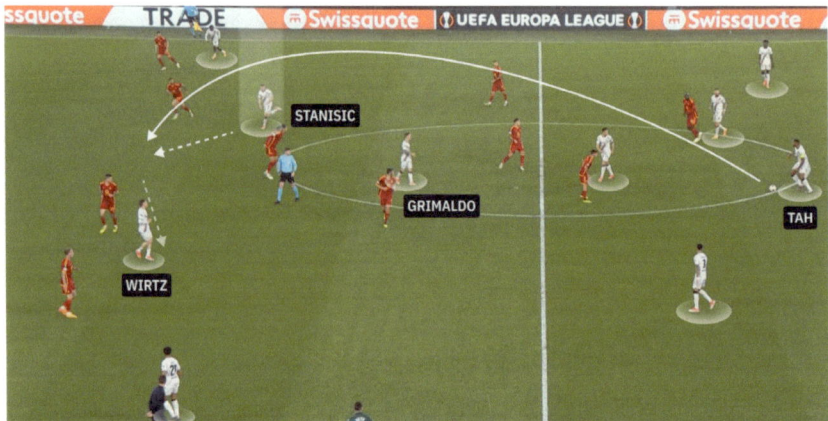

Leverkusen plays without a clear striker – not just with a false No. 9, but with players who constantly rotate into advanced attacking positions. Here, Stanišić, similar to the game in Dortmund, pushes forward into space vacated by Wirtz, who has dropped deep. Tah finds his right-sided center-back with a deep pass into the attacking zone. In addition, Grimaldo consistently shifts centrally when in possession of the ball to create a numerical advantage there.

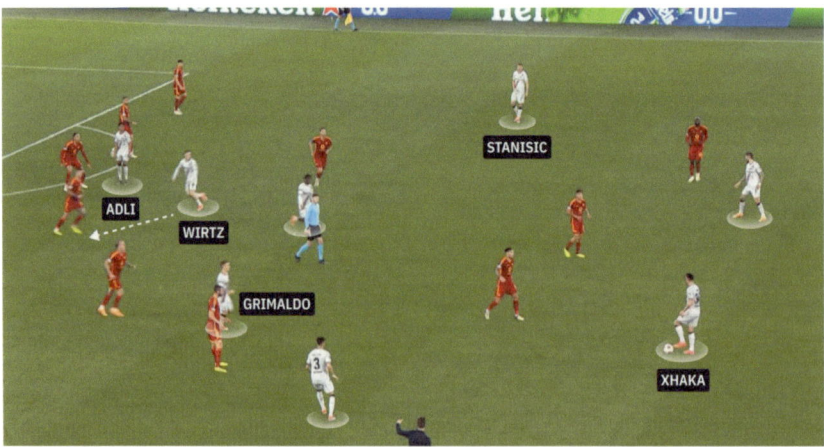

The Werkself execute a positional game of maximum fluidity. The players organize themselves around the ball at different levels to passing options at all heights. The original "position" of the players itself hardly plays a role anymore, as traditional roles blur; almost every player is in a different space, leveraging his strengths to interact prdoductively with teammates nearby.

Adli scans the field during buildup, monitoring two opponents within pressing range. Leverkusen's pressing is always about eliminating passing lanes and isolating opponents and, if possible, neutralizing multiple opponnents using fewer players.

Leverkusen remained active in the second half, even though the Werkself's bene- fited from a stroke of luck: Roma missed several top-class scoring opportunities that could have cut the deficit (like Abraham, who headed over the empty goal in injury time). Instead, Leverkusen is in maximum flow, where almost everything clicks, and Robert Andrich scores the highly deserved 2:0 with a dream goal in the 73rd minute. It's a top starting position for the second leg in Leverkusen.

Leverkusen presses high, but without overcommitting. Grimaldo challenges his oppo- nent and slows him down, allowing his teammates to anticipate the next move, cut off passing options, and recover ossession. In addition, Wirtz applies pressure from a higher position and ensures that the opponent faces both spatial and temporal pressure when in possession of the ball.

The initiation of the (decisive) 2:0 for Leverkusen: Xhaka in possession of the ball in midfield gains momentum after Leverkusen previously outplayed Roma's first line of defense through quick passing, numerical superiority near the ball, and a diagonal switch by Xhaka. Adli initiates a deep run and opens space for Grimaldo, who also pushes forward dynamically. As a result, Robert Andrich fires home the 2:0 with a spectacular long-range shot.

The next Bundesliga match against Eintracht Frankfurt will be played without Xabi. The usually highly controlled Alonso is absent due to a yellow card suspension and watches the game from the stands. Assistant coach Sebastian Parilla leads the team from the sidelines, which continues to play typical Leverkusen football despite many changes in the starting lineup (including the absence of Tah, Grimaldo and Wirtz).

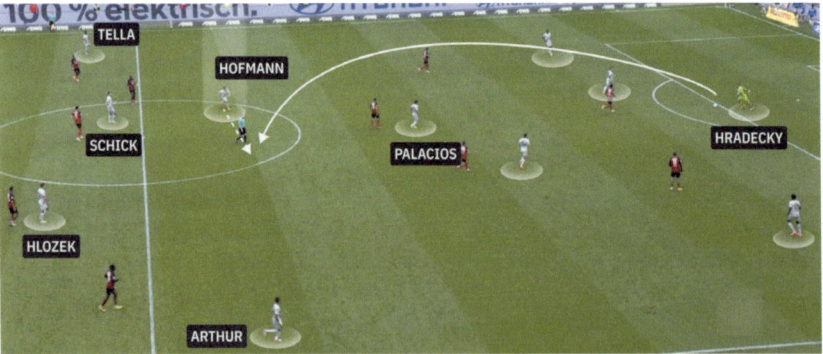

Frankfurt's defense gets stretched by four Leverkusen players (Tella, Schick, Hložek, Arthur) forcing them out of shape. Hofmann drops into the freed space and receives a lofted pass from Hrádecký. Hofmann lays off the ball to Palacios, who instantly progresses the attack. The following change of pace results in a penalty, making it 3:1 for the Werkself.

The coaching team has chosen a flexible 1-3-4-1-2 featuring Hložek and Schick as strikers, but its structure remains fluid and adaptable, as Tella plays more as a winger than a full-back. However, Kossounou operates a right-sided center-back rather than a full-back, which is why Hofmann takes on the role defensively, but positions himself as an advanced midfielder "between the lines" in attack. Tella and Hofmann act interchangeably in their roles, frequently adjusting based on the shortest distance, even though Tella assumes this position more frequently to exploit his dynamic advantage over the opponents during defensive transitions. In addition, there is an extreme amount of mobility, but this does not disrupt Leverkusen's passing rhythm.

With the first real chance on goal, Xhaka scores to make it 1:0 in the 12th minute with a well-struck, powerful shot from distance (113 km/h) at nearly 22 meters. Leverkusen maintains attacking intensity and creates several chances. But it is Frankfurt who finds the net, capitalizing on a short corner that leads to a precisely delivered cross for Ekitiké, who nods in the equalizer (32'). Leverkusen handles Frankfurt's ensuing pressure phase with disciplined defense, even though Frankfurt creates a top-class opportunity .

Just as Frankfurt's dominant spell fades, the Werkself strikes again: Xhaka delivers a cross into the penalty area. After a short clearance, Hložek retrieves the ball, setting up Hofmann for a precise cross, which Schick converts to restore Leverkusen's advantage (44').

Eintracht emerges out of the dressing room with a renewed energy and pushes for an equalizer, but it remains a game in which Leverkusen is comfortable even without possession and remains patient and focused, waiting to strike with maximum effectiveness at the opportune moments.

In the 58th minute, Palacios scores from penalty for 3:1 (after a foul on Tella). Frankfurt does not give up, but Leverkusen holds firm and stays clinical: A textbook counterattack makes it 4:1 (Frimpong, 77th); substitute Boniface scores again from 12 yards (after a foul on Frimpong) to make the final score 5:1 (89th). The victory is celebrated in style with stand-in coach Parilla, who receives a soaking from the players.

Alonso has a close bond with his staff, especially Sebastián Parilla. "He is a genius, a very important figure for Xabi," recalls Unai Veiga, a Real Sociedad youth player.[294] After a remarkable playing career and many experiences in Real Madrid's youth system, coaching across various age groups, he became assistant coach to Xabi Alonso's U14 team at Madrid.[295] Since then, there has been a close bond and a great deal of trust. Parrilla has a strong influence on tactics and the defensive aspect. Former *Sanse* players still remembers Parilla well: "He taught me a lot about defense, because Xabi was more focused on offense and structure." [296] The current players are also full of praise. Exequiel Palacios explains: "I am of course in close contact with 'Sebas'; we always talk about the Argentine league... what can be said about all the staff applies to him: they are all straightforward. They tell you everything to your face. I like things to be clear and transparent. And they are really good people."[297] Parilla is by far not the only key supporter within Leverkusen's coaching team, which also consists of Alberto Encinas (assistant coach), Ismael Camenforte (athletic coach; both with experience at FC Barcelona), Markus Müller (athletic coach), Jonas Rath (athletic coach), Daniel Jouvin (athletic coach), David Thiel (goalkeeper coach), Marcel Daum (assistant coach, analysis), Simon Lackmann (analyst) and Dr. Malte Krüger (head of sports science and athletics).[298] They all help ensure that the games run optimally, regardless of whether Alonso himself is on the bench or not.

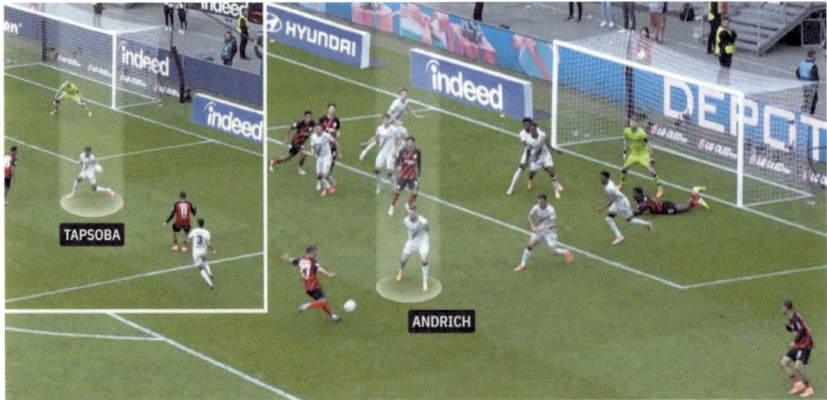

Defensive detail in Leverkusen's box defense: Following a corner, Andrich closes down the ball carrier , makes his body (and thus his potential target area for blocking) as large as possible and keeps his arms tucked in to prevent potential handballs within the penalty box.

295 Ibid.
296 Ibid.
297 Palacios quoted in SZ online, 14.04.2024.
298 bayer04.de / trainerstaff

All other players aim to put as much "body" as possible between the ball and the goal to increase the probability of blocking. The same applies to Tapsoba (see smaller picture) just like Andrich, who keeps his body as tall as possible and leans his body towards the ball to deflect the ball, as the danger of handball is averted by his hands bein tucked in.

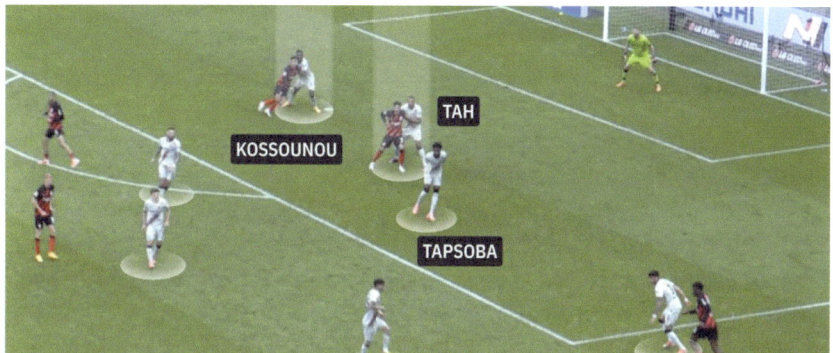

Leverkusen's box defense: At the moment of Götze's cross, both Tah and Kossounou are tightly marking to their direct opponents, who have no chance to time their way towards the ball, as they are effectively shielded.

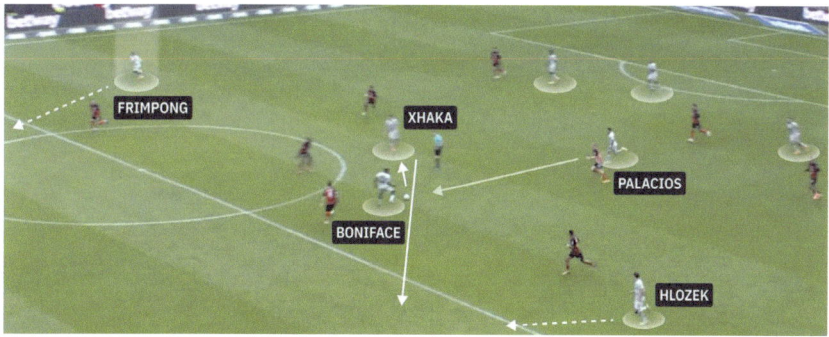

Leverkusen's picture-perfect counterattack to score the 4:1 goal by Frimpong: Tapsoba plays a release pass to Palacios, who finds Boniface as the deepest option ("find the deepest player"). The ball bounces off Xhaka, who immediately sends Hložek through on goal. Frimpong takes advantage of the subsequent cross and finishes clinically.

The Werkself go into the second leg at home against AS Roma with a comfortable 2:0 lead from the first leg. Alonso will initially be without the injured Wirtz, which is why Adli, Hložek, and Hofmann start in the front three. Leverkusen starts focused, alert, and by no means as if this game were already decided.

Although Roma are more active than in the first leg and try to develop more offensive power, Leverkusen stays true to the typical "Bayer style" and consistently attack the opponent's goal through possession and dynamism, even if Hložek remains unlucky this evening. After Roma's full-back Zalewski receives a yellow card, Frimpong throws himself even more into every offensive 1v1 duel with him; a testament to the team's overall greater maturity compared to last year in immediately exploiting such situations.

Roma tries to intensify its attacking efforts and, almost out of nowhere earns a penalty in the 41st minute, which Paredes converts to make it 1:0 (43'). Curiosity of the evening: apart from the fact that a second penalty would follow, the Werkself had only conceded one penalty in entire previous season including Europa League: In the 5:1 win against Qarabag. This statistic shows how outstandingly well Leverkusen has defended this season and how clean its challenges have been in key defensive moments. However, in this semi-final second leg, the number of penalties conceded so far would double. Up to this point in the game, Leverkusen has been already leading in shots on goal, 17:4.

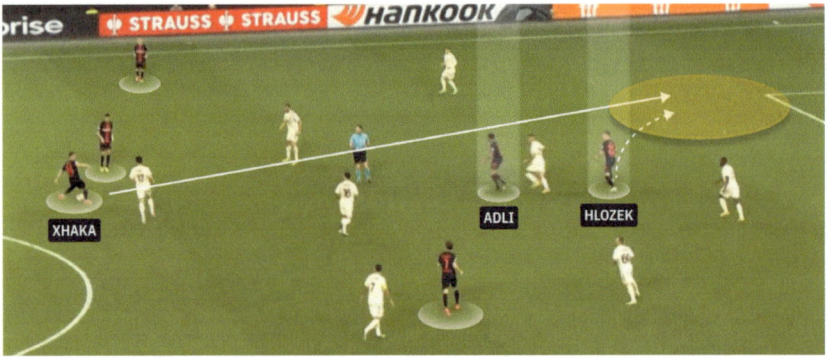

A good example of the concept of 'surrounding' ('*rodear*') opponents: Adli makes sure that his opponent follows him, while Hložek moves in the same axis and tracks Adli's opponent from behind. For a brief moment the Roma defender controls both Leverkusen players, until both initiate off-the-ball runs. At this point, the defender has to decide who to track, which is why – due to the 2-on-1 positioning (two Leverkusen players with one Roman) - one Leverkusen player automatically ends up free. Xhaka recognizes the free space and Hložek's intention exceptionally well and finds him with a pass into the open space.

The second half continues in a similar way: Leverkusen controls the game and attacks Roma's goal. However, a goal is scored for the visitors, this time after the VAR reviewed the play and determinded that Hložek had handled the ball in his own penalty area. Paredes scores the second penalty of the game (and the third overall this season against Leverkusen) to make it 2:0 and equalize the overall result. But the Werkself has faced similar situations during the season and once again responded brilliantly: In the 82nd minute, Mancini heads the ball into his own net after a Leverkusen corner (already goal No. 31 after the 80th minute this season), and in stoppage time, Leverkusen once again demonstrate its own invincibility: in the very last minute (90.+7), Stanišić even manages to equalize with a courageous move down the right. Leverkusen celebrates reaching the final of the Europa League. Xabi Alonso is satisfied after the game: "We wanted to play with more mobility and no clear positions. It was a very mature performance. Our counterattacks were highly effective with our attacking players."[299]

Until the end, 12.05.2024 - 18.05.2024

Despite the championship already being decided, the last two Bundesliga games did not degenerate into a exhibition match for the Werkself. The chance to crown an already historic season with a possible treble of Europa League and DFB Cup is too great. The next opponent Bochum also has a lot to do with that history, as it was Bochum almost a year ago against whom Leverkusen suffered their last competitive defeat (and the last red card they received in the Bundesliga). Leverkusen chooses a special approach for this game: Alonso sends the usual 1-3-4-3 formation onto the pitch, but with a fundamental asymmetry: Schick and Boniface start together, Tella prefers to cut in from the right and repeatedly appears with dynamic moves in different spaces. Therefore, Leverkusen plays with two center forwards and a right winger, while the space on the left side remains open.

The interpretation on the pitch is also very flexible: the two centre forwards are actively involved in the game; Schick often drops to the right, while Boniface moves into midfield more often to receive short passes. All this creates depth and space, which Tella tries to exploit through deep sprints. However, he not only sticks to the right side, but also repeatedly appears in the middle or even on the left side, which leads to the red card for Bochum's full-back Passlack in the 15th minute (professional foul). As a result, the entire dynamic of the game shifts to Leverkusen's side, while the efforts of the courageous Bochum team, who had actually got off to a good start to prevent their impending relegation, collapse.

299 Alonso quoted by kicker online, 03.05.2024.

When in possession of the ball, Stanišić takes on the role right that Grimaldo has often played on the left this season: He always positions himself centrally and is almost a right 8, who then runs from the center into deep areas. This movement is rarely picked up, especially in the attacking third.

It takes until the 41st minute for the Bochum to fall: Schick scores with a volley after a beautiful Arthur cross to make it 1:0. Shortly afterwards, Boniface increases the score to 2:0 with a penalty (after a foul on Tella). Against ten Bochum players, the German champions have no trouble controlling the game and at times allow the opponent to have some possession without running the risk of conceding scoring opportunities themselves. Instead, Leverkusen creates a variety of scoring opportunities and makes it 3:0 after a corner by Adli (76'). As a result, Bochum almost falls apart and concedes the 4:0 (Stanišić, 86') and 5:0 (Grimaldo, 90.+3).

And then finally comes the 34th matchday, the day everyone had longed for—at least since the victory against Werder Bremen: the last home game of the season against FC Augsburg, the festive day, begins with a hungry Leverkusen, bringing the 1:0 in the 12th minute after Adli's good effort in pressing and Boniface's ice-cold finish. Adli steals the ball from the Augsburg keeper inside the penalty area and lays it off for Boniface, who simply taps it in. The Werkself, playing without Xhaka and Wirtz, continues to play decisively and with composure in attack and increases the lead in the 27th minute after a corner to make it 2:0.

With their comfortable lead behind them, Leverkusen once again seems to want to control the game by dropping into a lower-possession phase; however, Augsburg comes back into the game, playing lively and even creatingscoring opportunities, even though Leverkusen goes into the break with a 2:0 lead.

In the second half, the Werkself are not particularly forceful for long stretches, and Augsburg shows that the team has not just come to congratulate: Mert Kömür scored in the 62nd minute to make it 2:1. However, there are no further goals. Augsburg shows that they could play an exciting role in the coming season under their new coach Jess Thorup. However, they fail to take advantage of the limited opportunities that arise, meaning that Leverkusen remains undefeated on matchday 34 of the Bundesliga and is able to celebrate the championship with three new points.

Bayer Leverkusen crowns a development that began a year and a half earlier with the home match against Schalke 04. Rafa Benítez, former coach of Xabi Alonso at Liverpool, has observed that Leverkusen has become a team that "always wants to be the main protagonist" and has "gained self-confidence and created a positive cycle" through victories, in which "positive interactions get reinforced" and the respective opponent suffers.[300] From Benítez's point of view, this is a clear credit to Xabi Alonso, whose team has developed a style reminiscent of Guardiola.[301] But the Werkself's journey this season is not over yet and will take them to two European capitals.

The very first time, 22.05.2024

"Dublin" marks the name of the first stop on Bayer Leverkusen's treble mission as they finally reach their first European final in 22 years (since losing against Real Madrid in the Champions League final). The opponent is Atalanta Bergamo from Italy, a team that has been playing the most exciting football in Serie A for several years under their experienced coach Gian Piero Gasperini. As in the past, Leverkusen opts for a very mobile 1-3-4-3 without a striker, with the option of attacking the opponent's man-marking through fluid play and many deep runs. But this evening Atlanta proves too disciplined and forceful. In an exciting final, the Werkself struggles to find their game and ultimately loses clearly and deservedly 3:0. The basic intention of countering the clear man orientation of the opposing defense with their own mobile and very dynamic forwards was absolutely logical and understandable. However, Leverkusen fails to establish contact with the strikers or find them in advantageous positions. The phases of possession are also noticeable short, compared to their season up to this point, and do not provide the expected balance and game control needed to utilize the strikers effectively. In addition, Ademola Lookman is in brilliant form and scored three outstanding goals.

The substitutions of Boniface and later Hložek and Schick fail to change the course of the match: Leverkusen fails to threaten the opposing goal and its first competitive match of the entire season - in game number 52 - unfortunately in the final of the Europa League against a top-class opponent.

300 Benítez in Cáceres 24.05.2024.
301 Ibid.

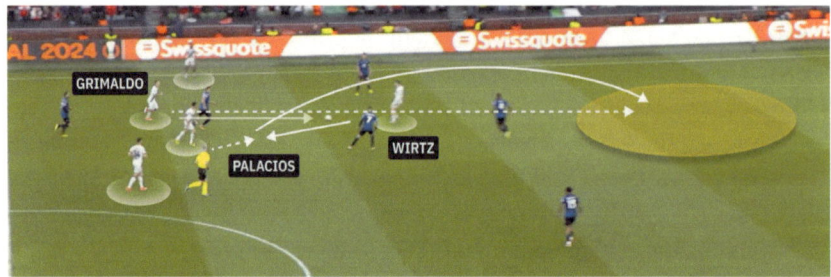

This is how it could have worked against Atalanta's man orientation: Wirtz receives the ball from Grimaldo who draws out his direct opponent. Grimaldo overlaps Wirtz and receives the pass from Palacios into the area. However, his lob is easily caught by the goalkeeper. With movements like these in combination with deep runs, Leverkusen repeatedly tried to open spaces behind the defensive line and attack against Bergamo's man-orientation.

After the game, Xabi Alonso looks back self-critically: His team had played "perhaps too many short passes", adding, "we had some problems. We didn't want to change our style. It didn't work." In his first European final as a coach, the coach of the new German champion had to admit: "We weren't at our best level, not even me. We must learn from this."[302] But even the defeat carries significance and, for Xabi Alonso this lesson is very clear after some time for reflection: "I am pretty sure this game makes me a better coach and manager than if we had won the treble," he said a few days later in a *CNN* interview: "You don't forget games like this and you can use that for the future. (...) Dealing with defeat is part of our job. It is not the first time and it will not be the last time."[303]

Double perfect, 25.05.2024

The last stop on the journey of an almost perfect season is Berlin. The 81st cup final in history takes place in the German capital. The last challenger of the season is 1. FC Kaiserslautern, who secured the last successful steps towards the cup final under their experienced coach Friedhelm Funkel. And this final also presents new challenges for Leverkusen unlike anything they have faced this season.

Leverkusen begins with the typically dominant start, even though Kaiserslautern shows from the beginning that they are not just lucky to be in the final. The first goal scoring opportunity actually comes from the second division team. The Leverkusen train starts rolling and takes a 1:0 lead with an outstanding long-

302 Alonso quoted in SZ online, 23.05.2024.
303 Alonso quoted according to SZ online, 05.06.2024.

range shot from Xhaka (13'). It remains a tight game with few clear goal chances until Kossounou receives a yellow-red card after just under half an hour. This is a first expulsion this season for Leverkusen – in the cup final of all things. Previously, in the Bundesliga and the Europa League, no players had been sent off, which speaks to the team's disciplined and well-structured defensive approach and overall performance.

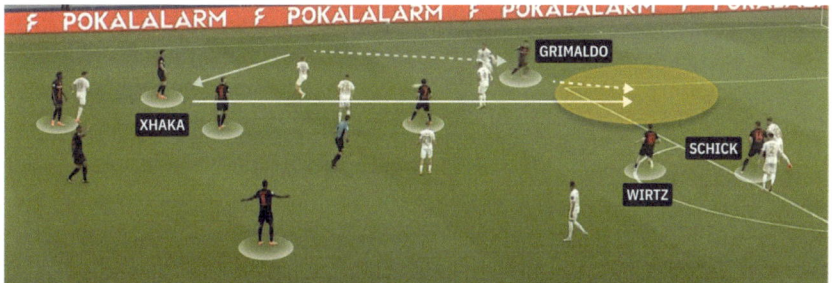

Grimaldo and Xhaka with the delayed one-two: Grimaldo passes to Xhaka, attacks into space, targeting the backs of his opponents. Leverkusen overloads the left side and thereby ties up multiple opponents there. Xhaka delays his pass a moment to lure his marker and give Grimaldo enough time before threading the ball perfectly through four opponents into the penalty area. At the same time, Schick pins down a central defender, freeing up Wirtz as the unmarked next ball receiver.

As a result, the Werkself succesfully defend their own goal in such a way that Kaiserslautern is limited to shots from outside the penalty area. At the same time, Leverkusen stays dangerous and has several opportunities to seal the game with a second goal. This doesn't happen, so it remains a tight and exciting game until the end, in which Bayer Leverkusen rightfully crowns itself the double winner. "I am proud and I am happy for the players," said Xabi after the game and gave an insight into the evening's plans: "Tonight I'm drinking German beer."[304] The pride of the successful Basque coach after this almost perfect season is immeasurable: "We were a great team with great energy all season, and we showed that again today. It was a dream season. We showed a great team performance with one man less and we were very disciplined. The team was ready to fight with ten men - and they did a great job." And in the end, it is "a great success for everyone here – for the fans, for the players, for the club – to win twice this season. We will always remember this in the future."[305]

304 Alonso quoted in SZ online, 26.05.2024.
305 Alonso quoted by kicker online, 25.05.2024.

Fortune favors the bold

The performance of this season by this Leverkusen team is very impressive - and it shines even more because everyone contributed to it: almost every player on the roster earned playing time, and coach Xabi Alonso frequently rotated his squad. The fact that every single player is important was not just an empty phrase, but proven by the coach's actions – and validated through the players' performance. In an interview with *kicker* in February, keeper Lukáš Hrádecký said: "Even those who didn't play much under him (...) praise him to the skies. That says a lot about Xabi – how he is in the dressing room and how he gets everyone on board. That's why everyone in the team is happy."[306] However, this satisfaction does not come at the expense of performance, but is a catalyst for further development. For Hrádecký, the team is not a prisoner of "a single style of play, the variability is there. With different team assembly constellations: With Jeremia Frimpong or Odilon Kossounou at right back, with Jeremia or Nathan Tella on the right wing – we have so many variations that we can offer for each game. It is the sum of these things that makes us successful."[307] All of these constellations are based on the same idea. In this process, Jonathan Tah once again highlights Alonso's training philosophy: "I think that [the feeling of being very good] only comes from training. By working hard together every day. That everyone is there in your head. That everyone wants to get better. This gives you self-confidence. Then you go into the game and say to yourself: I have implemented it every day in training and it has gotten better and better. Now I'm putting it into practice in competition. If that works, it will automatically happen again in the next game. That's how it is built up."[308]

Alonso is considered to be extremely professional and a perfectionist. An anecdote about Xabi as a player, told by Jorge Valdano, illustrates this perfectly: "I remember a game in Switzerland when we were leading 3:0 and a play came up in which he had to go in determinedly and injured himself. I was very angry. After the game, I went into the locker room and asked him if that was really necessary when the score was 3:0. He told me: If you have to keep your leg in, keep it in. I was really ashamed afterwards."[309] Bayer sports director Simon Rolfes confirms this basic attitude: "He is an incredibly hard worker. He is a top coach, but most importantly, his mentality has been passed on to the players. (...) He is relentlessly focused on the next game and always strives for improvement. As a former

306 Hrádecký in kicker online, 26.02.2024.
307 Ibid.
308 Tah quoted in Behnisch 2024.
309 Valdano quoted in SZ online, 12.04.2024.

superstar on the field, he knows what it takes to perform at his best every three days. He set an incredible example."[310]

The players are already very aware of their own game, as Jonathan Tah explains: "In the back three, I usually play in the middle. ((...)) I [am] often the one..., who distributes the balls or crosses the lines, and the others are the ones who then cross the lines after 'sucking in' the opponent. (...) [Question: What does 'sucking in' mean?] It's always about creating space for the team. If you play the ball without an opponent coming towards you, nothing happens. But if you attract him - maybe that's a better word - then maybe a space will appear behind him or beside him." [311]

Controlling the game is paramount: "He [Xabi Alonso] wants us to always be in control of the game. In every moment of the game. With and without the ball. (...) It's about being active and being conscious of what you do. That you know what to do with the ball when you capture it. You prepare for this with your positioning without the ball."[312] Alonso also repeatedly emphasizes the aspect of game control when he talks about his game idea: "Have control with the ball, be intense against the ball. Patient to find the space and create the space. In the Bundesliga it is important to control the counterattacks. We play in a controlled manner, but we also have to respect the qualities of our players. Grimaldo is a completely different quality than, for example, Frimpong."[313] As already explained with reference to the game model, the individual qualities of each player play a central role in the interpretation of the game idea.

Details play an important role, says national player Tah: "With the ball, it's all about attracting the opponent. That's what I'm doing, and we're simply doing it better as a team now. One thing that has improved significantly for me is box defense. (...) It's about access to the opponent. The coach attached great importance to this when he came. That's what he criticized, and he doesn't just show you a video or talk about it. Instead, he is very active and shows you how he imagines it. Then he demonstrate it on the training ground That's how you have to be!"[314] A central theme, especially after he took office in fall 2022, was

310 Rolfes quoted in The athletic online, 14.04.2024.
311 Tah quoted in Behnisch 2024.
312 Ibid.
313 Alonso on SKY SPORT, 05.02.2024.
314 Tah quoted in Behnisch 2024.

improving the defence. For Edmond Tapsoba, who like almost all players has taken a huge step forward under Xabi Alonso, this is mainly due to Alonso's focus on team structure and the many small-sided training games. He's tough in defense. We work a lot on positioning - that seems to be an important part of Spanish training - and also on not getting the ball between the lines and being prepared for the pressure," the central defender gives interesting insights.[315] The details are by no means limited to the defense. Granit Xhaka, who was coached by Alonso's childhood friend Mikel Arteta at Arsenal London and has now experienced how Alonso works, compares the former world-class players and current coaches, who once played together in their youth: "Mikel showed me a whole new way of looking at football by focusing on the basics - the things you might have forgotten as a teenager. Pressing. The posture. Positioning. Movement. Coming out of someone else's shadow. Communication on the field. Xabi is similar. I think the Spanish see football differently than others. When I first heard Xabi talk about his ideas, I thought: 'I've done that before, under Mikel'. It's a different coach, but the same philosophy."[316] The topic of positioning comes up repeatedly in the players' stories, as Germany international Florian Wirtz explains when he talks about his individual development under Xabi Alonso: "It was also the coach who showed me positions on the pitch where I can be even more dangerous. He sort of shifted me around in certain game situations. He explained to me exactly which direction I should run in certain situations, which makes it easier for me. And you can see that I now score more goals and provide more assists than before. I am very happy to have a coach with such an understanding of football from whom I can learn a lot."[317]

Xabi Alonso benefits from his background and approach, as he himself explains: "I think that as a number six back then, my job was to make the players around me better, to make the game easier for them. As a coach, it's a bit the same. You try to take a step back and put yourself at the service of others, trying to implement the shared vision and improve the overall quality."[318] Pep Guardiola expresses a similar view about the role of central players: "Midfielders are intelligent, because they have to think about the team as a whole. They are unselfish and understand the game better than others, and the more midfielders you have, the

---

315 Taposba cited in The athletic online, 30.07.2023.
316 Xhaka quoted in The athletic online, 19.12.2023.
317 Wirtz in SZ online, 06.06.2024.
318 Alonso in TV interview with Jorge Valdano, 07.12.2023.

easier it is to fill other positions with them."[319] Xabi Alonso continues: "As a mid-fielder, you are generous towards the team: you don't play for your own personal glory. What did I want as a player? To have better players around me and help them improve. Because if I was the best, then the playmaker, the inside player [No. 8] and the winger were not so good. I wanted to give them good balls so they could do what I couldn't. If I can make the players better now, I can also be a better coach. The technical and tactical details come later. To come here and be an iron-fisted general? No! I like discipline and basic professional standards, but I don't want to be a tyrant. If I have to play the role of the bully, of course I will put on my jacket and be a bully... You have to be able to play different kinds of music."[320] The idea of selflessness, improving others, and enabling them to shine remains central to Alonso, even as a coach. He acts as a mediator and supporter rather than a dictator seeking to predetermine every little detail. Observers got an impression of what this looks like on the training ground during the 2023/2024 championship season. "Two touches," he encourages his team to play quickly, look for space inside and attack the far ('weak') side with a switch of play. "Push up," the loud call for the team to press high and keep the lines together, is undoubtedly the most frequently repeated expression. "Two meters in the penalty area is a lot," you can hear him shout.[321] Overall, Alonso is very active, as Granit Xhaka confirms: "He runs more than some other players and wants to show his team how to do certain things on the pitch."[322] Xhaka sees Alonso's coaching as a key factor in his continued improvement; under Alonso as well as under his previous coach Mikel Arteta at Arsenal London, as both master "the art of being a central midfielder" and are now passing it on to him.[323]

For the team, it is by no means a matter of being a silent accomplice to the coach's idea: "I help them, but then they have to develop the intuition to make their own decisions," says Alonso,[324] who is particularly keen to develop that intuition: "As a player, I liked to read the games, prepare them and try to control them, and as a coach I also want my team to adapt to the games and be dynamic."[325]

319 Guardiola quoted in Cox, 2020.
320 Alonso in Torres, 2023.
321 Alonso quoted by Marca online, 27.07.2023.
322 Xhaka quoted in The athletic online from 19.12.2023.
323 Ibid.
324 Alonso quoted by Marca online, 27.07.2023.
325 Alonso quoted by Marca online, 09.07.2019.

Xabi Alonso developed his own approach to "reading the game" early on. In 2017, in an interview for Martí Perarnau's, now unfortunately discontinued digital magazine, *The tactical room*, when asked what he first looks at in a game, he explained: "The systems and how we have to attack them right from the start, from the first phase [first game phase; in the sense of opening the game, author's note], the second phase [transition to attack, author's note] and the third phase [finalising and exploiting, author's note] and how we can eliminate them in the first phase, the second phase and the third phase. For me they are very clear. (...) That's how I break the game down as a player. The better you defend, the better you attack, and the better you attack, the better you defend. And the better you get the ball into play, the better you attack, because you control the passing game much better."[326] The topic of "control" is fundamental for the novice coach Xabi Alonso from an early stage: "I think you have to adapt to the players, but I like control. I want to be able to balance the team well. You need players who create balance and players who create imbalance, and then you have to find the balance between them. I want to have good players and then I will find a way to work with them. Ultimately, you depend on the players and the secret is how to lead them in a way that makes them feel committed."[327]

In most cases, Alonso said he would prefer his team to play two or three short passes rather than one long pass so that his players can stand compact and defend as a unit if they lose the ball. "When you play long passes, your players have a lot more distance between them," explains Alonso, "and if they lose the ball, it's harder to get it back because they can't press together "as well."[328] The 2017 interview with *The Tactical Room*, conducted by Isaac Lluch and Martí Perarnau, offers deep insight into the mindset of future coach Xabi Alonso. In order to control the game, the team must also determine the rhythm of the game, which in turn can be challenging to dictate. It also comes into play here that the Spanish word *'ritmo'* can be translated not only as "rhythm" but also as "tempo." The term is often used in the context of football, as it is about finding the right "rhythm" for the game. On the subject of "rhythm", Alonso answers in that interview: "The tempo depends on the emotions you have and also on the emotions of the audience. I remember the second leg of last year's Champions League semi-final against Atlético de Madrid [03.05.2016, author's note]: With

326 Alonso in Perarnau 2017.
327 Ibid.
328 Alonso in Sports Illustrated online 2016.

the tempo we set in the first half, against a team that is one of the best organized in modern football, and they couldn't get to it, they couldn't get to it... We
gave them a pace that was emotional because we needed it, because we said
we wouldn't mess them up if we didn't give them that pace. Just as we didn't get
a chance in the first leg at the Calderón because the ball wasn't circulating as
quickly, here in the first half you could see that everything was running at speed
of thousand miles an hour."[329] And even today, after the end of his career, Alonso
the coach still masters the topic of "rhythm" as before, as Alejandro Grimaldo
marvels: "There are only a few in the world who can pass a ball as well as he can.
Every time he is involved in a tactical exercise, a 'possession game,' he speeds up
the rhythm so that the team sees the rhythm we have to play in."[330]

Another topic is Alonso's attitude towards tackles and sliding tackles. Even as
a Liverpool player, it was a real culture shock for him that players described
their core competency by this ability.[331] For him, tackling while sliding across
the ground was always the very last option when nothing else worked: "Tackling is one thing and a duel where you have to take tough action is another. I call
the tackle a 'broom', where you throw yourself to the ground, because it is a last
resort, a situation where you either win or get beaten. It's like a knockout. But to
get into this situation, something has to happen first. In the midfield or central
midfield position you can intervene before such a situation occurs. To me, you
made a mistake along the way that led to the tackle. If you had been in a better
position beforehand or used your body better or planned ahead, you wouldn't
have had to make the tackle... That's why tackling is not so important to me."[332]
Alonso refers to good positioning, which is essential for midfielders. It is important to be well positioned, and that means anticipating what could happen. "So
if it happens, you're well positioned. And if it doesn't happen, it's because the
ball was intercepted beforehand. For me, the midfielder must be constantly connected to the game and constantly anticipate situations that could arise. If these
situations arise, you are well positioned, and if they do not arise, it is because
you have already intercepted them. I have always said that the best tactical
players I know are Sergio Busquets and Philipp Lahm. They do everything they
can to gain a tactical advantage, especially when making quick decisions. They

329 Alonso in Perarnau 2017.
330 Grimaldo cited in The athletic online from 02.03.2024.
331 Alonso in The athletic online from 02.04.2024.
332 Alonso in Perarnau 2017.

are very good. While others are more of a talent and grab the ball and dribble as they please, these two grab the ball and say, 'I'm going to do this to achieve that.' That's intelligence and knowledge of the game."[333] For Alonso, this is a characteristic of the best players: making good decisions, "knowing what to do. If you have the technical and physical qualities to do more things, you are even richer. To me, the great player is the one who is good in one-on-one situations, but also the one who can dribble well to seek superiority and give his teammate an advantage."[334] His midfielders in particular should therefore "go into the game (...) with the idea that the pitch is a map. You have to control the zones – and know where numerical superiority can be created. You must always know how many players are to your left and right. If there are six on one side, there are three on the other side. If there are six there, there are three here. Only one striker up front? [Then] I have to look more forward. There are two in front? [Then] I have to be prepared to help my central defenders a little more. In a way, it's a constant counting to know how to take the next step."[335] In this permanent orientation process, it is important to make the best decisions.

This happens by combining and playing together, like Bayer Leverkusen has progressively demonstrated more and more often over the last one and a half years. A tactical means frequently used was to "win the backs" ('ganar espaldas') and to position the offensive players in the gaps. This is because for Alonso, the pass is more dangerous when it is played behind the opponent. "But then that pass has to have another pass in the back of the defense. If the one who comes behind the midfielder is the striker, who goes behind the defense? This last line must be attacked with the striker, with the eight, with the winger or whoever. But this last line must be attacked. Or you have to be well prepared for losing the ball. You can prepare systematically or reactively. Against a well-organized defence, it is often the case that they get confused when the ball is lost and then situations are created."[336] Good, compact positioning when in possession of the ball helps to ensure optimal preparation for possible counter-pressing. During a game, there are always moments in which the team controls the game from a well-structured defense, allowing them to attack together with the ball again in the next step. The organized cooperation of several position levels through shared intentions is a basic prerequisite for achieving collective success.

333 Alonso in Perarnau 2017.
334 Ibid.
335 Alonso in Torres 2023.
336 Alonso in Torres 2023.

Excursus: Shared Intentions

"It is important to understand that the 'affordances' [possibilities for interaction] perceived in one context cannot be directly transferred to another context. People learn to use new affordances in different contexts. In short, we do not learn to move because of the environment, but we learn how to move because we are in a process of constant adaptation [to the environment]."[337]
    KEITH DAVIDS

"Playing and sharing an interpretation of the game with teammates near [intervention space; see concept of stage spaces; author's note] and far from the ball [cooperation space; see concept of stage spaces; author's note] does not consist in mastering predetermined responses. It's not about having automated behaviors that are triggered when the game environment meets certain characteristics. Rather, it is about behavioral structures that enable players to adapt to the situation or propose specific responses and to network appropriately with their fellow players to achieve a common goal. This interpretation of the game must be discovered by the players and demonstrated by the coach in training."[338]
    CARLOS LAGO

In the specialist literature, a literal translation of the term '*affordances*' is often avoided because it is difficult to find a precise, all-encompassing and situation-independent translation. As a rule, they are understood as "*opportunities, invitations or requests for an action*," but are always dependent on "*the relationship between certain environmental characteristics and the effectiveness of the person carrying them out.*" [339] So the "opportunities for interaction" mentioned in Keith Davids' quote are highly accurate, although the bigger picture must be taken into account: In our culture and the way we grow up in Germany, for example, we usually see chairs primarily as an opportunity to sit. However, if we imagine that a person grows up with the understanding that chairs are only used for standing on to reach a higher leveled surfaces (e.g., a cupboard), and this is not only demonstrated by those around them but also exclusively experienced by them, then we can imagine that this person will not perceive the chair as a place to sit. This means that we respond to opportunities for interaction according to our abilities, experiences, characteristics, and intentions, and that these abilities, experiences, characteristics and intentions are not the same for all people. For further comprehension, we define the term '*affordance* as an opportunity or

337 Davids, 2020.
338 Lago, 2021.
339 Torrents, Ric, Hristovski, Torres-Ronda, Vicente, Sampaio, 2016.

possibility for interaction (especially in relation to team games in sports), carrying a certain inviting character. In sport and specifically football, these are opportunities or "invitations" to interact with game dynamics that arise through the coordination of our intentions and constraints.[340] In terms of game tactics, a hierarchy of interaction possibilities can also exist if certain spaces on the pitch are prioritized over others. This requires a coordinated perception of the game by all players at the same time – ideally based on the same (common) interpretation of the game. Game situations are not simply solved – they are played. The jointly defined goals serve as a compass in the interpretation of the game (game concepts for the realization of the game goal, both situational and overarching), which acts as the basic orientation for the interpretation of the game. This in turn, after appropriate training, can lead to a coordinated perception of the players in competitive play. The shared intentions simplify the team's interaction in order to achieve, maintain and change its approach to of the "hybrid organization over time."[341] The players act collectively on their common goals through the "specific ecological framework" and through their experiences in joint training.[342] Not only that, the adaptable organization of the team itself creates ever-changing opportunities to execute their current game plan.[343]

The "three I's" are fundamental to this: information, intention and interaction.[344] Perception plays a central role here, as "looking" allows us to recognize the possibilities "that I have to act as my teammates and I (...) [wish, regardless of the moment of the game] striving to overcome the actions of the opponents."[345] What is crucial here is that the individual action is clearly related to the team's goals, wishes and needs and thus pursues a collective intention. To achieve this, the third "I" appears: the interaction of all those involved and their mutual influence on one another.[346] The elements that influence our decision-making based on our intentions are the ball, the opponents, the teammates (and the information they all provide), as well as the gaps and spaces that are perceived.[347]

340 Vaughan, 2021.
341 Seirul·lo, 2024.
342 Ibid.
343 Ibid.
344 Ibid.
345 Ibid.
346 Seirul·lo, 2024.
347 Vaughan, 2021.

"The best always have one second more on the ball. You gain more time through positioning and ball control. They make the ball they were given a better one. How? By passing it on with a message: 'I'm giving it to you so that you do this or that', 'I'm playing it into this foot so that you can control it or pass it on' ..."[348]
    XABI ALONSO

A player's perception cannot be analyzed in isolation without taking into account his motor skills. It is possible for a player to perceive an option within the game but not have the technical ability to implement that option. Therefore, when analyzing the decision-making process, it is important to consider both the precondition ("before") and consequence ("after") "of each player (in terms of perception) and to take into account not only the specific action itself, but also his physical execution.

High efficiency in coordinated perception enables players to perceive the smallest body movements that provide information about a teammate's intention - often milliseconds before the opponent can identify it. The result is "assertive, motor communication based on emphatic resonance." This ensures that players can not only anticipate the behavior of their teammates, but also feel like them.[349] In football, one can speak of an almost "blind" understanding, which is scientifically proven from a research perspective, but also creates a competitive advantage through the players' and coaches' own varied experiences. Luis Enrique's long-time assistant coach, Rafel Pol, and his colleagues discuss the advantages of the synergies that arise when a wide range of different skills (i.e., a group that is as diverse as possible in terms of abilities) are used cooperatively within a team and through (internally) predictable behavior emerges: "Especially in sports such as football, where the stability and reproducibility of game situations is rare, teams and players constantly have to deal with a highly unstable, non-cooperative environment. In such contexts, survival (in the tournament, championship, or league) is defined by positive competitive outcomes, which are better achieved through a higher diversity potential."[350] It is important to emphasize that while the predictability of behavior within the group prevails (for example through shared tactical intentions), it must at the same time remain sufficiently unpredictable for the opponent. This also affects the structure and the design of training: "Due to the interrelationship of the conditions influencing the player, there is no need to reduce the training unit to individual players

348 Alonso in Cáceres, 2023.
349 Seirul·lo, 2004; Guerrero, Damunt & Lopez, 2017.
350 Pol et al. 2020.

in team sports or to a subsystem in individual sports. The cooperative qualities of the team, such as discovery, deviation, synergy, and synchronization, which develop in challenging and varied environments, vary individual behavior in corresponding ways."[351] A central goal of training is therefore to generate synergies among players through varied, challenging, and ideally unpredictable contexts in order to prepare them for the game's demanding characteristics.

Xabi Alonso explains this in a TV interview with Jorge Valdano: "We often work [in training] with the position lines and then we put them together in different phases. When we have more time, we also work on connections, because often it is not possible to execute in a collective game what has to happen with two or three players simultaneously"[352] Valdano then raises the concept of "small communities" or "small societies" *('pequeñas sociedades')*, a term coined by former Barcelona and Argentina World Cup-winning coach César Luis Menotti. Historically, the term goes back to the colonial era, when "small communities" were founded as precursors to villages and cities, thus securing the basis for communal life and survival.[353]

Menotti uses this term to describe "partnerships" that arise naturally from playing together, citing, for example, the connection between former Real Madrid strikers Di Stéfano and Puskás, who worked as a congenial duo. These "communities" or "partnerships" within football enable an understanding of one another "without looking at one another."[354] It is a gathering of players with "complementary talents" who, when "come together, can perform at a very high level. Everything, of course, for the good of the team."[355] Menotti underlines the importance of the coach who must "support and promote their potential" and continues: "They never detract from the collective spirit of the team, even if they seem to be more sought after between the two 'partners'."[356] The coach is also responsible for making it clear to the team that this "constant search" represents a very important contribution to the team.[357]

Although the coach can suggest the creation of these "communities," these connections often develop organically, as they depend on the players' instinct and thus their relationships with each other. Menotti emphasizes: "It is not as easy

351 Ibid.
352 Alonso in Valdano, 2023.
353 León in La Ciencia Pop podcast, 2023.
354 Cappa & Menotti, 1986.
355 Ibid.
356 Ibid.
357 Ibid.

to form a small partnership as some people think. It's not just about bringing two great players together. They must also interpret and complement each other: one is a receiver and the other a creator, one distracts and the other completes. In other words, one reinforces and completes the other, and both together increase the effectiveness of the other."[358]

Paco Seirul·lo calls this connection between players an "implicit complicity that creates 'a world of its own within the team.'"[359] In football, it is synonymous with a "blind understanding of the game," which brings a decisive competitive advantage. However, it is important to consistently train the connections between the players and to bring the players together on the pitch so that they can "connect" with each other. The concept does not end there: once a "small community" (or a 'duo') has been made to work effectively, the coach's goal is to "harmonize" it with another: "The team will reach a high level of efficiency when all the players know exactly the functions of each of their teammates, and when it is time to put them into practice, which is the most difficult thing to do."[360] For Paco Seirul·lo, they are essential components of "great teams": "They function like a clock in a team and add something that is more than just the sum of its parts. They behave well, understand everything, play well and win championships."[361] We also find connections in many areas of life that complement each other enormously (and thus can therefore be considered "small communities"), such as in cinema, where Martin Scorcese and Robert de Niro formed an outstanding, successful duo from their very first film together.[362]

> "I pass the ball to you a meter forward so that you can better connect with the next player, I pass the ball to your far leg because you have the advantage there, I pass the ball to you on your near leg, or with less tension to tell you to repeat the pass and lure opponents."[363]
>
> **CARLES MARTÍNEZ**

In summary, intentions can be perceived as an open door through which we must go in order to achieve our goal. Shared intentions arise when we perceive this opportunity together with our teammates. If we now make efforts, based on our position and situation, to move through this door together, we can speak

358 Ibid.
359 Seirul·lo, 2017.
360 El Gráfico online, 2021.
361 Seirul·lo in El Gráfico online, 2021.
362 León, 2023.
363 Martínez in Ballesteros, 2020.

of so-called "skilled intentionality", the "skillful response to several interrelated and nested possibilities simultaneously within a form of life."[364] If we succeed in creating a collective intention within the team and, as a result, an almost "blind" understanding of the game by forming and honing "small communities," we will generate a decisive competitive advantage for our team.

364 van Dijk & Rietveld 2017, quoted in Vaughan, 2021.

Position profiles of the Game Model

The impressive aspect about Bayer Leverkusen's game model is that almost every player is capable of bringing it to life and seamlessly incorporate his own characteristics and strengths. The roles on the pitch remain identical for the most part, but are sometimes assumed by different players within a game, adding an extra dimension to the position. In the right-winger role, for example, we have seen the dynamic Frimpong and Tella throughout the season, but also Hofmann, Adli and Stanišić (who is probably the most conservative and defensive option of all). Each of these players, some of whom interacted perfectly along the right flank, has added something distinctive to the game: Frimpong, with his dynamic approach focused on giving assists; Tella, who arrived at Leverkusen from the English Championship after scoring 39 goals for Burnley and is more of a finisher; Hofmann, who feels particularly comfortable operating between the lines; Adli, who plays as a lively, agile striker with a desire to play deep and constantly rotates; and Stanišić, who funcitons as a half-back in the build-up, but also repeatedly takes on a No. 6 role from the wide position—or remains in a more conservative width and provides crosses from the right with slightly less dynamism. The variability within the game model while maintaining a clear framework greatly helps the team a lot in terms of their orientation and interpretation of the game.

Here, we recognize the importance of the coach's idea of giving space to the individual player to express his own characteristics and abilities.
In football, the individual appears where the ball is. The player is able to do something concrete because others have already created something before him. In the subsequent action, which follows his action, he as an individual adds something new to the game situation shaped by his talent and his individual characteristics and features within the complexity of the interactions with the other players.[365] It is essential to understand the nature and character of the player in beforehand: What does he perceive? How does he see and evaluate a situation? What is his intention? Basically, it is about efficiency in an action. At the same time, it should be considered whether a player is acting based on his own intuition or merely responding to what he believes the coach expects at that moment.

365 Seirul·lo, 2007.

Quite often, an ideal situation arises in football when a player does something unexpected—which usually happens intuitively and is rarely explicitly instructed by the coach.

"There are beautiful players and good players. Beautiful is the one who does beautiful things, but that is not efficient. Why is Messi great? Because he knows how to make a simple pass: he gives it to the player in the best position. That means being good, not always doing the most brilliant thing. Florian does that. That's why he's so good."[366]
XABI ALONSO ABOUT FLORIAN WIRTZ

In football, every team has players with unique characteristics and skills that—if used strategically—can be game-changers. With all these players, the question always arises: Who activates the players with the individual talent? Who makes the other players better through their presence? In the case of Bayer 04 Leverkusen, Granit Xhaka, Florian Wirtz and, to some extent, Alejandro Grimaldo form the backbone of Xabi Alonso's team and whose absence was hardest to compensate for over the course of the season.

"Granit is a glue for this team." [367]
LUKAS HRÁDECKÝ

Certainly, over the course of the season and the team's evolution (see the progress of Tah, Andrich, etc.), other players have emerged to elevate their teammates (such as Palacios, Andrich, Adli, Hofmann). However, the negative impact was most evident in the games in which neither Xhaka (as metronome and provider of rhythm) nor Wirtz (as creative playmaker and instigator in crowded spaces) were on the pitch. It is this duo who orchestrate everyone and everything else around them, who dictate the game's rhythm and who, through their skills, elevate all the players around them to a higher level.

If we look at the key statistics from the past season, the first thing that catches our eye is a big notable surprise: According to the calculation of *expected points (xP - i.e., the points that the team was projected to earn based on their theoretical performance),* Bayer Leverkusen trails Bayern Munich by only 0.7 points, even though Bayern actually only finished third in the end.[368] So the Werkself

366 Alonso in Torres, 2023.
367 Hrádecký in kicker, 26.02.2024.
368 cf. understat.com

not only did many things right last season; they also had the necessary good fortune on their side, which—although not statistically or scientifically quantifiable—may nevertheless have been a result of many other well-executed steps that the team took in its development.

In addition, we can draw conclusions from the data of the past season regarding Bayer Leverkusen's tactical approach, game model and the requirements for each position. The distribution of goals is relatively typical for a top team, both in terms of shot location (inside/outside the box) and in terms of the individual moments of the game. It is logical that all teams with a dominant, possession-based game are more likely to be dangerous in front of goal from inside the box. In fact, top teams can also be assessed based on the number of completed passes in the opponent's penalty area.

Within the statistics, goals from set pieces are of course important, with the Werkself being successful from corners a total of 21 times in all competitions. Taken together, the numbers have the same influence as scoring a goal after a ball recovery followed by a counterattack. Looking at the value of *xG (expected goals) —i.e.,* the value that indicates how many goals the team was expected to score based on the quality of their goal-scoring opportunities - it is evident that Leverkusen has a slightly positive overperformance here (+4).[369] On average, spectators witnessed at least two goals from the Werkself in Bundesliga matches.[370] The team's leading goal-scorer was Victor Boniface (14 goals), who, according to *the xG metric,* had an expected goal tally of 16.[371] The combination of *xG* and *xA (expected assists)* per 90 minutes in the Bundesliga shows the extreme impact of the Nigerian striker on the Werkself's attacking output; statistically, at least one goal contribution (assist or goal) was expected per match.[372] Granit Xhaka and Edmond Tapsoba posted impressive numbers in terms of their progressive passing and deep build-up involvement, which directly contributes to chance creation. The same applies to ball progression and possession control for Florian Wirtz, again Granit Xhaka, Alejandro Grimaldo, Jeremie Frimpong and Jonas Hofmann.[373] These players clearly make the game more fluid through their participation, making it easier for their teammates. In Grimaldo's case, this is not only evident in his scoring output (the nominal left-back scored ten goals): he is also the Werkself's best assists provider (leading with 13 assists).[374]

369 cf. theanalyst.com
370 cf. footystats.org
371 cf. theanalyst.com
372 cf. understat.com
373 Ibid.
374 Ibid.

Goal distribution Bayer Leverkusen

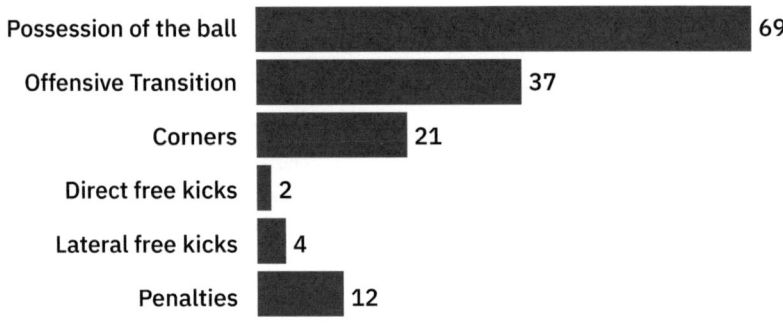

Possession of the ball	69
Offensive Transition	37
Corners	21
Direct free kicks	2
Lateral free kicks	4
Penalties	12

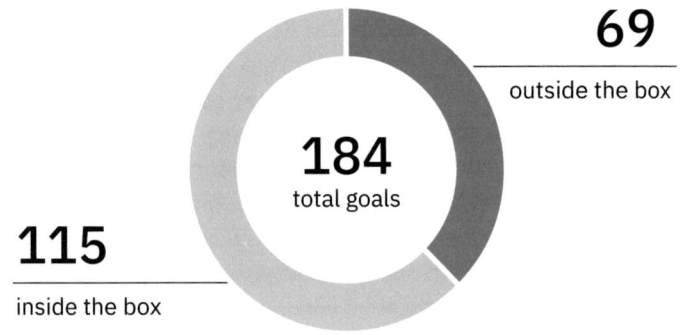

69
outside the box

184
total goals

115
inside the box

If you look at the passing accuracy of all Bundesliga players last season, the top three most accurate passers all came from Leverkusen. The positions of these players also provide insight into the structured build-up play of the Werkself: Jonathan Tah (96.47%), Granit Xhaka (92.72%) and Edmond Tapsoba (92.7%) are the players maintain high passing accuracy and are primarily responsible for Leverkusen's build-up phase.[375] However, this isn't just about many of these passes break lines and bypass multiple opponents and carry an inherent risk of losing possession. The passing accuracy of the entire team is also one of the best in the league (almost 90%) despite having the second-best possession percen-

375 cf. bundesliga.com

tage.[376] The Werkself always dictated the tempo in their games, as their coach intended and played the most passes per possession sequence. Bayer Leverkusen is the team that has by far most frequently played sequences of 10+ passes (740 times) and initiated build-ups from the back (197 times).[377] The total time in possession is only surpassed by Bayern Munich, although Bayer registered more passes per possession phase than the record champions.[378] This held true to almost all areas of the pitch where the Werkself had more possession sequences than their opponents. The only exception was the opponent's penalty area – a sign of the team's absolute superiority throughout the campaign.[379]

Even the most unfortunate attackers were in their ranks: Florian Wirtz hit the post five times and Alejandro Grimaldo hit the post four times, leading the Bundesliga in this statistic.[380] Consequently, Bayer Leverkusen was also the team that struck the woodwork most often (17 times).[381]

Although Bayer's offensive department was "just" the second-best in the league (behind Bayern Munich), their defensive record told a different story, which conceded the fewest goals (24) and was therefore the best. In addition, goalkeeper Lukáš Hrádecký was able to keep a clean sheet 15 times, which is also the best value in the past Bundesliga season.[382]

The Werkself conceded the fewest high-quality chances, but also benefited from the fact that goalkeeper Hrádecký made seven saves on shots classified as "unsaveavle" by *xG* models.[383]

A key factor behind Leverkusen's defensive success was their pressing. Of all the teams in the Bundesliga, the Werkself recovered possession and converted turnovers into shots and goal-scoring opportunities the most.[384] However, Bayer was still not fully clinical in capitalizing on these situations (only seven goals). Leverkusen allowed their opponents an average of 13 passes (so-called *ppda value*, which describes the number of passes allowed to the opponent per defensive action).[385] This puts them among the top ten in the Bundesliga, but also reflects a tactical style that isn't solely dependent on constant high pressing. Rather, these

376 see bundesliga.com
377 see theanalyst.com
378 Ibid.
379 Ibid.
380 see bundesliga.com
381 Ibid.
382 cf. footystats.org
383 cf. theanalyst.com
384 Ibid.
385 Ibid.

statistics confirm the behavior we have seen throughout the season: Dictating the game by altering defensive rhythms and varying the level of pressing to keep opponents off balance.

Interestingly, the Werkself ranked second to last in Bundesliga duel win percentage last season (ahead of Darmstadt 98; leader: VfL Bochum), and also committed the fewest fouls.[386] From this we can infer that Bayer regains the possession primarily through clever anticipation and intercepting passes rather than engaging in direct duels. Werkself's most successful tackler was actually Florian Wirtz.[387] In fact, Bayer Leverkusen was the only Bundesliga team not to concede a single penalty (the only three penalties against them came in the Europa League) and also avoid a red card (neither a yellow-red nor straight red; the exception was the DFB Pokal final).[388] If you factor in that the Werkself was the team which had the most ball recoveries in the Bundesliga, but registered the fewest tackles (and had one of the league's lowest tackle success rates), it highlights the team's remarkable defensive organization.

With regard to the game of football as a whole, there are certain fundamental requirements[389,] which should be fulfilled in almost every tactical setup, regardless of position and task. These include:

386 cf. bundesliga.com
387 Ibid.
388 cf. transfermarkt.de
389 according to Fran Beltrán, 2022.

9
Boniface
Schick
B. Iglesias

10
Wirtz
Adli
Hlozek

7
Hofmann
Tella
Frimpong

11
Grimaldo
Arthur
Hincapié

6
Xhaka
Grimaldo

8
Palacios
Andrich
Puerta

2
Frimpong
Stanisic
Tella

3
Tapsoba
Hincapié

4
Tah
Andrich

5
Kossounou
Tapsoba
Stanisic

1
Hradecky
Kovar
Lomb

Defensive

1. Everyone defends; everyone works off the ball (RUN).
2. Movement starts the moment the ball moves.
3. We all stay in front of our opponent against direct / high play (*pre-defen-ding / defending forward*).
4. Positional adjustments depend on the ball's location..
5. Sprint through defensive transitions (recover shape or counter-press actively).
6. Shield the central areas (stay between the ball and the goal).
7. Stay on your feet; avoid sliding tackles.
8. Avoid overcommitting inside the box.
9. No fouls in our defensive half.

Offensive:

1. Every player has a role (task) – We stay connected.
2. Always be available (and playable) for a pass.
3. If receiving isn't possible, reposition (re-location).
4. Constant scanning: assess space, opponent's movement, and distance.
5. Organize / position around the ball: maintain in shape for possible counter-pressing and control bypassed opponents.
6. Overload / surround defenders ('*rodear*' concept: create threats ahead, behind, and on both sides).
7. Maintain compact shape (short distances), even when not directly involved in the attack.
8. Move in sync with the ball's trajectory during medium or long passes.
9. Keep possession - protect the ball (dominate 1v1, win duels, shield under pressure, manage to play covered - despite under pressure).
10. Pass while in motion; receive and drive forward simultaneously.

In addition, certain universal, high-probability behaviors can be implemented and reinforced for individual, frequent in-game scenarios, but they fall beyond the scope of this section.

The role-specific profiles and key attributes for each position at Bayer Lever-kusen during the 2023/24 season can be outlined as follows below (without claiming to be exhaustive or exclusive). Furthermore, it is essential that play-ers master all relevant fundamental principles in both offensive and defensive play, along with situational awareness in fundamental, recurring game moments (such as 1v1 defending, behavior against balls played from the outside, penalty area defense, behavior in man-marking situations, etc.).

Goalkeeper:

In addition to all position-specific actions and qualities such as shot-stopping, aerial command, and penalty area control, which are undoubtedly paramount in this position, the following skills are also required:

→ Defensive organization & communication
→ Game reading & anticipation: Predict second-ball situations and read threats before they develop
→ Focus & mental resilience: Stay engaged even in low-activity phases
→ Numerical awareness & spatial understanding: Evaluate overloads, positional balance & build-up decision (short vs. long distribution)
→ Technical ball-playing ability: Initiate controlled build-up play; confident distribution with both feet
→ Positional adjustments: Maintain optimal positioning relative to team shape
→ Personality & leadership: Composure under pressure & vocal leadership

Central defender:

A remarkable statistic about Jonathan Tah: The national player is among the top 15 fastest players in the Bundesliga with 35.81 km/h, which makes it easier for him to defend in a high defensive line as he can use his speed and anticipation effectively. According to statistics, he is ranked second among Bundesliga center-backs in sprint speed last season.[390]

→ Core defensive skills, including

   ↳ Defending short passing combinations / double passes: Prevent being pinned by quick passing exchanges; stay mobile & block passing lanes

   ↳ 1v1 defensive ability: Controlled body positioning – dictate opponent's options; stay on feet, active footwork, use your arms, body leverage in physical duels; push your body between the ball and your opponent when there are two "long" touches.

   ↳ Defending wide-area passes & crosses: Cover central zones or mark the greatest occuring danger; prioritize clearances over controlled touches; maintain ground contact for balance, lateral positioning.

   ↳ Penalty area defending: Body positioning blocks attacking runs; maintain 45° defensive angle with physical contact; clear danger decisively

→ Cover / protect / supports / closing - Spatial behavior

→ Blocking & Shot Prevention: Preventing shots through compact positioning; keep legs closed & hands behind back to avoid handball

→ Winning Duels: Engage in physical duels assertively; control contact intensity based on game situation (dosage / body technique)

→ Adaptive Positioning: Adjust position dynamically based on ball, teammates & nearest opponents

→ High Defensive Line Awareness: Maintain high defensive line if required; rely on anticipation & timing for proactive defending

→ Body Orientation & Awareness: Optimize body positioning to maximize field awareness

→ Anticipating Opponent Intentions: Anticipate / "read" opponent's body cues to predict next move

→ Marking & Aerial Coverage: Track unmarked attackers & provide cover for aerial duels; drop back to prevent deep runs

→ Situational Sweeper Role: Act as last-man defender or "libero" when necessary

→ Leadership & Mentality: Take responsibility with strong positional discipline & leadership mentality

→ In possession of the ball and especially in the moment of build-up:
  ↳ Beating Pressure with Passing: Break opponent's press with composed passing under pressure
  ↳ Disguised Passes: Disguise passing intentions to mislead defenders
  ↳ Directional Play: Exploit opponent's momentum with passes against their movement
  ↳ Passing Through Compact Defenses: Thread passes through high-density defensive setups
  ↳ Initiative in Build-up: Take proactive initiative in dictating game tempo
  ↳ Consistent Passing Outlet: Always provide a passing option as a stable build-up point
  ↳ Switching Play: Switch play diagonally to exploit open spaces
  ↳ Defensive Anticipation: Read potential turnovers & maintain defensive security

→ Set-piece Threat: Provide aerial threat in attacking set-pieces

Half-back:

→ Advanced Positioning: Positioned aggressively high in Leverkusen's system

→ Right-Side Build-up Focus: Preference to build-up through the right; position himself high to bypass opponent's first pressing line based on their structure

→ Line-Breaking Passes: Plays progressive passes early to break lines (similar to central defenders)

→ Compact Field Control: Maintain compact spacing in possession; ensure constant connectivity; option to create a threat by overlapping, crossing, shooting.

→ **Defensive and offensive abilities as before** (see center-back profile; largely the same responsibilities)

→ Do not attack without coverage

→ Defend shots (don't stand sideways, make yourself tall, legs closed, don't jump, stand upright)

→ Ability to control more than one player; "defend in between" (recognize the opponent's orientation, speed and time to anticipate the follow-up action)

→ Regain space if beaten by the opponent

→ Key position in rest defense (don't attack an opponent who has time and space; defend the next pass (already direct the opponent); prevent turns; block deep runs before the opponent can get fast, etc.)

Central midfielders:

A statistical value that is not surprising in this position is the number of kilo-meters run, which puts Granit Xhaka in the top three of the past Bundesliga season.[391] With regard to football-specific skills, the following are particularly required:

→ Permanent option in possession of the ball (always wanting to have the ball), in particular:
  ↳ Use the cover shadow of the pressing opponent to be an offer / available passing option for the central defenders
  ↳ Occupy *"BASE"* permanently; dominate the center
  ↳ Change pass line to be an offer (different heights & axes in positioning)
  ↳ Positioning in the gaps, attacking the opponent's back
  ↳ Demand the ball to repeat passes and attract opponents
  ↳ Diagonal passing direction first; hidden passes (disguising hiding intentions; opening feet and hips late, feinting) and passes against the direction of the opponent

391 see bundesliga.com

↳ Situationally drop next to central defenders to form a three-man back-line in the build-up phase player opening

↳ Moving sidewards in certain situations to create a numerical advantage

↳ Look into the depth / perception, orientation, and scanning; play in all directions when possible

↳ Permanent play & go ("pass & offer solution"); stay connected and anticipate actions

↳ Expansive dribbling; "dividing" opponents

↳ Identify himself as the "fourth player" of a pass (target player; increase instead of "third player", preferring to play one more pass to capture the opponent's attention) to receive the ball in a higher space on the pitch and further accelerate the game

↳ Anticipate the next action and position accordingly (follow the ball's trajectory)

→ Superior: providing rhythm and structure to the game

→ Connector & networker; "sharing the ball" with others

→ Quick decision-making

→ Keep an eye on the open playing position or the next direct passing option (orientation)

→ Threatening opponents with deep passes

→ If the situation allows: deep runs into the space behind the opponents

→ Threatening the goal with long-range shots

→ Balance your own team – create balance; monitor the situational needs of your own team

→ Anticipation; intercepting passes; defending in advance

→ Position between opponents, anticipate the next pass and defend accordingly

↳ Identify the orientation and speed of the ball possessor

↳ Anticipate follow-up action (possible passes)

↳ Close down the opponent at the same time as the pass

↳ Defend from the inside out and from back to front

↳ Avoid being pinned down by a potential passing target; force predictability in the opponent's play and anticipate to defend aggressively

→ Stay compact and avoid being bypassed by the opponent

→ Protect your own goal, slow down the opponent, block close to goal with the largest body surface possible and keep hands behind your back

→ Maintain connection between all parts of the team

Outside players:

Jeremie Frimpong's pace has been an exceptional factor in every game and has certainly had an impact on creating individual, qualitative,
 and dynamic advantages for his team. However, if you look at the Bundesliga statistics, you realize that Frimpong was only the tenth fastest player in the league (at 35.96 km/h) (Alphonso Davies reached 36.41 km/h).[392] However, Frimpong's speed was regularly utilized by his team, allowing him to maximize on these qualities. In terms of the number of sprints, Frimpong ranked among the top three of the past Bundesliga season.[393]

Both wingers, Grimaldo and Frimpong, are also in the top 10 for the number of crosses delivered; a tool that was used time and again by Alonso's team to create goal-scoring threats and often targeted toward the corresponding playing partner on the other wing at the second post.[394]

Regarding the role-specific requirements of the wingers, it should be said in advance that this position was interpreted differently depending on the player: While Frimpong embodies a classic, dynamic winger profile, often deployed as a high and wide winger or even as a striker in certain situations, Grimaldo adjusts his interpretation based on the game situation and opponent. The Spaniard appears frequently in the center, sometimes occupying the interior spaces (like

392 see bundesliga.com
393 Ibid.
394 see bundesliga.com

a No. 6 or No. 8) and then acting as a winger again. As discussed earlier in the book, it is the unique characteristics of the players that add something special to the game model and usually pose major challenges for the opponent. Other players who have played in this position (e.g., Stanišić, Tella, Arthur) have also brought their own qualities, depending on their profile. Irrespective of this, the following requirements can be summarized, even if there is no absolute distinction to be made between other roles or positions in the interpretation of the players:

Offensive:

→ Responsible for maintaining width
→ Create positional and relational advantages through interplay with half-back and No. 8 or supporting striker
→ Occupy optimal spaces ("squares") depending on the situation; never position yourself on the same axis as other players (except when surrounding an opponent)
→ Positional flexibility (change into No. 6, No. 8, or striker) possible depending on game flow and tactical needs
→ Always maintain an maintain anopen passing line (*stage space: cooperation or immediate support*); adapt to the needs of your own team; engage and challenge / threaten opponents through positioning
→ Permanent pass-and-move sequences (pass & offer solution); win the opponent's back
→ Identify oneself as the "fourth" player (target player in the passing sequence) and anticipate the passing sequence of one's team to arrive / appear at the optimal moment
→ Connections through passing sequences from wide-wide-central and wide-central-wide; maintain optimal spacing / width
→ Beat opponents by dribbling
→ Well-timed double passes and deep runs (between center-back and half-back or wing-back); attacking depth (right moment and execution)
→ Drop deep before making a run in behind (or vice versa)
→ If the opponent is behind one's back: cross the trajectory
→ Threaten opponents with a decep a deceptive first touch (disguise / hide intent)
→ Linking actions with subsequent plays

→ In the box: attack the second post
→ Crosses:
   ↳ From the corner of the penalty box: low cross between defenders and
      goalkeeper
   ↳ Middle of the penalty area: driven ball (opposite to defensive
      momentum)
   ↳ Baseline: Cut back to the second post or edge of the box
   ↳ Avoid crosses from extreme wide positions

Defensive:

→ Defend one-twos (leave ball carrier and passing options outside)
→ Engage in 1v1 defensive duels (see defensive principles)
→ Arrive with the ball at the opponent (timing)
→ "Blind side" attack: Press from an opponent's blind side
→ Anticipate, defend forward
→ Use body positioning to guide and control the opponent; anticipate ball
   carrier's intentions
→ Cover passing lanes between multiple opponents (access to more than one
   opponent)
→ React and pivot quickly to disrupt pass-and-move plays
→ Sharp directional changes to stay with the opponent (crossing feet)
→ Press only with adequate defensive support
→ Diagonal trajectories to shut down passing lanes
→ Prioritize space by blocking potential runs (contact!) instead of blindly
   following movement (possible feint)

Attacking Midfielder / Hanging Striker:

Florian Wirtz ranks in the top 5 for intensive runs during the last Bundesliga season.[395] This role can be divided into a typical No. 8 / No. 10 profile (e.g., Wirtz,
Hofmann) and more mobile, depth-seeking second forwards (e.g., Adli, Hložek,
or Tella). This position requires, among other things:

---

395 see bundesliga.com

Offensive:

→ Occupy space between the lines / "squares" / dynamic pockets of space; engage the last defender while staying one step behind the offside line) / exploit space behind the defensive line / win backs

→ Temporarily drop into deeper positions to facilitate buildup (occupy *BASE)*

→ Constant awareness of teammates' positioning and constant interaction with nearby attacking players: strikers, wide attackers / wingers, and central midfielders. Goal: Adapt positioning relative to ball movement and teammates' actions to manipulate space for oneself and others (e.g., dropping deeper to create space behind)

→ Use off-ball movement to drift out of sight and reemerge in dangerous spaces ("Disappear" & "Appear")

→ Connect and share the ball, play the decisive ball, maintain compact passing distances

→ Together with striker: surround defender (*'rodear'*)

→ Consistently threaten goal-scoring opportunities, play & go into the box by positioning as a finisher inside the penalty area

→ Permanent intention to destabilize / disorganize the opponent and disrupt their structure

→ Overload spaces and create a numerical advantage; recognize and anticipate the "needs" of your own team (orientation & perception)

→ Interchange positions dynamically

→ Ensure vertical and horizontal staggering to maintain passing options at all times

→ Attack central spaces especially targeting gaps between central defenders and full-back

→ Stay positioned to receive passes efficiently (open body profile); control the ball while maintaining speed or let it roll through turning for an immediate directional first touch

→ Ability to play both on and off the ball in tight spaces

→ Quick decision-making (cognitive speed) and permanent orientation

→ Feinting before receiving the ball, especially close to the goal (e.g., feint a deep run before dropping short, or vice versa)

→ Change in rhythm by ball reception or dribbling action

→ Position at second post / Stay active inside the penalty area / Occupy box

→ Attack the space behind the defense again and again

→ Use circular off-ball movements to reposition effectively after bypassing a defender

→ Provide an inside passing option from wide areas

→ Anticipate potential involvement as a fourth passing option and position accordingly

→ Delay revealing intentions with subtle body movements

→ Anticipate defenders' reactions and manipulate positioning to create space

→ Adjust, giving "optimal" width based on tactical role and team shape

→ Always engaged in play; lurking & anticipating possible errors from the opponent

→ Connect actions

Defensive:

→ Make the opponent's game predictable through positioning and posture, robbing options

→ Time challenges perfectly: intercept or tackle simultaneously as the ball arrives, capture balls

→ Defend persistently when needed (deep in own half) and support the next player

→ Stay available for passes after ball recovery; push play forward and follow up after passing

Striker:

Leverkusen has several central "9s", who occasionally played together last season (a front two of Boniface and Schick, plus Tella and at times Hložek). In other games, the profile of the traditional striker was deliberately left out in favor of a flexible striker with high mobility who constantly makes deep runs. The profile of the target man can be combined; however, the Werkself most often operated with one fixed forward (at the beginning of the season mostly Boniface, later Schick).

The requirements for this position include:

→ Clinical finishing, appropriate behavior; intelligent movement in and around the box to remain a constant threat
→ Use varied positioning: body-to-body duels in 1v1s, occupying gaps between defenders (tying up defenders), or standing offside to disrupt defensive lines
→ Adapt role based on tactical setup: hold defenders, make off-ball runs, drop deep to link play, or create space for teammates (blocking opponents)
→ Off-the-ball runs targeting gaps behind defenders
→ Work with teammates to generate superiorities (positional advantages, overloads, numerical advantages, pinning defenders to free up space, etc.)
→ Position laterally to maintain vision of both ball and goal
→ Stay diagonally aligned to the ball for optimal passing angles
→ React instantly when the ball moves past to stay involved in play
→ Unpredictable movement; dominate in final-third duels and decisive actions
→ Combining in the box (playing slightly diagonal from behind to the opponent; occupying different heights in the box, changing tempo, etc.)
→ Shield and control the ball effectively; use arms before first contact to maintain balance and space
→ Manipulate defensive structures through intelligent positioning
→ Guide pressing structure; dictate defensive movements and anticipate the game proactively; make the game predictable
→ Apply pressure on ball carriers; arrive at the same time with the ball (timing); anticipate passes, tackle decisively, and cut off passing lanes (steal options)

The position profiles presented are intended to provide an insight into the possible level of detail of the players' interpretation and thus an orientation for which movements and actions should be harmonized, synchronized and subsequently implemented together. It is neither necessary for all players to know everything (about every position), or for each individual player to know everything about his own position, since the actions do not necessarily require knowledge of the overall context, but can also be carried out intuitively. The aim is to address essential information that the coach can convey to his players during training sessions in order to implement his game idea. Some of these contexts are provided in the training proposals section.

CHAPTER 4

Outlook

What will happen next for Bayer Leverkusen and Xabi Alonso – after an (almost) perfect season? We can assume that the hunger for more and the obsession with achieve an even greater level of perfection will not diminish. The Champions League brings a more demanding level of competition for which the team seems ready. Xabi Alonso himself has not given this much thought during the current season. At the moment of the DFB Cup triumph, the Basque has no thoughts about the future: "I need a bit of time now to accept and process what kind of season this has been. Everything we have experienced and now being able to celebrate here on the last day is something special."[396]

These thoughts will surely arise during the summer break, when there is time to reflect and process the countless impressions – and then the staff will continue to challenge the team with renewed energy, inspiration, and further tactical refinements and prepare them as best as possible for the next challenges. We will probably then also experience what is it like when Bayer Leverkusen loses. However, it is also likely that this will not be the case too often. Already during his time as coach of *Sanse* in San Sebastián, Alonso spoke about the great difficulty of maintaining a successful level: "Winning a Copa is very difficult, but the most difficult thing is to maintain the level - not just to win and then be relegated, but to stay close to the next victory[397]

---

396 Alonso quoted by kicker online, 25.05.2024.
397 Alonso quoted in Corrigan, 2021.

Looking at the development of the team under Xabi Alonso since he took office in the autumn of 2022, becomes clear that after establishing a defensive framework and an offensive basic structure, the team has shown increasingly fluent positioning and more dynamic interpretations of its own game in recent months. It is expected that this trend will continue in the coming season. In addition, the game model will continue to evolve with incoming players (including Aleix García from Girona), and each new player will add his own unique nuance and interpretation. The Champions League also represents the next challenge for Alonso's team: to play their own "Bayer football" at the absolute top level week after week, continuously improving and navigating dry spells while still achieving good results. The fact that Xabi Alonso's team has mastered both pragmatism and high-level combinational football has already been proven in the last two seasons. Now we look ahead to the further development of one of the most exciting teams in European football.

CHAPTER 5

Training Considerations

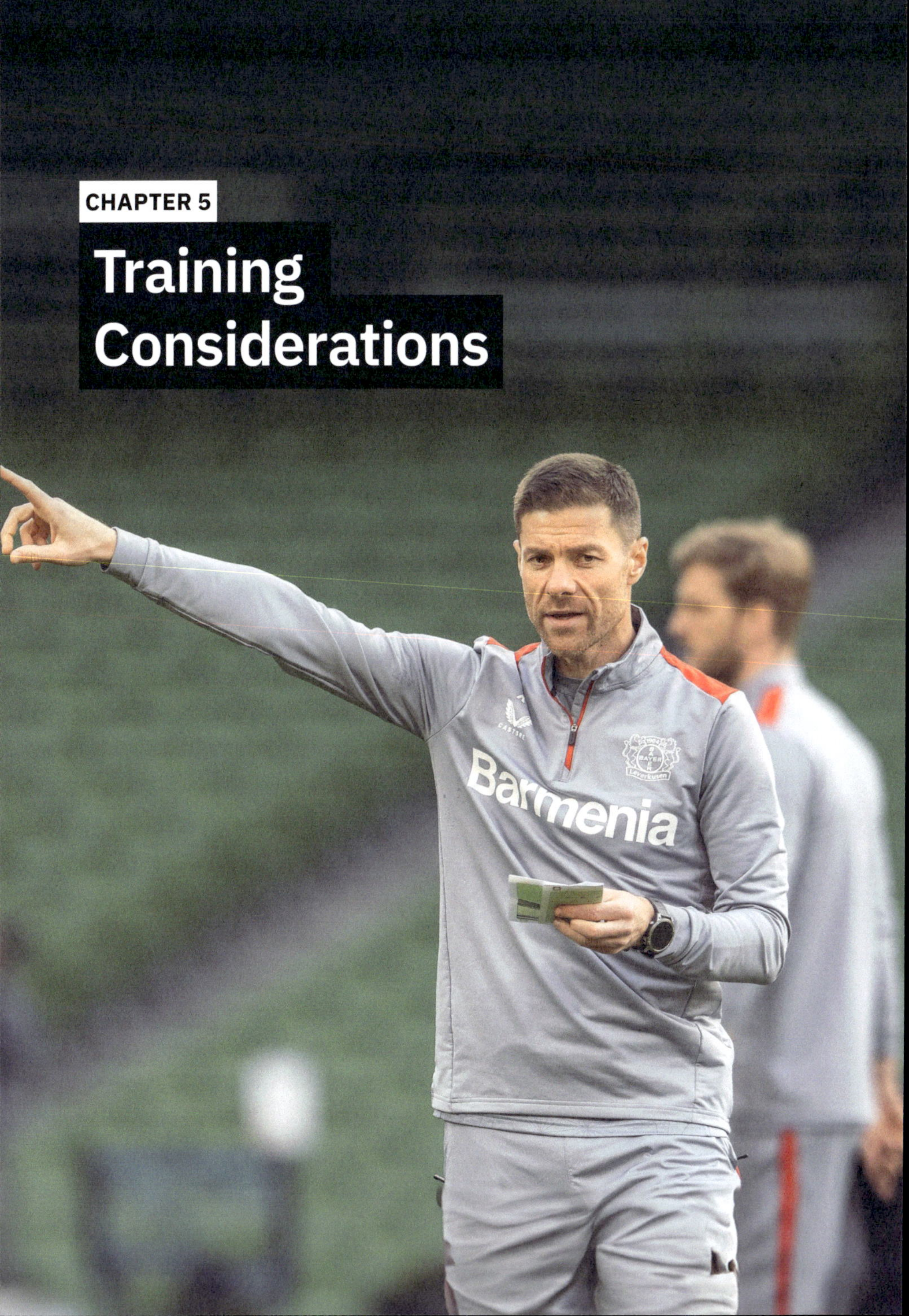

"I think it's very important to understand the game. You have to understand where the spaces are, how to use your teammates and how to get the most out of the game."
XABI ALONSO

"The coach should choose the daily training formats with his team in mind."
CÉSAR LUIS MENOTTI

This chapter is not about blindly copying specific training contexts under the assumption to be a recipe that will help any team play the same way as Bayer Leverkusen under Xabi Alonso last season. Rather, it's about training ideas and suggestions that serve as inspiration to adapte, refine and make them suitable for your own team - ensuring that they align with the coach's philosophy, the club's specifications and requirements and, most importantly, the abilities of your players. It is therefore essential to emphasize that each exercise focuses primarily on the underlying intention, the methodological approach and the specific tactical principles. However, these exercises also require careful adaptation in detail to match the unique needs of a team. In football, a key responsibility of the coaching team is to "develop training methods that reflect the context and conditions of competition, with the aim of achieving maximum transfer from training to competition."[398] Training serves as the primary "communication channel to the athlete in order to interact; to modify motor, cognitive, conditioning schemes; to change behaviors and, ultimately, to optimize the athlete."[399]

A coach should be passionate about designing training, enjoy the competition and understand not only the sport itself, but also the underlying structures and needs that arise, shape and define the player.[400] And all this in a dynamic, non-linear, and complex context like football.
So when we look at training, we see the coach and his coaching staff proposing a training context that enables varied interactions between the players and thereby optimizes the team's relationships and cohesion. Training should be an engaging and enriching process in which the coach acts as a supporter and facilitator by offering the player new perspectives to the players. During training, situations are created in which different options and solutions are discovered

398 Pinder et al. 2011.
399 Serrés Lara 2017.
400 Ibid.

through exploration. In the professional segment, this is not always possible: considering the players' characteristics and the limited training time available, it can be helpful for a team to rehearse concrete solutions on the pitch. At the same time, in an unpredictable, chaotic game like football, the scope for ready-made solutions is always rather limited. In fact, it is worthwhile to use subtle changes (such as adjustments in positioning or height) to create concrete, high-impact opportunities and to help players develop instinctive behaviors that are characteristic of "our game". The emergence and discovery of new solutions is a constant in football training. Technique and tactics are inherently connected, as both develop together. When understanding training, methodology and the planification of training, it should not be forgotten that every session is a very lively process in which each individual player and the team as a whole interacts dynamically with the coaching staff's suggestions and interprets them in relation to the existing (explicit or implicit) intentions and tactical context.

Also part of Xabi Alonso's coaching staff is fitness coach Ismael Camenforte, who, in addition to his extensive experience at FC Barcelona, has also written a research paper on the specificity of football training in collaboration with other fitness coaches from the Spanish professional sector. It examines criteria that can be used to assess how football-specific a particular exercise is. The specificity of football training is considered the most important characteristic[401], which, as an "increasingly recognized training principle", shapes the athlete's adaptive responses within the proposed contexts.[402] Camenforte et al. present a list of 100 training exercises, evaluated according to their specificity, with those formats that have more characteristics of competitive play (e.g. involving two goalkeepers, fixed playing direction, offside, etc.) being considered more specific.[403] The exercise that most closely represents match conditions is an 11v11 game, although even a distinction must be made between the requirements of an official match and a training game.[404] The training session therefore forms a controlled "simulated match scenario, which we [as coaches] manipulate ito either reach the player's optimal engagement threshold more easily or to stimulate it excessively. We give priority to those aspects that are of particular interest to us at a given moment."[405] However, this does not mean that we should only play in

401 Tarrago et al. 2019.
402 Gamble 2006; Issurin 2010; Vilar et al. 2014.
403 Camenforte et al. 2021.
404 Ibid.
405 Serres Lara & Massafret 2017.

full 11v11 contexts, as certain behaviors and details may be more prominent in other, smaller contexts and are therefore easier for players to recognize and internalize. Former Real Madrid U18 coach Fran Beltrán explains the value of varied training contexts as follows:

"The didactic means used to achieve this degree of coordination and harmony must be varied. Openly speaking, one must have a very high level of competence, (...) so that (only) from game situations and contexts of maximum uncertainty, respecting entire game cycle [all moments of the game, like possession, transition, etc.; Author's note], players are able to pay attention to certain stimuli, of which they were previously not aware and which cause more individual questions and interactions, that are defined in such a way to recur repeatedly for ten minutes [during a proposed training context; Author's note]..

I believe in training that addresses the game and the player on all possible levels and integrates individual tactics into group contexts. [Training is about] provoking situations that force me to interact in stressful situations and with opponents in the way I consider useful, working occasionally without direct or active resistance, paying attention to criteria of distance, possible relationships, coordinated movements, reproducing many times in a very short time an response to a specific question (...).

The player does what he knows in contexts of uncertainty, so I don't think it's wrong to take questions from the game, present them, make them conscious and work on them. (...) Just one thing? Just the other thing? No! These are non-linear processes in which there is a relationship between all the elements of the construction that is intended, and if we declare ourselves to be mediators, we must act on the players in the most appropriate way and not always in just one way." [406]

Nevertheless, it remains evident that "the ultimate goal is to play. And if that is the goal, training can only have one purpose: to achieve it in a playful way."[407] The core focus within the training process is therefore clearly on game-based situations where the players apply their skills and immerse themselves in realistic game situations. This is a non-linear, dynamic process.[408] On the one hand, this relates to how the human brain learns: it processes information in contexts (concepts). We collect different experiences linked to the same concept, or the same concept becomes transferabe to different and previously encountered experien-

406 Beltrán in Ballesteros 2020.
407 Amiero quoted in Cano 2010.
408 O'Sullivan et al. 2021.

ces. The emotional connection to the experience can be a decisive 'catalyst' (or 'barrier') within the learning process.[409] Learning takes place "when the learner is immersed within the learning environment, and [...] knowledge [is acquired through] [...] interactions between the learner and the environment.[410] This occurs through constant adaptation to achieve the variable goals proposed by the coach.[411] The training context should include "representative [specific] information", "invite players to explore learning opportunities" while guiding their attention toward specific areas.[412] The players do not act as passive consumers but engage actively in the training process, as they contribute to the interpretation and especially determine *how* to implement the training. They can "learn through their development process" and be directly involved by the coach.[413] The coach helps players direct their attention to specific stimuli in the training context, making it easier for them to identify common opportunities for interaction and to cultivate shared intentions.[414] Within this process, the coach should not forget "that we do not all learn in the same way within the same proposed training situations."[415] In the continous interaction of the training context, it is therefore important for the coach to regularly check whether the training form, they have designed, provides optimal learning opportunities for each player and how they can further support this process. However, being attentive to the individual does not mean training players in complete isolation, as Óscar Cano notes: "Tailor-made exercises for each player without taking the others into account prevent 'social intelligence from staying alive', when the great aspiration is finding out what we can do together effectively so that everyone expresses their greatest potential."[416] The same applies to predictability within training: "If you already know what is going to happen, it is not training for intelligent beings."[417] Paco Seirul·lo underlines this:

"[I] confirm what science says, namely, that isolated practice produces selfishness and aggressiveness. But it is even more destructive because it has been said to block executive attention and inductive-deductive thinking, leading to slow and

409 Damunt & Guerrero 2021, Balagué 2021.
410 Chow 2013.
411 Damunt & Guerrero 2021.
412 O'Sullivan et al. 2021.
413 O'Sullivan et al. 2021, Balague 2021.
414 Ibid.
415 Massafret 2017.
416 Marina quoted in Cano 2010.
417 Balagué 2021.

generally complicated decision-making. On the contrary, cooperative practice itself, whatever it may be, generates immediate 'rewards' for its participants, as studies indicate that it activates all the so-called 'frontal brain regions' responsible for environmental knowledge and the complex functionality that distinguishes us as intelligent human beings - with all that this entails. And when this exercise is performed in a 'reduced space', these values are optimized exponentially."[418]

In fact, specific and individual training is done in a playful way, "by attacking in natural spaces, based on my characteristics, in alignment with those who complement me best and in a way that defines our common goals."[419] This fosters "indestructible" bonds that significantly increase mutual respect and pride in belonging to the group, as the players' understanding that they must always contribute for the group is further developed.[420] This is particularly true for a collective, cooperative, and socio-affective interpretation of football as a team sport.

To adapt to the context, the player must collect relevant information from the overall context (environment, game situation, and himself), understand the game, and know the effects of his actions within the context (intentional information). The result of the training is both a higher number (increase in executable actions) and quality (better calibration – situation-appropriate execution) of the technical possibilities.[421]

Training enables the player to gain extensive experience related to a single concept. The player should experience diverse contexts with varied stimuli (in terms of fellow players, opponents, rules and space, etc.) in order to be able to apply the concepts flexiby. At the same time, there is never just one isolated concept alone, but ideally all of them at the same time, albeit with different emphasis. One concept, for example, might be to form passing lines, another to network with the teammate who is currently in the most advantageous position. This occurs in the team context, whereby within the development process it is essential to learn "in the team context" (*'en equipo'*) (which benefits the individual player), but even more to learn *as* a team (*'como equipo'*), since this emphasizes realizing shared intentions and coordinating collective actions - essentially syn-

418 Seirul·lo 2024.
419 Cano 2010.
420 Seirul·lo 2024.
421 Damunt & Guerrero 2021.

chronizing them.[422] This plays a crucial role, especially in all areas that depend on seamless teamwork on the field.

"Football is located in a subzone between order and transformable chaos and therefore belongs entirely to the realm of complexity. It follows that information and interactions are the most important emerging factors." [423]

PACO SEIRUL·LO

The essence of the game is based on the connections and dynamic interactions promoted by the coach, which enable creative play as long as the group identifies that it must act and perform collectively as a team. All actions that enable the player to perform in a particular facet of the game should always contribute to the implementation of the team's shared intention. Within this team dynamic, the synergy between the players are an important element. From Abel Mourelo's perspective, these dynamics should be developed through games "in a [structured and] didactic way", and in such a way that "the coach's observation power provide valuable information. For us, the first player to move was always the one closest to the ball. Depending on what he did, the next person was challenged. The key is to create a context of 'certainty' where the boys know which spaces to occupy and what role to assume depending on where they are. The potential receiver halts to tie up the opponent so the next player can take advantage, and then when he [the first receiver] gets the ball, I'm the potential [next] receiver... Therefore, it is a game of interrelations, not just relationships. When I have the ball, I function one way and you function another. But the moment I give it to you, the way we function changes. I no longer have possession of the ball, but not in relation to you but in relation to someone else. It is important that the player recognizes himself in this dynamic and helps shape our style of play, which is why the understanding of 'who' plays which role is so important."[424] For this reason, the composition in training is an important tool within the didactic process, since this is where decisive decisions are made about team dynamics and the relationships between players. The coach may choose to group as many different players as possible during training to promote team's adaptability or to strengthen specific relationships ensuring these players develop a seamless understanding of each other in competition. For instance central defenders may be trained together possibly paired with the central midfielders, while

---

422 Seirul·lo in Benedetti 2024.
423 Seirul·lo 2010.
424 Mourelo in Ballesteros 2020.

strikers could work in tandem with the attacking wingers and so forth. Anyone who spent countless hours with their best friend on the football pitch as a child may remember that over time a near-telepatic understanding developed. This stemmed from many shared experiences on the pitch, playing, communicating, and anticipating each other's movements. The team that develops such a deep understanding of the game gains a significant advantage over its opponent. It is this kind of intuitive connection that Paco Seirul·lo calls a "socio-affective advantage" or "relational advantage".[425]

Within the training process, we aim to create certain "habits" through systematic repetition of our game, enabling players to play "in harmony" with the others.[426] Fran Beltrán even adds: "Football is only effective when you stop thinking. That's why I have to turn everything I want to do on the pitch into a second nature beforehand."[427] However, a "habit" should not be confused with a "automatism", as Paco Seirul·lo explains, expressing skepticism about this term in football: "We build variations into the repetition. Because if I keep doing the same thing to you, you'll figure it out by the third time at the latest. (...) We need to create game situations where automatic repetition is of no use. We need to reduce the number of 'automatisms'. Because if the game is too automated, I won't need ten seconds to understand what your automatisms are. Instead, we need to figure out how two players interact most effectively with each other, and then we need to train that. (...) The interactions between players are the basis for success in football."[428]

For Abel Mourelo, the coach is the key figure in this process: "the ability to see, to recognize... and knowing the responses our players give. There can be three kinds of responses: the autonomous one, the spontaneous one and the one we do not know how to respond to. The autonomous response is the one where you notice that the player repeats it again and again because of his talent. He is able to maintain it over a longer period of time by performing it consciously. Our job is to identify these responses and strengthen them."[429] Here, Mourelo emphasizes the importance of valuing the player's intention, regardless of successful execution, as this can be optimized together. "Then there are the spontaneous reactions. (...) He does everything from the subconscious. He doesn't know why, where or how he did it. Our help consists in identifying these behaviors and con-

425 Seirul·lo 2024.
426 Mourelo in Ballesteros 2020.
427 Beltrán in Perarnau 2016.
428 Seirul·lo in Perarnau 2016.
429 Ibid.

nections for the player, giving them names and training them to bring them from the unconscious into the conscious. After all, it is the reactions that he does not recognize or perform that can help expanding this palette. The process of perception – decision – execution does not exist. The player acts. Everything is based on what came before."[430] At this point I would like to add that it is usually not crucial for the player (or for the team) whether he knows what he is doing, as long as he acts appropriately in the game situation, since intuitive action is linked to the feeling of the game and can therefore often be carried out much faster than if it were consciously thought about beforehand. In his book *Thinking, Fast and Slow,* psychology professor Daniel Kahneman describes the distinction between two cognitive systems: System 1 and System 2. System 1 is what we can describe as intuitive action or intuitive reaction and assumptions; it "works automatically and quickly, largely effortlessly and without conscious control."[431] When we mentally operate in this system, we act quickly. This is different with System 2, which "directs attention to mental demanding tasks. (...) The operations of System 2 are often accompanied by the subjective experience of power to act, freedom of choice and concentration."[432] As we can all imagine, we act more slowly in these moments. In football, where quick (correct) decisions are a key to success, it is advisable to use System 1. To do this, the player must be trained to act intuitively and appropriately to the game situation.

The difference that Mourelo mentions in his commentary describes an intermediate stage within competence development. In the model of "competence level development"[433] a distinction is only made between "conscious incompetence" and "conscious competence" on the way to "unconscious competence". In football, however, players may already be "unconsciously competent", but lack the necessary stability due to uncertainty in their decision-making processes. For the coach, this process is not about overloading the player's perception with excessive information but rather about highlighting the vaue of his actions. This allows the player to recognize, execute, and time these actions more consciously and effectively. If this succeeds, the player is '*performing*' in the moment, as Mourelo puts it - he is acting. At this stage, the player can reach a state known as "*flow*".

430 Ibid.
431 Kahneman 2011.
432 Ibid.
433 Maslow / Burch.

The ability to "flow" puts the player into an emotional state that enables high performance during a game. The player is driven by emotions to achieve speed and efficiency in decision making.[434] At this moment the player acts completely intuitively and without conscious thought. The concept of flow goes back to psychology professor Mihály Csíkszentmihályi, who defines flow "as a state of mind in which performance is optimal without the need for great mental effort and in which the person is fully engaged in the activity for its own sake."[435] One is no longer aware of oneself or of the passage of time, since "every action, movement or thought (...) inevitably arises from a preceding action, movement or thought.[436] We can often see this behavior in everyday life in children playing, who forget everything around them while playing and are only "in the moment".

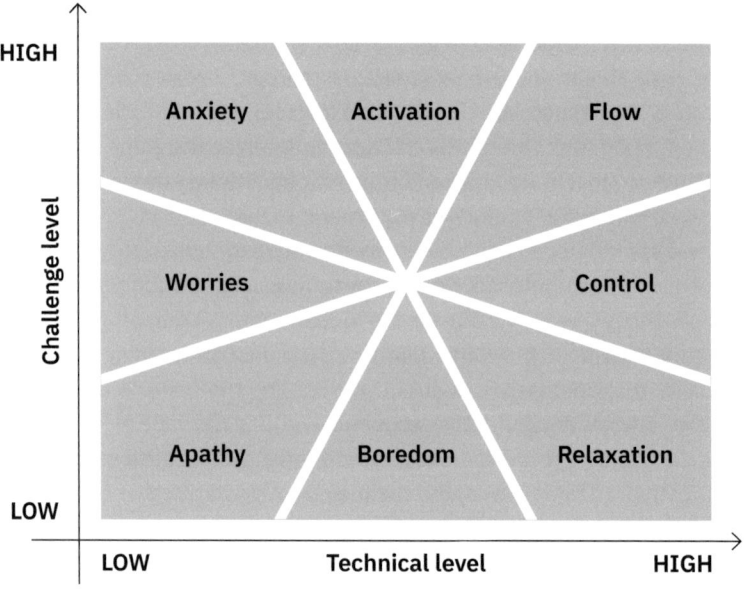

Graphic: Finding flow according to M. Csíkszentmihályi (1997). Own illustration.

434 Damunt & Guerrero 2021.
435 Ibid.
436 Ibid.

For someone to get to this state, a balance must be established between the challenge of the task and the player's skills. The tasks must be motivating and focus the player on the task itself or its goals rather than on himself; they must also not be based on commands or reasoning, as these can lead the player back to a state of consciousness." [437]Flow arises from the optimal relationship between demands and challenges and one's own abilities. If a task is perceived as too easy, it creates boredom; if a task is perceived as too difficult it can lead to fear or even apathy.

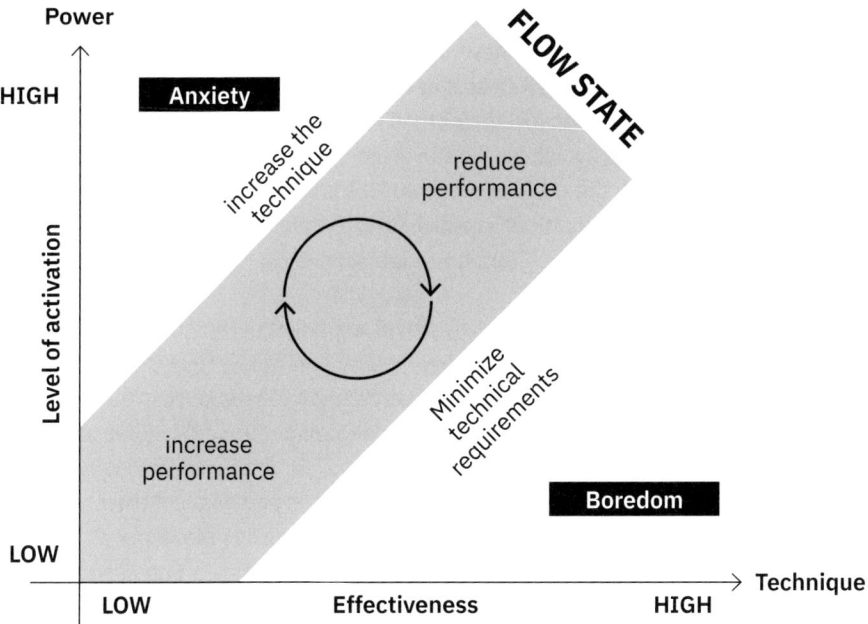

Graphic: Finding flow according to M. Csíkszentmihályi (1997). Own illustration.

437 Ibid.

For the coach, training is about getting his players "into the flow", which is why he should suggest tasks and training contexts that maximize player activation and present them with engaging challenges. This can be achieved by gradually increasing the demands during training, while ensuring they remain in optimal proportion to the players' abilities. At the same time, the coach will receive very quick feedback if the task is perceived by most of the team as too difficult or too easy so training context can be adapted accordingly. The coach should be aware of his role and not interrupt the flow of his players through his behavior, but support it.

Since the player is "in action" in this state, it is impossible to reach this state through prescribed procedures. Instead, players should train in such a way that they can deal with the "unpredictability and variability of situations". We achieve this through implicit learning, which is "based on discovery learning."[438] Andrés Iniesta explains it like this: "These are situations that you have experienced so many times that your brain must have somehow stored them so that when you come into that situation again, it does it automatically or intuitively, otherwise it is very difficult to explain because in football there are no seconds to think."[439]
This happens in a group, which is why the socio-affective structure of the players has a crucial role in the training process. This is always optimized "when he [the player] experiences situations in which he is emotionally involved with other individuals - individuals with whom he must necessarily cooperate, compete, accept, or reject."[440]
The game situation is the reality that a player experiences, and interacts with, in any socio-affective space (in any stage space) and at any time during competition or training. The motor communication experienced during training is therefore more likely to be recognized by the teammate during the game and to appear again. Training the team's relationships and "football empathy" can help players better interpret and understand the intentions and goals of their teammates. This is based on mutual support. Football is always played in a team, with the aim of overcoming the opponent, who also acts as a group to prevent this. The need to train situations in the game context arises precisely from this: it is the permanent context of interaction with one's own teammates, but also with the opponent. Paco Seirul·lo explains the impact on competition: "You can play well and win more often than you lose if you manage to be a team in which

---

438 Damunt & Guerrero 2021.
439 Iniesta in Damunt & Guerrero 2021.
440 Seirul·lo 2017.

most expectations converge and harmonize, in which the feeling of conscious [mutually respectful] identity takes precedence over any individual interest."[441]

"Create an atmosphere in which players' talent can flourish."[442]
   PAT RILEY

The coach should therefore design training formats whose elements are oriented towards the needs of the game and the players. The training exercises are complex, but not complicated, as they function as a simulation of the game.[443] In this way, preferred game simulation situations (abbreviated in Spanish as SSP) are created, which offer to the player(s) the necessary variability to promote the emergence of new collective synergies, which in turn help them self-organize and thus work together in a synchronized way. This happens in unity with the collective goal: to share the ball and win! In the training scenarios, it is important that the game identity is expressed in a specific way. The "SSP" ["simulated preferred situation" > training context derived from the game, author's note] are "the communication channel of the instructor-trainer to transmit the objectives of the practical work to the athlete. This takes place in a context specific to interactive sport in a shared space."[444] The "SSP" come close to the reality of the game and promote tasks "in which players constantly adapt to new situations."[445] The coach creates a context with a task to be completed. In relation to the training goal, this should lead the players as naturally as possible to "perform actions and interactions that the coach intends to optimize."[446] This should be done implicitly rather than explicitly so that game-like experiences can be gained organically. This allows the player to "firstly, identify the intentions necessary for understanding the game and secondly to discover possible courses of action through a process of perceptual tuning that will make him more precise in perceiving and handling the information received, and more flexible in the face of the requirements posed by the context, while at the same time making him more stable in his motor responses."[447]

441 Ibid.
442 Riley quoted by Seirul·lo 2017.
443 Seirul·lo 2024.
444 Massafret 2017.
445 Damunt & Guerrero 2021.
446 Ibid.
447 Ibid.

The perception process takes place in four dimensions:

→ *View:* Body profile, body orientation, head and eyes positioned with the intention of expanding the field of vision.

→ *Perception:* Recognizing situations, neighboring spaces (with reference to the concept of stage spaces; e.g., space of mutual support); distant spaces (cooperation)

→ *Analyze and understand situations:* Fixation of gaze, peripheral vision. Detect spaces that are opening or closing. Anticipate the next step.

→ *Decide:* Choose the best option for the team.

Before the ball reaches the player, he should already have processed all this information. The more intuitive this process is, the faster the player can act.

Each player needs a certain amount of time to interpret the key spatial or temporal aspects when trying to achieve what the coach has asked of him. Jonas Hofmann explains this himself in a podcast[448] from *kicker* and *DAZN*: There were training days after which he always noticed how he had made clear steps forward in his development. He also highlighted the value of competitive matches in the development process of the team and each individual. This sounds logical: only the game itself allows the player to optimize his performance in a competitive context.

Being successful is a positive incentive that facilitates the connection between movement and emotion. The coach's expectations must be aligned with those of the player, as these are closely linked to his motivation. One aspect can be optimized when the coach gets to know the player better (e.g. his interests, needs, as they are key to determining our imagination). During training, players are usually given guidelines or reference points to think about or orient themselves by, helping them structure their actions. This activity strengthens the player's motor and cognitive skills. During competition, real game situations provide no fixed guidelines – there are only a few reference points to orient himself with. These should be internalized through specific training so that the player can make the optimal and best decision in each game situation based on the shared intentions of the team.

448 Hofmann in KMD podcast April 1, 2024.

The following training proposals build on this foundation and serve as ideas, suggestions and inspiration to reflect Bayer Leverkusen's game based on the intentions they show. They are by no means a recipe for always winning - as no such formula exits in football or any other sport - nor are they a universally "best" form of training. Within the training proposals, the coach can also (re-) evaluate the role of the neutral players. Central midfielders are often selected for this role. The central midfielders are the connectors of the team. Not only are they extremely important for the rhythm of the game, but they are also close to every player. When selecting neutral players, the coach should consider in advance: Who do I want to position next to him? How will the positioning of the joker affect the game (where is the numerical advantage)? The same applies to team composition in order to decide which relationships should be optimized in which context.

The smaller the spaces in training, the higher the action density: the pressure on the ball is more intense, the players have less time and space to make decisions, and have to orient themselves better. At the same time, it is important to keep the specificity of the training in mind. This is achieved, as already mentioned by Beltrán, by the optimal mix of various training proposals based on the needs of each team with regard to the information that the coach wants to give implicitly or explicitly to the players.

Paco Seirul·lo formulates the following tips and guidelines for coaches:[449]

→ I am clear and unambiguous; I communicate what I want with the certainty that they will understand, because that is how we have trained.

→ I am honest because I offer them alternative solutions so that we can help each other in one way or another.

→ I am responsible for ensuring that our exchange takes place the way you, I and the team want it to, at this time and in this game situation.

→ I increase collective fine-tuning through convincing synchronization of collective impulses to achieve immediate success at desired moments of the game.

449 Seirul·lo 2017.

→ I understand that motor assertiveness is a process and not a state, that you always have to pay attention to how you communicate and learn to do it in different ways to adapt it to the situation in which you are practicing with other teammates.

In football, the focus is on joint action, which is based on good relationships with each other, motor communication and a good "care of each other" approach: "Every team needs this shared sensitivity for its teammates, to be a place where personal talents are put at the service of the group, where success and failure are truly the achievements of the team, as is its happiness."[450]

450 Ibid.

Training Proposals

The training exercise accessible digitally via This approach helps keep
both the production costs and, consequently, the book's sales price
reasonable—especially considering the full-color presentation.
Enjoy exploring them online!

Training exercise available as a downloadable PDF:
https://is.gd/4N8BQo

Acknowledgements

Just like a championship, it is a great achievement done by teamwork that this book project is in your hands today:
A huge THANK YOU to everyone who supported and helped bring this book to life. Starting with my wife and children, who were a constant source of inspiration and strength, ensuring I took much-needed breaks and found moments of distraction. My "first editors" since time immemorial—my parents—without whom my writing would not have found its precision and depth. You showed me the beauty of language! Robin—what is supposed to work without you? Stephan—a permanently supportive inspiration! Marwin—for the thoughts and the constant exchange, especially about training! Stephanie—for all the thoughts and support you share and your watchful eyes! Frank—for the gift of critical feedback! Lukas—I have rarely had a greater personal hero! You are made of pure gold! My coaching staff—because without you, nothing would be possible! Thanks to Nils for the support and good news! Thanks to Damir for the perfect pictures! And of course, a heartfelt thanks to everyone who put their time and energy into this "crazy project" to ensure it reached an extraordinary conclusion! You are true champions!
Muchas gracias, Fran—aprendí tanto de tí. Abel—la inspiración viene de tu parte! Isaac y Xavi—el juego de ubicación no solo es una exploración sino también una realidad! Gracias a todos los entrenadores españoles que han compartido sus conocimientos conmigo! Obrigado por tudo ao Filipe e a toda a família "Periodização Táctica", mesmo que não se trate de um livro sobre Periodização Táctica.
... and thanks to all the unnamed heroes, who through their daily dedication, passion, knowledge, conversations, and love for the game, enrich football and the world—your impact has reached me too!

Bibliography

Contents from the Master in Tactical Periodization by Vítor Frade

→ Notes from the online conferences, especially from Vítor Frade, Miguel Lopes and Jorge Reis.
→ Transcripts from presentations and personal exchanges during the presential phases in 2021, 2022 and 2023 (including with Vítor Frade, Vítor Matos (then Liverpool assistant coach), Sergio Ferreira (then SC Braga assistant coach), and many more

Contents from the Master in Dirección de fútbol (Universidad Europea de Madrid & Real Madrid)

→ Notes from the lectures, especially from the presentation of the Real Sociedad San Sebastián youth academy by Luki Iriarte on May 6, 2022.
→ Personal exchanges with Real Madrid's youth coaches during my internship in Spring 2022, particularly with Fran Beltrán including training observations with him and other coaches from the Real Madrid Academy.

Content from the Master en fútbol professional (INEF Barcelona, Barca Innovation Hub & FC Barcelona)

→ Balagué, Natalia (2021): Various lectures on complex systems and their implications for football training
→ Damunt, Xavier (2021-2023): Various lectures on Barca's methodology and the concept of "stage spaces"
→ Fernandez, Daniel (2023): Various lectures on optimizing the defensive behavior of the team
→ Fernandez, Jordi (2022): From the team to the player: shared affordances and creativity
→ Giraldez, Jonatan (2022-2023): Various lectures and practical examples on the methodology of FC Barcelona using the example of the 1st team (Women FC Barcelona), including, in addition to overarching aspects of the game model, micro-aspects, and scenarios of maximum challenge
→ Personal observation at the 1st team (women) of FC Barcelona in Spring 2023
→ Gonzalez Garcia, Adrian (2022-2023): Learning processes within a team
→ Guerrero, Isaac (2022-2023): Various lectures on the rondo and positional play

↳ Personal observation and exchange in the youth academy of AC Venice, which is based on the game concept of the *"Juego de Ubicación"* (Game of Spaces organized in Autumn 2022)

→ Peris, Albert (2022-2023): Various lectures on the stage spaces and methodological tendencies of FC Barcelona in the youth sector

→ Pol, Rafel (2022): Methodological tendencies in football derived from the game & training methodology

→ Ric, Ángel (2021 / 2022): Tactical training in football

→ Vila, Joan (2023): Another Idea: The Game, the Player and the Ball

→ Various lectures by FC Barcelona's responsible coaches and training observations at "La Masia" between 2022-2024

Online lectures

→ Fore Front Football (2023-2024) by Marc Quintana & Xavier Damunt: El Juego de Ubicación

→ Guerrero, Isaac (2020): El Juego de Ubicación / Location game (as part of the Barca Innovation Hub *Sports Tomorrow* congress)

→ IDE University Rey Juan Carlos (online):

↳ Bretones, Andrés (2023): Espacios indefendibles

↳ Cano, Óscar (2020): El Juego de Ubicación

↳ Vila, Joan (2023): El Fútbol. Juego de los Espacios

→ Vaughan, James (2021): Sociocultural constraints and skilled intentions in football

Scientific articles and books

→ Amiero, N. (2005): Defensa en zona en el fútbol. MCSports, Barcelona.

→ Balagué, N. & Torrents, C. (2011): Complejidad y deporte (Rendimiento deportivo). Barcelona: INDE.

→ Balagué, N.; & Torrents, C. (2014): Aceptar la complejidad en el fútbol: Una tarea compleja. FútbolLibro.

→ Balagué N., Pol R., Torrents C., Ric A., Hristovski R. (2019): On the relatedness and nestedness of constraints. https://doi.org/10.1186/s40798-019-0178-z.

→ Balagué, N.; Torrents, C.; Pol, R.; & Seirul·lo, F. (2014): Entrenamiento integrado. Principios dinámicos y aplicaciones. Revista Apunts.

→ Ballesteros, A. (2020): PEP táctico. librofutbol.com

→ Bermúdez Hernández; J. A. (2018): Lillo y Pep. Convicciones sobre la cultura del juego. librofútbol.com

→ Camenforte, I.; Casamichana, D.; Cos, F.; Castellano, J. & Fernandez, J. (2021): Diseño y validación de una herramienta de valoración del nivel de especificad de las situaciones simuladoras preferenciales en fútbol. https://doi.org/10.5232/ricyde2021.06306
→ Cano, O. (2010): El modelo de juego del FC Barcelona. Barcelona: MCSports.
→ Cano, O. (2012): El juego de posición del FC Barcelona. Barcelona: MCSports.
→ Cappa, A. & Menotti, C. L. (1986): Fútbol sin trampa. Muchnik Editores. Barcelona.
→ Capra, F. (1996): The web of life. Harper Collins Publishers London, UK.
→ Castellano, J. (2000): Observación y análisis de la acción de juego en el fútbol (Tesis doctoral inédita). Universidad del País Vasco.
→ Castellano, J. (2008). Análisis de las posesiones de balón en fútbol: Frecuencia, duración y transición. European Journal of Human Movement.
→ Castellano, J. (2009): Conocer el pasado del football para cambiar su futuro. Acción motriz. Tu revista científica digital.
→ Castellano, J., Perea, A. & Álvarez, D. (2009): Transiciones en la posesión del balón en fútbol: de lo posible a lo probable. Apunts. Educación Física y Deportes.
→ Castelo, J. (1994): Modelo técnico-táctico do jogo. Lisbon: Ediçoes FMH.
→ Castelo, J. (1999): Fútbol: estructura y dinámica del juego. Barcelona: Paidotribo.
→ Chow, J. (2013): Nonlinear learning underpinning pedagogy: Evidence, challenges, and implications. National Association for Kinesiology in Higher Education.
→ Costa, I., Garganta, J., Greco, P., Mesquita, I., & Maia, J. (2011): Sistema de avaliação táctica no Futebol (FUT-SAT): Desenvolvimento e validação preliminar. Revista Motricidade.
→ Couto Reis, J. (2018): Periodización Táctica. La sustentabilidad del morfociclo patrón. MCSports.
→ Cox, M. (2020): The Mixxer (German Version). Suhrkamp.
→ Damunt, X. & Guerrero, I. (2021): El entrenamiento sistémico based en las emotions. FDL.
→ Delgado, J., & Méndez-Villanueva, A. (2012): Tactical Periodization: Mourinho's best-kept secret? Soccer Journal.
→ Enrich, A. (2024): Meditaciones de entrenador. [Coaching Meditations]. Amazon.

→ Frade, V. (1985): Alta competiçao no futebol-que exigencias do tipo metodológico? Faculty of Sports at the University of Porto, Porto.

→ Frade, V. (2004): Entrevista and P. Leal (2004). Different entendimentos, different orientações metodológicas. Faculty of Sports at the University of Porto, Porto.

→ Freitas, S. (2004): A especificidade que está na concentratedração táctica que está na ESPECIFICIDADE… no que deve ser uma operacionalização da Periodização Táctica [monografía]. University of Porto, Porto.

→ Garganta, J. (2016): The humanización del entrenamiento y la competition será la gran revolución del fútbol. Fútbol holístico. Recuperado de https://fholistico.wordpress.com/2016/04/06/julio-garganta-la-humanizacion-del-entrenamiento-y-la-competicion-sera-la-gran-revolucion-del-futbol/ (accessed December 2018).

→ Garganta, J., Maia, J., & Basto, F. (1997): Analysis of goal-scoring patterns in European top level soccer teams. In: Bangsbo, J., Reilly, T., & Williams, AM (1997). Science and football III. London: E & FN Spon.

→ Garganta, J., & Pinto, J. (1998): O Ensino do Futebol. In: Graça, A., & Oliveira, J. (Eds.), O ensino dos jogos deportivos, 3a Ed. (pp. 95 – 135). Porto: Centro de Estudos dos Jogos Desportivos. Faculty of Sports at the University of Porto, Porto.

→ Gamble, P. (2006): Periodization of training for team sports athletes. Strength and Conditioning Journal. https://doi.org/10.1519/1533-4295(2006)28[56:POTFTS]2.0.CO;2

→ Guerrero, I.; Damunt, X. & López, J. (2017): The creation of a non-verbal communication code. Working a proposal for improving decision making in youth football. Valencia University.

→ Guindos, D. (2015): Construcción metodológica del modelo de juego. Madrid: Futboldlibro.

→ Hristovski, R. & Balagué, N. (2020): Theory of Cooperative-Competitive Intelligence: Principles, Research Directions, and Applications. doi: 10.3389/fpsyg.2020.02220

→ Issurin, V. (2010): New horizons for the methodology and physiology of training periodization. Sports Medicine. https://doi.org/10.2165/11319770-000000000-00000

→ Kahneman, D. (2011): Thinking, Fast and Slow. Penguin Publishing.

→ Lago, C. & Seirul·lo, F. (2021): La dirección del entrenamiento y del partido en el Fútbol y los Deportes de Equipo.

→ Lopez, J. (2004): Modelos tácticos y sistemas de juego: elaboración y

entrenamiento integrado. Seville: Wanceulen.
→ Mallo, J. (2020): Complex football. From Seirul·lo's Structured Training to Frade's Tactical Periodization. 2nd Edition.
→ Marina, J. A. (2009): La recuperación de la autoridad. Versatil Ediciones. Barcelona.
→ Martín Acero, R. & Lago, C. (2005): Deportes de equipo. Comprender la complejidad para elevar el rendimiento. INDE Barcelona.
→ Martin-Barrero, A. & Martínez-Cabrera, F. I. (2019): El modelo de juego en el fútbol. De la concepción teórica al diseño práctico. Federación Española de Asociaciones de Docentes de Educación Física (FEADEF) ISSN: Edición impresa: 1579-1726. Edition Web: 1988-2041 (www.retos.org)
→ Martín-Barrero, A. (2018): ¿Cómo construir el camino desde el fútbol de la calle al fútbol profesional? Madrid: Abfutbol.
→ Moreno, R. (2018): Mi "receta" del 4-4-2. FutbolDLibro.
→ Morin, E. (1982): The Enigma of the Human. Basic Questions of a New Anthropology. Piper Verlag.
→ Morin, E. (2000): La mente bien ordenada. Seix Barral Barcelona.
→ O'Sullivan, M.; Woods, CT; Vaughan, J. & Davids, K. (2021): Towards a contemporary player learning in development framework for sports practitioners. DOI: 10.1177/17479541211002335
→ Oliveira, J. G. (2004): Conhecimento Específico em Futebol. Contributos para a definição de uma matriz dinâmica do proceso ensinoaprendizagem/ treino do jogo. Faculty of Sports at the University of Porto, Porto.
→ Oliveira, B.; Amieiro, N.; Resende, N. & Barreto, R. (2007): Mourinho, ¿por qué tantas victorias? MC Sports.
→ Perarnau, M. (2011): Senda de campeones: De La Masia al Camp Nou. Salsa Books CAS.
→ Perarnau, M. (2016): PEP Guardiola. The Germany Diary. Red Bull Media House.
→ Pinder, A.; Davids, K.; Renshaw, I., & Araújo, D. (2011): Representative learning design and functionality of research and practice in sport. Journal of Sport & Exercise Psychology. https://doi.org/10.1123/jsep.33.1.146
→ Pol, R. (2011): La preparación ¿fisica? En el futbol. El proceso de entrenamiento desde las ciencias de la complejidad. MC Sports.
→ Pol, R.; Balagué, N.; Ric, A.; Torrents, C.; Kiely, J. & Hristovski, R. (2020): Training or Synergizing? Complex Systems Principles Change the Understanding of Sport Processes. https://doi.org/10.1186/s40798-020-00256-9.

→ Pol, R. (2021): Entrenamiento deportivo y complejidad: actualizando supuestos teóricos, prácticos e hipótesis de investigación. Tesis doctoral.

→ Ric, Á. (2017): La complejidad en el fútbol: dinámica exploratoria y emergencia de comportamiento táctico. Tesis doctoral.

→ Seirul·lo, F. (2003): Sistemas dinámicos y rendimiento en deportes de equipo. 1st Meeting of Complex System and Sport. INEFC- Barcelona.

→ Seirul·lo, F. (2004): Estructura socio-afectiva. entrenamientodeportivo.org

→ Seirul·lo, F. (2010): Las competencias en el alto rendimiento. entrenamientodeportivo.org

→ Seirul·lo, F. (2017): El entrenamiento en los deportes de equipo. Mastercede. In it:

 ↳ Figure "Finding Flow" according to M. Csikszentmihalyi (1997).

 ↳ Espar Moya, X.: La complejidad en la toma de decisiones y conocer el juego.

 ↳ Massafret i Marimon, M.: La proyección del movimiento deportivo específico en el juego.

 ↳ Seirul·lo, F.: La emotividada en la toma de decisión.

 ↳ Serrés Lara, R. & Massafret i Marimon, M.: La estructura coordinativa.

→ Seirul·lo, F. (2024): ADN Barca. Roca Editorial.

→ Silva, B.; Garganta, J.; Santos, R., & Teoldo, I. (2014): Comparing tactical behavior of soccer players in 3 vs. 3 and 6 vs. 6 small-sided games. Journal of Human Kinetic. https://doi.org/10.2478/hukin-2014-0047.

→ Silva, M. (2008): O desenvolvimento do jogar; segundo a Periodização Táctica. MC Sports.

→ Silva P., Garganta J., Araújo D., Davids K., Aguiar P. (2013): Shared knowledge or shared affordances? Insights from an ecological dynamics approach to team coordination in sports. Sports Medicine.

→ Silva, P.; Vilar, L.; Davids, K.; Araújo, D., & Garganta, J. (2016): Sports team as complex adaptive systems: manipulating player numbers shapes behaviors during football small-sided games. https://doi.org/10.1186/s40064-016-1813-5

→ Tamarit, X. (2010): ¿Qué es la periodización táctica? Barcelona: McSport.

→ Tarragó, J. R.; Massafret-Marimón, M.; Seirul.lo, F., y Cos, F. (2019): Entrenamiento en deportes de equipo: el entrenamiento estructurado en el FCB. Apunts: Educación Física y Deportes. https://doi.org/10.5672/apunts.2014-0983.es.(2019/3).137.08

→ Torrents, C.; Ric, A.; Hristovski, R.; Torres-Ronda, L.; Vicente, E. & Sampaio, J. (2016): Emergence of exploratory, technical and tactical behavior in small-sided soccer games when manipulating the number of teammates and opponents. PLoS One.

→ Vaughan, J.; Mallett, C. J., Potrac, P., López-Felip, M. A. & Davids, K. (2021): Football, Culture, Skill Development and Sport Coaching: Extending Ecological Approaches in Athlete Development Using the Skilled Intentionality Framework. doi: 10.3389/fpsyg.2021.635420

→ Vaughan, J.; Mallett, C. J.; Potrac, P., Woods, C., O'Sullivan, M. & Davids, K. (2022): Social and Cultural Constraints on Football Player Development in Stockholm: Influencing Skill, Learning, and Wellbeing. doi: 10.3389/fspor.2022.832111

→ van Dijk, L., & Rietveld, E. (2017): Foregrounding sociomaterial practice in our understanding of affordances: the skilled intentionality framework. doi: 10.3389/fpsyg.2016.01969

→ Vilar, L.; Duarte, R.; Silva, P.; Chow, J.Y., & Davids, K. (2014): The influence of pitch dimensions on performance during small-sided and conditioned soccer games. Journal of Sport Science. https://doi.org/10.1080/02640414.2014.918640

Newspaper Articles and Online Media

→ BILD online. Mail from Wagner (11.02.2024): Dear Xabi Alonso. https://www.bild.de/politik/kolumnen/franz-josef-wagner/post-von-wagner-lieber-xabi-alonso-87123180.bild.html (Accessed February 2024).

→ Bundesliga online (www.bundesliga.de);
  ↳ Publicly available statistical data of individual players and clubs for the entire season, as well as for individual matches.
  ↳ Online article (unattributed author) from 15.04.2024: Guarantee of success from the Basque Country: Xabi Alonso and his masterpiece with Bayer 04 Leverkusen.

→ https://www.bundesliga.com/de/bundesliga/news/bayer-04-leverkusen-xabi-alonso-trainer-geschichte-aufnahme-deutscher-meister-24999 (Accessed June 2024).

→ Culemania Homepage: Malo, Víctor and López, Artur (21.03.2024): Entrevista a Paco Seirul·lo: de los orígenes con Núñez, Valero y Cruyff al Barça de Xavi y Laporta. https://cronicaglobal.elespanol.com/culemania/culemaniacos/20240321/entrevista-paco-seirullo-valero-cruyff-barca-laporta/839916145_0.html (Accessed March 2024).

→ El Gráfico online: Editorial (22.10.2021): LOS SECRETOS DEL FÚTBOL: LAS PEQUEÑAS SOCIEDADES HACEN EL GRAN EQUIPO. https://www.elgrafico. com.ar/articulo/%C2%A1habla-memoria!/33514/los-secretos-del-futbol-las-pequenias-sociedades-hacen-el-gran-equipo (Accessed April 2024).

→ El mundo (online): Romero, Abraham (04.12.2021): Entre Zubieta y Valdebebas, los dos caminos de Xabi Alonso: "Está preparado para la élite". https://www.elmundo.es/deportes/futbol/2021/12/04/61aa-4e97fc6c83532f8b456d.html (Accessed April 2024)

→ El país online:

  ↳ Pons, Sergi (10.10.2010): REPORTAJE:EXTRA HOMBRE Xabi Alonso. https://elpais.com/diario/2010/10/10/eps/1286692024_850215.html (Accessed May 2024).

  ↳ Torres, Diego (14.01.2023): Xabi Alonso: " El Mundial no mostró la evolución del fútbol". https://elpais.com/deportes/2023-01-14/xabi-alonso-el-mundial-no-mostro-la-evolucion-del-futbol.html (Accessed March 2024).

  ↳ Torres, Diego (09.12.2023): Cinco entrenadores guipuzcoanos agitan Europa. https://elpais.com/deportes/futbol/2023-12-09/cinco-entrena-dores-guipuzcoanos-agitan-europa.html (Accessed March 2024).

→ El Periódico Online: Guasch, Albert (05.04.2024): Paco Seirul·lo decons-truye el ADN Barça: "Cruyff fue una ventana de aire fresco cada vez que estuve con él". https://www.elperiodico.com/es/deportes/20240405/paco-seirul-deconstruye-adn-barca-100552092 (Accessed April 2024).

→ 11 Freunde (#267). Behnisch, Ilja (Februar 2024) im Interview mit Jonathan Tah: „Man muss lernen, Fehler zu lieben".

→ 11 Freunde (#268). Biermann, Christoph (March 2024): Baskisches Wunder.

→ France24 online: Unattributed author (24.11.2023): Xabi Alonso, un estilo de juego que se impone en Leverkusen y crea unanimidad en Alemania. https://www.france24.com/es/minuto-a-minuto/20231124-xabi-alonso-un-estilo-de-juego-que-se-impone-en-leverkusen-y-crea-unanimidad-en-alemania (Accessed December 2023).

→ GOAL.com: Jones, Neil (29.01.2023): Future Liverpool manager? Xabi Alonso shows Reds fans why Bellingham's not the only Bundesliga story to follow. https://www.goal.com/en/news/future-liverpool-manager-xabi-alonso-bellingham-bundesliga-story/blt7478daf4a7bf5139 (Accessed March 2024).

→ Kicker (Print edition) from 26.02.2024: von Nocks, Stephan in an interview with Lukas Hrádecký: "We are not prisoners of Tiki-Taka".

→ Kicker Online:

↳ Elspaß, Leon (01.04.2024): Bayers Andrich und die Tore: „Das ließ ihn fast verzweifeln". https://www.kicker.de/bayers-andrich-und-die-tore-das-liess-ihn-fast-verzweiln-1007845/artikel (Accessed April 2024).

↳ Mag (27.01.2024): „Das nächste Mal die Dinger reinschießen": Leverkusen hadert nach 948 Pässen. https://www.kicker.de/das-naechste-mal-die-dinger-reinschiessen-leverkusen-hadert-nach-948-paessen-992764/artikel (Accessed January 2024).

↳ Mag (26.05.2024): Xabi Alonso zwischen „Traumsaison" und „deutschem Bier". https://www.kicker.de/xabi-alonso-zwischen-traumsaison-und-deutschem-bier-1027680/artikel (Accessed May 2024).

↳ Unattributed (15.03.2024): 20 für Bayers Selbstverständnis: Leverkusens Tore nach der 80. Minute. https://www.kicker.de/20-fuer-bayers-selbstverstaendnis-leverkusens-tore-nach-der-80-minute-1002617/artikel (accessed March 2024).

↳ Without author information / Excerpt from KMD podcast (01.04.2024): Hofmann and the secret of "Laterkusen". https://www.kicker.de/hofmann-und-das-geheimnis-von-laterkusen-1007835/artikel (Accessed April 2024).

↳ Schindler, Ulrich und von Nocks, Stephan (12.04.2024): „So krass war es selten": Bayers 2:0 gegen West Ham als Spiel der Extreme. https://www.kicker.de/so-krass-war-es-selten-bayers-2-0-gegen-west-ham-als-spiel-der-extreme-1013336/artikel (Accessed April 2024).

↳ Von Nocks, Stephan (14.12.2023): Xabi Alonso: „Hoffentlich sind wir nicht so dumm". https://www.kicker.de/xabi-alonso-hoffentlich-sind-wir-nicht-so-dumm-984554/artikel (Accessed December 2023).

↳ Von Nocks, Stephan (19.04.2024): Nicht nur bei Kossounou: Xabi Alonsos Klarheit rettet Bayer. https://www.kicker.de/nicht-nur-bei-kossounou-xabi-alonsos-klarheit-rettet-bayer-1017000/artikel (Accessed April 2024).

↳ Von Nocks, Stephan (03.05.2024): Nach bestandener Reifeprüfung: Funktioniert Bayer auch ohne Xabi Alonso? https://www.kicker.de/nach-habener-reifepruefung-funktioniert-bayer-auch-ohne-xabi-alonso-1021349/artikel (Accessed May 2024).

→ MARCA Online:
  ↳ Badallo, Òscar (09.07.2019): Xabi Alonso: I was comfortable in Madrid, but at Real Sociedad I can improve at home. https://www.marca.com/en/football/real-madrid/2019/07/09/5d24c5f3ca4741300b8b45d5.html (Accessed December 2023).
  ↳ Rubio, Alberto (26.07.2023): Xabi Alonso a MARCA: "¿El Madrid? Cada cosa a su tiempo, lo que tenga que venir en un futuro ya se verá " https://www.marca.com/futbol/futbol-internacional/2023/07/26/64c11e2046163fa9138b4583.html (accessed January 2024).
  ↳ Rubio, Alberto (27.07.2023): El método Alonso: así es un 'entreno' de Xabi en el Bayer Leverkusen. https://www.marca.com/futbol/bundesliga/2023/07/27/64c195c6ca4741d7018b456d.html (Accessed January 2024).

→ MEDIUM Online:
  ↳ Gagliardi, Antonio (24.03.2024): English translation of the article from L'Ultimo Uomo: Is the era of the Position Game coming to an end? https://medium.com/@toni_Gagliardi/is-the-era-of-the-position-game-coming-to-an-end-b5a341011017 (Accessed April 2024).
  ↳ Hamilton, Jamie (27.03.2023): What is relationism? https://medium.com/@stirlingj1982/what-is-relationism-c98d6233d9c2 (Accessed June 2023).

→ Neue Zürcher Zeitung online: Haupt, Florian (14.02.2024): Kleiner Landstrich, grosser Zusammenhalt: Das Baskenland bereichert den europäischen Fussball. https://www.nzz.ch/sport/fussball/europaeischer-fussball-was-hinter-dem- Success-des-baskenlands-esten-ld.1807387 (Accessed March 2024).

→ Neunzigplus online: Weber, Florian (12.10.2022): Neuer Bayer-Coach Xabi Alonso: Mehr Pep Guardiola oder José Mourinho? https://neunzigplus.de/bundesliga/neuer-bayer-coach-xabi-alonso-mehr-pep-guardiola-oder-jose-mourinho/ (Accessed March 2024).

→ New York Times online: Smith, Rory (26.04.2017): Cybernetics, Cesarean Sections and Soccer's Most Magnificent Mind. https://www.nytimes.com/2017/04/26/sports/soccer/cybernetics-cesarean-sections-and-soccers-most-magnificent-mind.html (Accessed July 2019).

→ Notiziario del Settore Tecnico (No. 2, 2024): Gagliardi, Antonio and Bordin, Francesco: A new era. PDF document.

→ Rasenschach online. Provision of article & interview Juanma Lillo from 2011. https://rasenschach-10.de/juanma-lillo-der-virtuose-unter-den-fussballphilosophen/ (accessed May 2024).

→ Relevo online:

  ↳ Blaya, Albert (03.10.2023): "XABI ALONSO ES UN OBSESO DEL TIEMPO Y EL ESPACIO": ASÍ JUEGA SU BAYER LEVERKUSEN. https://www.relevo.com/futbol/bundesliga/xabi-alonso-bayer-laverkusen-wirtz-20230309063809-nt.html (Accessed May 2024).

  ↳ Lavín, June and P, Rodra (14.04.2024): ASÍ ES LA BRIGADA DE MODA QUE ESCOLTA A XABI ALONSO EN LEVERKUSEN: TODO EMPEZÓ CON UN INFORME DE VALDEBEBAS. https://www.relevo.com/futbol/bundes-liga/cuerpo-tecnico-xabi-alonso-bayer-20240224140229-nt.html (Accessed May 2024).

→ Spiegel online: Saller, Josef (29.10.2023): Der Mann, der Leverkusen (und die Bundesliga) verzaubert. https://www.spiegel.de/sport/xabi-alonso-der-mann-der-leverkusen-und-die-bundesliga-verzaubert-a-6b3c34e8-bdf4-4983-a7da-0e428ef16b97 (Accessed May 2024).

→ SPOX online: SID (24.01.2024): Granit Xhaka über möglichen Abgang von Xabi Alonso: „Es wird der Tag kommen, wo er vielleicht den nächsten Schritt machen möchte". https://www.spox.com/de/sport/fussball/bundes-liga/2401/News/xabi-alonso-abgang-von-bayer-leverkusen-irgendwann-wird-der-tag-kommen.html (Accessed February 2024).

→ Süddeutsche Zeitung online:

  ↳ Cáceres, Javier (06.10.2022): Ein Trainer, für den Abstiegskampf ein unbekanntes Wort ist. https://www.sueddeutsche.de/sport/xabi-alonso-leverkusen-trainer-1.5670019 (Accessed January 2024).

  ↳ Cáceres, Javier (16.01.2023): Interview mit Xabi Alonso: „Fußball ist auch eine Frage von emotionalen Zuständen". https://www.sueddeut-sche.de/sport/xabi-alonso-interview-leverkusen-1.5731948 (Accessed April 2024).

  ↳ Cáceres, Javier & Selldorf, Philipp (12.04.2024): Meister der Effi-zienz. https://www.sueddeutsche.de/sport/bayer-leverkusen-europa-league-xabi-alonso-meisterschaft-1.6545317

  ↳ Cáceres, Javier (15.04.2024): „Man muss die großen und exzellenten Spieler gut behandeln". https://www.sueddeutsche.de/sport/exequiel-palacios-leverkusen-championship-interview-rolle-team-1.6553875 (Accessed May 2024).

↳ Cáceres, Javier (24.05.2024): „Xabi war das perfekte Puzzleteil". https://www.sueddeutsche.de/sport/alonso-benitez-liverpool-pokalfinale-1.7331803 (Accessed May 2024).

↳ DPA in SZ online (05.06.2024): Alonso: Als Trainer von Europa-League-Niederlage profitieren. https://www.sueddeutsche.de/sport/bundesliga-alonso-als-trainer-von-europa-league-niederlage-profitieren-dpa.urn-newsml-dpa-com-20090101-240605-99-280983 (Accessed June 2024).

↳ Hellmann, Frank (15.10.2022): Systemabsturz der Werkself. https://www.sueddeutsche.de/sport/bundesliga-bayer-leverkusen-xabi-alonso-eintracht-frankfurt-1.5675645 (Accessed February 2024).

↳ John, Ulrike; Schmidt, Holger; Mies, Jan & Richter, Arne; dpa (26.05.2024): Darauf ein „deutsches Bier": Alonso macht Double perfekt. https://www.sueddeutsche.de/sport/fussball-darauf-ein-deutsches-bier-alonso-macht-double-perfekt-dpa.urn-newsml-dpa-com-20090101-240525-99-159940 (Accessed May 2024).

↳ Kneer, Christoph & Schneider, Philipp (06.06.2024): „Ich habe vieles im Wohnzimmer gelernt". https://www.sueddeutsche.de/sport/florian-wirtz-dfb-em-interview-lux.V4mYwLU7wHcWQYf7tM7K1u

↳ Selldorf, Philipp (26.01.2024): In jedem Pass steckt eine Botschaft. https://www.sueddeutsche.de/sport/leverkusen-alonso-xhaka-bayer-bundesliga-1.6339631 (Accessed February 2024).

↳ Selldorf, Philipp (09.02.2024): „Wir sind auf einer ganz guten Spur, um die Tyrannei zu beenden". https://www.sueddeutsche.de/sport/Hrádecký-leverkusen-bayern-interview-bundesliga-1.6346682 (Accessed February 2024)

↳ Selldorf, Philipp (23.05.2024): Einsichten in die eigene Fehlbarkeit. https://www.sueddeutsche.de/sport/leverkusen-atalanta-europa-league-xabi-alonso-kritik-1.7296199 (Accessed May 2024).

→ The Athletic Online:

↳ Corrigan, Dermot (11/17/2021): I have ambition to manage an elite team, but I am in no hurry' – Xabi Alonso happy to learn at Real Sociedad. https://theathletic.com/2943017/2021/11/17/i-have-ambition-to-manage-an-elite-team-but-i-am-in-no-hurry-xabi-alonso-happy- to-learn-at-real-sociedad/?access_token=15461426# (Accessed March 2024).

↳ Corrigan, Dermot (28.09.2023): Guipuzcoa, the tiny Spanish province big in the Premier League and beyond. https://theathletic.com/4904302/2023/09/28/arteta-emery-iraola-premier-league-guipuzcoa-managers/ (Accessed March 2024).

↳ Corrigan, Dermot (02.03.2024): Bayer Leverkusen's Alex Grimaldo: 'I'd have loved to have a coach like Xabi Alonso at 20'. https://theathletic.com/5309751/2024/03/02/alex-grimaldo-leverkusen-xabi-alonso/ (Accessed March 2024).

↳ Garrick, Omar (05.10.2022): Xabi Alonso appointed head coach of Bayer Leverkusen as Gerardo Seoane departs. https://theathletic.com/3659771/2022/10/05/xabi-alonso-bayer-leverkusen/ (Accessed March 2024).

↳ Honigstein, Raphael (19.12.2023): Granit Xhaka exclusive: Staying at Arsenal, leaving and being 'calmer' at high-flying Leverkusen. https://theathletic.com/5125452/2023/12/19/granit-xhaka-arsenal-interview-arteta/ (Accessed March 2024).

↳ Honigstein, Raphael & Stafford-Bloor, Sebastian (14.04.2024): How Bayer Leverkusen won the Bundesliga: Alonso magic, breaking up cliques and clever transfers. https://theathletic.com/5411110/2024/04/14/bayer-leverkusen-xabi-alonso-bundesliga/ (Accessed April 2024).

↳ Hughes, Simon & Honigstein, Raphael (02.04.2024): Xabi Alonso, the coach who said no to Liverpool and Bayern Munich. https://theathletic.com/5375366/2024/04/02/xabi-alonso-liverpool-bayern-real-madrid-profile/ (Accessed April 2024).

↳ Millar, Colin (23.02.2024): Xabi Alonso hails resilient Leverkusen as win over Mainz sets German unbeaten record. https://theathletic.com/5296039/2024/02/23/xabi-alonso-leverkusen-unbeaten-record/ (Accessed March 2024).

↳ Muller, John (28.01.2024): Xabi Alonso's Leverkusen tactics and Liverpool's squad are not a natural fit. https://theathletic.com/5231341/2024/01/28/xabi-alonso-liverpool-manager/ (Accessed April 2024).

↳ Pearce, James; Ornstein, David & More (30.03.2024): What happened with Liverpool and Xabi Alonso - and where does the club look now? https://theathletic.com/5377617/2024/03/30/liverpool-xabi-alonso-manager-what-now/ (Accessed April 2024).

↳ Stafford-Bloor, Sebastian (30.07.2023): Xabi Alonso, Granit Xhaka and plotting for the Bundesliga: Inside Bayer Leverkusen's pre-season camp. https://theathletic.com/4731113/2023/07/30/bayer-leverkusen-alonso-xhaka/ (Accessed March 2024).

→ The coaches voice homepage. Xabi Alonso's coaching career analyzed. https://www.coachesvoice.com/cv/xabi-alonso-bayer-leverkusen-liverpool/ (Accessed March 2024).

→ The players tribune: Robles, Sam with Alonso, Xabi (13.06.2024): To Leverkusen. https://www.theplayerstribune.com/posts/xabi-alonso-bundesliga-leverkusen (Accessed June 2024).

→ The Tactical Room:
  ↳ Beltrán, Francisco Ruiz (2013): Madrid micro, Madrid macro (in Perarnau Club#7)
  ↳ Benedetti, Ignacio (2020): Entrevista con Carles Martínez (in TTR 61).
  ↳ Fernandez, Daniel (2012): El juego de posición. https://www.martiperarnau.com/el-juego-de-posicion/ (Accessed May 2021).
  ↳ Perarnau, Marti & Lluch, Isaac (2017): Entrevista con Xabi Alonso (in TTR 31).

→ transfermarkt.com: Bienkowski, Stefan (26.01.2024): 'I'm Basque, with a big German influence' - Why Alonso is Europe's most in-demand head coach. https://www.transfermarkt.com/im-basque-with-a-big-german-influence-why-alonso-is-europes-most-in-demand-head-coach/view/news/430238 (Accessed January 2024).

→ VAULT sports illustrated online: Si staff (27.06.2016): Master of space and time. https://vault.si.com/vault/2016/06/27/master-space-and-time (Accessed May 2024).

→ WELT Online: Hesse, Axel & Arens, Phillip (19.04.2024): Nach dem Dortmund-Spiel platzte die Wut aus Xabi Alonso heraus. https://www.welt.de/sport/fussball/bundesliga/bayer-leverkusen/plus251051236/Weg-zur-Championship-Nach-dem-Dortmund-Spiel-platzte-die-Wut-aus-Xabi-Alonso-heraus. html?notify=success_subscription (Accessed June 2024).

→ **For the statistics on Bayer Leverkusen (especially numbers from the Bundesliga; besides bundesliga.de):**
  ↳ understat.com
  ↳ theanalyst.com
  ↳ footystats.org

→ TV show: "UNIVERSO VALDANO". Interview by Jorge Valdano with Xabi Alonso from December 7th, 2023.

→ YOUTUBE: Xabi Alonso's first press conference. Retrieved February 2024.
→ YOUTUBE: Ecos del balón. La mirada de un mediocentro: Xabi Alonso. From December 13, 2017. Retrieved October 2023.
→ YOUTUBE: Press conference with Juanma Lillo from 2016.
→ Video clip on X: Xabi Alonso in a report about the Bundesliga for a US broadcaster about his approach (further details cannot be identified).
→ Kicker TV: Recording of press conference from April 14, 2024 (title win after victory against Bremen).
→ PODCAST: Mi fútbol by Ignacio Benedetti (02/19/2024). Entrevista with Paco Seirul·lo (part 1). Retrieved February 2024.
→ PODCAST: La ciencia pop by Gabriel León (November 3, 2023). The small societies. Retrieved April 2024.
→ PODCAST: Kicker meets DAZN (KMD): Episode with Jonas Hofmann from April 1, 2024.

About the author

Tim Stegmann (*1989 in Hamburg) currently works as a football coach and coach educator in the Regional Football Federation of Hamburg. He also gained experience in professional football as assitant coach at FC Würzburger Kickers.

Tim Stegmann stands out as the only coach in Germany holding three master's degrees in football. He was the first German to complete the *Master in Tactical Periodization by Vítor Frade*, focusing on the Portuguese methodology of tactical periodization. Driven by his passion for Spanish football, Tim Stegmann decided to study two additional master's programs conducted in Spanish:

In 2022, he graduated at the top of his course from the *Master en Dirección de Fútbol*, a program jointly offered by *Universidad Europea* and Real Madrid in the Spanish capital. This course focuses on successful models in youth football. As part of this program, Tim Stegmann also spent six months working within Real Madrid's youth development department.

In 2023, he completed the *Master en Fútbol Profesional*, offered by FC Barcelona. During this course, he acquired in-depth knowledge of the content, methodology and philosophy of FC Barcelona.